BITTER EMBRACE

MAGGIE SIGGINS

BITTER

EMBRACE

WHITE SOCIETY'S ASSAULT ON THE WOODLAND CREE

M&S

To the memory of Philip Ratt and Dr. Harvey Christiansen

Library and Archives Canada Cataloguing in Publication

Siggins, Maggie, 1942-
    Bitter embrace : white society's assault on the Woodland Cree / Maggie Siggins.

ISBN 0-7710-8060-3

1. Cree Indians – Saskatchewan – Pelican Narrows Region – History. 2. Cree Indians – Saskatchewan – Government relations.   3. Pelican Narrows Region (Sask.) – History.   I. Title.

E99.C88S44 2005   971.24'100497323   C2004-906834-2

We acknowledge the financial support of the Government of Canada through the Book Publishing Industry Development Program and that of the Government of Ontario through the Ontario Media Development Corporation's Ontario Book Initiative. We further acknowledge the support of the Canada Council for the Arts and the Ontario Arts Council for our publishing program.

The poems on pp.5, 51, 94, 99, 133, 173, 207, 253, and 283 are from Glen Sorestad's *Jan Lake Poems* and *Hold the Rain in Your Hands*. Reprinted by permission of the author.

The excerpt on p.156 is from *Kiss of the Fur Queen* by Tomson Highway. © Tomson Highway 1988. Reprinted by permission of Doubleday Canada.

"A Race for Life" on p.141 is from *The World of the Wetiko: Tales from the Woodland Cree* by Marie Merasty. (Saskatchewan Indian Cultural College, 1974.)

All photos courtesy of the author, unless otherwise indicated.

Frontispiece: Pelican Narrows in 1922. The Hudson's Bay Company post was the heart of the community.

Typeset in Sabon by M&S, Toronto
Printed and bound in Canada

This book is printed on acid-free paper that is
100% ancient-forest friendly (40% post-consumer recycled).

McClelland & Stewart Ltd.
The Canadian Publishers
481 University Avenue
Toronto, Ontario
M5G 2E9
www.mcclelland.com

1 2 3 4 5   09 08 07 06 05

CONTENTS

ACKNOWLEDGEMENTS

I am indebted to many people for their help in researching this book. Gordon Peter Ballantyne and his family were my eyes and ears in the Pelican Narrows community. Phil Ratt, with his superb memory, added important historic interpretations. The co-operation of Chief Ron Michel was greatly appreciated, as was the linguistic expertise of Keith Goulet.

Yaya Siggins laid down the foundation of this project and Carmen Pauls Orthner did an excellent job in interviewing and researching the contemporary scene. Rachel Knudsen's sleuthing among the archives was invaluable. Without her help the book could not have been written.

I would also like to express my gratitude to those who made my life in the north so much more comfortable: Phil Poiron, Christina and Don Pomeroy, Kjell Nasselquist, and Betty and Fred Brown.

Finally, I would like to give a special thanks to my editor, Pat Kennedy, and to my husband, Gerry Sperling, who became an expert hewer of wood and hauler of water, and, as always, my first reader.

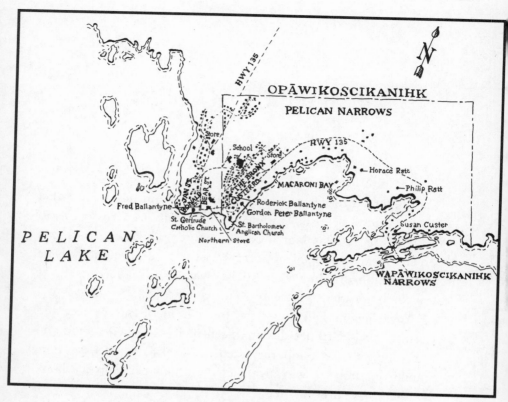

The community of Pelican Narrows

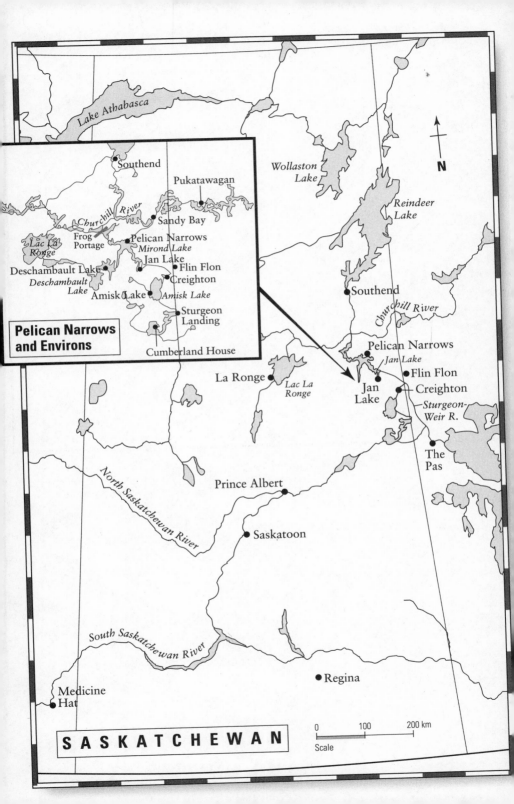

Lake Athabasca

N

Wollaston
Lake

Reindeer
Lake

Pelican Narrows and Environs (inset map)

Southend

Pukatawagan

Churchill River

Sandy Bay

Frog
Portage

Pelican Narrows
Mirond Lake

*Lac La
Ronge*

Jan Lake

Flin Flon

Creighton

Deschambault Lake

*Deschambault
Lake*

Amisk Lake

Amisk Lake

Sturgeon
Landing

Cumberland House

**Pelican Narrows
and Environs**

Southend

Churchill River

Pelican Narrows

Jan Lake

Flin Flon

Jan
Lake

Creighton

*Sturgeon-
Weir R.*

La Ronge

*Lac La
Ronge*

The
Pas

Prince Albert

North Saskatchewan River

Saskatoon

South Saskatchewan River

Medicine
Hat

Regina

| 0 | 100 | 200 km |
Scale

SASKATCHEWAN

PROLOGUE

I met him at a dinner party given by Phil Poiron, the proprietor of Miniquay Hotel in Jan Lake, north-central Saskatchewan, on a lovely summer day in 2002. Deeply absorbed in a television program about mating whales on the Discovery Channel, he hardly acknowledged the introductions offered, and I thought him ill-mannered and self-absorbed. He was a short, portly man in his fifties, whose dress was not so much casual as shabby – baggy dung-coloured shorts, an ill-fitting T-shirt, so faded the lettering had all but disappeared. But, as the evening wore on, and he deigned to talk with us, I began paying close attention.

Michael Bomek was a lawyer with both the Saskatchewan and Manitoba bars. He had a busy practice in Flin Flon, involving everything from family to corporate law. He himself preferred the cut and thrust of criminal proceedings, and travelled the circuit, mostly to Indian reserves in northern parts of the two provinces. He asked me if I would like to see him in action. I replied, I wouldn't miss it for anything.

Early next morning we drove to Pelican Narrows, an Indian reserve forty-four kilometres from Jan Lake cottage country. The so-called courthouse – in reality a dilapidated community hall and bingo parlour – was already packed with the nervous accused, their families, and court staff, including the judge, Gerry Morin, who was anxious to get on with business. Bomek quickly changed from his beggar's outfit to the more appropriate slacks, dress shirt, and wrinkled tie, although he never did manage to get his shoes on during the day's proceedings.

The entire miserable underbelly of the community paraded through the courtroom that day – the wife beaters, the drug dealers, the petty thieves, and drunks all quietly submitted to whatever punishment was meted out. It became obvious very quickly that Michael Bomek did more for his clients than the legal-aid lawyer, who sat with his pile of unread cases balanced perilously in front of him. Bomek tried to bolster their spirits, joking with them, listening patiently as they attempted to explain themselves, counselled their wives or parents, and most important, did as much legal preparation as possible. During the actual trials, he fought hard for these demoralized, poor people. He claims he won 70 to 80 per cent of his cases.

This was a "Cree court" set up so those with little English would feel comfortable. As it turned out, the judge and prosecutor were fluent in Cree, but none of the defence lawyers were. A makeshift translation process was in effect, the court clerk whispering in the ear of the attorney. Bomek was the only one who took the trouble to have the evidence repeated if he felt the translator had been mistaken. He was also the only one to challenge facts presented by the RCMP, the only one to cross-examine the Crown's witnesses with skill and vigour, the only one not to acquiesce to the dictates of the court. By the end of the day, he had risen immeasurably in my esteem.

Back in Regina a month and a half later, my husband was drifting in one of his two-hour baths, when he suddenly cried out. The radio had just reported that a lawyer by the name of Michael Bomek had been arrested and remanded to the Prince Albert Penitentiary.

Some time later Bomek would tell me what had happened. He had arrived at Pelican Narrows early in the morning of September 16, 2002. He was meeting a former client, a high-school teacher who fifteen years before had pleaded guilty to sexually assaulting a ten-year-old boy. The man had maintained a clean record since, and Bomek thought he might be able to arrange a job for him at the reserve's Opawikoscikan School.

Bomek sauntered into the RCMP depot, the agreed-upon meeting place. What greeted him was a menacing silence. Suddenly Mounties surrounded him. One read him his rights. Three others bundled him into a police van and drove the short distance to the courthouse.

In handcuffs and shackles, he waddled past the half-dozen or so of his clients waiting for him to deal with their cases. Their mouths dropped open as they took in the spectacle. "If ever I wanted to die, that was the day. I never felt as low as I did that moment," he confessed. Standing in front of his old antagonist, Judge Gerry Morin, James Michael David Bomek was arraigned on sixteen counts, all involving sex crimes against young Cree men living on the reserve.

By December the charges against the fifty-three-year-old lawyer had piled up – forty-one counts of sexual assault, soliciting for the purpose of prostitution, and obstruction of justice, all but two involving young men, seventeen to twenty-two years old, all but one his clients.

The people of Pelican Narrows were shocked and then outraged by the crimes that the lawyer had allegedly committed. Once again a white authority figure had infiltrated their community, full of promises, bloated with best intentions, only to despoil and debauch. I began to see reflected in the Bomek case the entire sad history of white-Indian relations. So many do-gooders had arrived to impose their ways, always so sure of their sincerity, their superiority, their infallibility. In the process, the Cree livelihood, their society, their artistic expression, their religion, and most tragic of all, their belief in themselves were destroyed. A struggle now rages to cure the terrible hurt these people have suffered, to put their lives back together.

How far has the healing process progressed? My husband and I own a cabin at Jan Lake Recreation Area and I decided to spend seven months there, easy driving distance to Pelican Narrows, not to write another dismal account of reserve life, but rather to try to appreciate this unique culture, to sympathize with the Woods Cree plight, and above all, to listen.

All during this time I kept thinking of Michael Bomek (the last time I saw him he was selling hot dogs for a living in Prince Albert's downtown park) and all the others who came before him. I concluded that all my white society can do now is stand aside and give what is asked.

SAMARITANS ON THE HANSON LAKE ROAD

The car crouches motionless on the approach.
It is past midnight. A figure
on the roadside hails us; we stop.
The Woods Cree tells us his battery
is dead and he can't start the car
without a push. The silent Ford
has two windows boarded with plywood.
We pile out, all six of us
and the avalanche catches him off-guard.
At his suggestion we push
the car backwards, roll it
slowly, then pick up speed.
He throws the clutch,
the engine engages with a roar
and he fishtails wildly backwards
in a spray of gravel, a spatter
against the forest darkness.
He slams the brakes, guns
the motor, rockets ahead
while we leap and scatter
from his single-mindedness.
A terse blare of horn
and he is gone. We watch
his tail-lights fade
like tiny red fireflies
until darkness takes over again.

Glen Sorestad
Jan Lake Poems

1
pēyak

THEY MEET

KĪ NAKISKĀTOWAK

For months Gordon Peter* Ballantyne had looked forward to the fish derby. He had dug deep to come up with the $150 entry fee for both him and his wife, Susan. The stakes were high, first prize a brand new half-ton, second prize ten thousand dollars cash. But at eight-thirty in the morning, as he was launching the shabby little boat he had borrowed, he noticed the crowd starting to gather. The power-crafts slithered off their trailers like partying Jackfish. There'd be more chance of cashing in on Jumping Jackpot Bingo than delivering the winning pickerel, Gordon Peter concluded.

He firmly believes that, where there are small fish, there are large fish. Just a while back a friend had won a new Chevy in a similar derby. He had settled in the same spot all day, every now and then pulling out the kind of specimen others laughed at. Then, just before the finish, he snagged the fat grandfather lounging on the bottom and won the competition. This was Gordon Peter's model. He found a spot where a couple of two- and three-pounders

---

* Gordon Peter is called Gordon off the reserve and Peter on the reserve so I am using both names.

7

were landed and he had wanted to park there. But after an hour or two his wife had grown restless. "Not getting anything here," Susan said. "Let's try another spot."

"You have to be patient when you're fishing," he kept saying, until Susan finally lost patience. They quarrelled. She had walloped him on the cheek with her fishing rod.

Lots of pickerel were caught (and thrown back – a rule of the derby), but they weren't that big. So right up until the last moment, everybody, including Susan and Gordon Peter, felt they had a chance. Then, ten minutes before the closing, a young woman from Amisk Lake pulled out a seven-pound-three-ounce fish. Goodbye shiny red truck.

So far this has not been the luckiest year for Gordon Peter. For the first time in twenty years he hadn't been called up by the band council to work as a foreman on construction. No money to build houses, they announced. All spring he'd had to scramble. Tired of waiting a year for a bathroom door to be replaced or a broken window fixed, reserve folks, who admired Gordon Peter's skill and hard work as a carpenter, asked him to renovate their houses, but often they forgot to pay him. "The end of the month," they'd say, and he knew the pelicans would have come and gone before he'd see his money.

There'd been more disappointment. In the spring Gordon Peter had run for band councillor and had lost. His seventeen-year-old son announced that he was quitting school and that his girlfriend had just had a baby. And then a cousin, Leland Ballantyne, had been hit on the head with a baseball bat while he was partying in Saskatoon. During the funeral at St. Gertrude's Church, Gordon Peter's heart had gone out to Leland's wife and four children. He may have felt gloomy about all this, but he certainly wasn't surprised. Life on this reserve is always an unpredictable soap opera. "It's worse than *All My Children*," says Darlene McKay, one of the reserve's comedians. "Erica Kane would feel right at home."

Scribbled along Pelican Lake on the west, past Church Point, and continuing east along Macaroni Bay until Wapāwikoscikanihk (Narrows of Fear), where the bush takes over once again, Pelican Narrows Reserve sits atop granite rock amidst the gorgeous scenery of deep boreal forest. Located just south of the Churchill River, for a hundred years the village was a convenience stop on Canada's busy fur-trade highway.

In the old part of the community, the houses, all stamped from the same cookie-cutter design, unimaginatively mass-produced by the Canadian government, are strewn every which way, a leftover from the time when wigwams, and then log cabins, housed Cree fur trappers and their families. In the new part of the village, the streets are straight or curved in cul-de-sacs, suburban-like, with names such as Sunset Drive. But homes here are still versions of the same cut-costs design; the residents call them "disposable houses" because they fall apart so quickly. Or, in a flash, burn to the ground.

Gordon Peter, his wife, Susan, their five children, Vanessa, twenty-one, Peter Junior, nineteen, Ronald, eighteen, Scott, sixteen, and Melissa, thirteen, and their two grandchildren – Vanessa's kids, Andrew, four, and Arwin, three – live in the old part of the reserve near the Anglican Church, in what is called – nobody knows for certain why – the Bronx. Once they moved permanently in from the bush in the 1920s, this strain of the Ballantyne clan all settled here. The houses of Oscar and Anson, Gordon Peter's brothers, are located only a few yards away. His sister, Linda, a teacher of Cree language at the local school, lives nearby. On the road running up a hill that splits the community in two is the neat house of the patriarch of this clan, Gordon Peter's father, Roderick Ballantyne, a retired fur trapper and fishing guide. Still living with Roderick is a daughter, Laurie, a beautician, and Roderick's youngest child, George the Talker, whose idea of heaven is to camp deep in the forest, much as his ancestors did. In a roomy new house in the suburbs (its windows were recently smashed by vandals) lives another son, Philip, and his four children. Gordon

Peter's fifth brother has moved to the big city of Prince Albert (population 40,000), although he returns every summer to Pelican Narrows to fight forest fires.

Highway 135 runs through the reserve on the way to another community, Sandy Bay, seventy kilometres north. A provincial government responsibility, it remains unpaved as are all the roads in Pelican Narrows under band control. Merasty Street, Bear Street, Chachakew Street, Custer Road, Jan Street, Michel Street, are choked with potholes and debris; they look like the main arteries of some Middle East war zone. In the summer, dust is thick in the air, coating everything, giving the place a feel of fatigue and forlornness. This is only exacerbated by the hundreds of rez dogs, many of them feral, who lie panting on the road. Pelican Narrows has a healthier, more vigorous spirit in the frigid winter, when the kids are skating on the outdoor rink, and there's ice fishing on the lake. There's more hope in the air then.

It's hard to keep track of the population, because it is expanding so fast, but somewhere around 2,800 people live here. The ramshackle band office, the medical clinic, the Napoleon Merasty Arena, the two modern schools, the two old churches, and the RCMP depot dominate the landscape. There's a Northern Store that replaced the old Hudson's Bay post, the band's gas bar, Charles Confectionery, Pearson's Enterprises, which sells mostly potato chips, in fact 2,400 bags a week – and Medicine Rapids, a restaurant that is too expensive for most people, and that's it. No hairdresser, no ladies' dress shop, no bookstore, no dentist, no florist, no sports-equipment outlet, no funeral home, no hotel, no shoe store, no video arcade, no jeweller, no coffee shop, no movie theatre, and no bank. Try and pay your telephone bill without a bank account when the closest Sasktel outlet is 110 kilometres away and you don't have a car. Some people do have bank accounts – in the Ballantyne family, Susan is the only one who has opened one – but the half-dozen cash-disposal machines available on the reserve are always out of money at precisely the moment when people have it: at the end of the month on pension or social-assistance days. The machine at Charles Confectionery has a forty-dollar limit on each transaction, and each transaction costs two dollars.

There are, of course, charming features to living at Pelican Narrows – sandy beaches where the children play in the summer, dense bush not far away for moose hunting, neighbouring lakes full of fish, and all the friends, relatives, and gossip you could ever wish for. These things must be important since few people leave the reserve, and those that do, often come back.

The place is not as isolated as it used to be before the road was cut in – Jan Lake, a summer holiday resort, is fifty minutes away by car, the nearest city, Flin Flon, in northern Manitoba, 110 kilometres – but still it's not a place which tourists, or anybody else, accidentally stumble across. And despite the satellite dishes perched cockily on almost every roof, with their hundred-something channels beaming into the living rooms, it remains a world unto its own.

For Gordon Peter's family, an excursion into the larger society usually consists of a weekend at Prince Albert. Not only does the wholesale food outlet have fantastic sales – fifty pounds of potatoes for ten dollars, whereas the Northern Store charges eight dollars for ten pounds – but the bingo halls offer up really big prizes – an $8,000 all-terrain vehicle, say. (Neither Gordon Peter nor his wife have ever cashed in such magnificent prizes, although Susan once won $2,500 at a Pelican Narrows bingo jamboree. That bonanza cleaned up all the outstanding bills, she says.) The Ballantynes usually stay with relatives at the Prince Albert Reserve, often just taking over the living-room floor for the night. Family among these First Nations people is like an intricately plaited spiderweb. For those trying to escape reserve life, it can seem as confining as a link chain. For most it is comforting, inviting, and full of drama.

Pelican Narrows is the largest of eight communities that make up the Peter Ballantyne Cree Nation. Other reserves include Amisk Lake, Sturgeon Landing, Southend, Kinoosao, Prince Albert,

Sandy Bay, and Deschambault Lake. With a population of 7,300, more than half of whom live on these reserves, the rest in cities, it is the second-largest band in Saskatchewan. Located just north of the 55th parallel, the populated reserves are dotted over thirteen hundred square kilometres of forest. It takes the chief a week to visit his entire domain.

For Gordon Peter his birthplace has special historical significance. The band is named after his great-grandfather. He often asks himself a very disturbing question: is my life any better from that of the original Peter who was elected chief 100 years ago?

The scholar Anthony D. Fisher once called the Cree the most important aboriginal group in Canada because of their "central historic position . . . geographic extensiveness . . . contemporary significance."[1] At present about two hundred thousand Cree live in five provinces from northern Quebec westward to Alberta. They range north to the Athabasca River and southward to the Dakota states and Montana.

All speak a soft, sibilant language that belongs to the Algonkian branch of the Algonkian-Wakashan linguistic stock. Tomson Highway, the brilliant playwright, novelist, and musician, who grew up in Brochet, Manitoba, north of Pelican Narrows, describes his mother tongue as "physical, visceral, the language of nature." Elvena Pearson, who lives in one of the most modern and stylish homes in Pelican Narrows, says, "I love the language; it's so descriptive. When you say something in Cree, it's way more funny than in English." The Cree penchant for naming birds as they sound enchanted the American traveller P.G. Downes writing in the 1930s – his favourites: *piskwa* for nighthawk, *cah-cah-kāýow* for red-winged blackbird, *ōhōw* for owl, *mākwa* for the loon. Joseph F. Dion, a Cree writer, also points out how beautifully descriptive his language is. English has only one word for snow, he writes, but Cree has the following: snow generally is *kona*; falling snow, *mispon*; melting snow, *sasken*; drifting snow, *pīwon*;

snowdrifts, *papēskwacistin*. And the language can be embarrass-ingly direct. Those prissy euphemisms used by English-speakers – washroom, bathroom, water closet, the place where one powders one's nose – when directly translated from Cree come up "shit-house." One of Gordon Peter's favourites is the word for a television set – *cikāstēpaýihhcikan* – "a movie with a small screen." The Cree language is built of tiny poems, each conjuring up a clear, often funny, image. There are several dialects of Cree, and the speech of Pelican Narrows people is quite distinct. A word like *me* is pronounced with a *th*, *niitha*, while the Plains Cree use the *y* sound, *niýa*. Other Cree groups use *n* and *l*, for example, *niina* or *niila*. The *th* speakers are variously called Rock, Rocky, Stony, or Missinippi Cree.*

The word "Cree" derives from the Kenisteniwuk Indians, who lived south of James Bay in the seventeenth century. This particu-lar band has disappeared into the mists of time, but the French derivation of their name, Kiristinon, later contracted to Cri (Cree in English), has stuck. Cree is a clumsy word for a Cree-speaker to pronounce, and most use it only when speaking English. The name they call themselves is a logical one – *nēhiýaw*, meaning "those who speak the same language."

Gordon Peter Ballantyne's relatives were not the stuff of Hollywood westerns – the painted warriors who galloped across no man's land and partook of Sun Dances. Those were the Plains Cree, who became infatuated with horses and the relatively more secure and prosperous life of hunting buffalo on the prairies until these animals suddenly disappeared in the 1870s. Gordon Peter's ancestors, now called Woodland, or Woods, Cree, stayed in the northern forest, gathering plants and berries, hunting large game

---

* Rock Cree bands in Manitoba include Pukatawagan, Nelson House, Brochet, South Indian Lake, Hughes Lake, Granville Lake, Southern Indian Lake, and Churchill. In Saskatchewan Lac La Ronge, Lac Wollaston, Sandy Narrows, Sandy Bay, Sturgeon Landing, Island Falls, Pelican Narrows, Southend, and Deschambault Lake.

– the moose is to the Woodland group what the buffalo is to the Plains people – fishing, and trapping various fur-bearing animals. It was a life that persisted right up to the 1970s when the Brigitte Bardots of the world turned the wearing of fur coats into a mortal sin.

The Pelican Narrows Cree refer to themselves as *asinīskā-wiýiniw*, or a people of the place where there is an abundance of rocks. In this country that could only be the great Canadian Shield.

Some twenty thousand years ago huge ice sheets began a battering retreat, scooping out lake basins, shovelling away most of the soil, gouging and scarring the crystalline bedrock below. What was laid bare was the Precambrian Shield, a shell of granite and rock formed about 600 million years ago. In Pelican Narrows country, 45 per cent of the terrain consists of exposed bedrock, 25 per cent is covered with water, and only 30 per cent has any soil at all. But what grows on this thin covering of earth is amazing. Although often straggly and undernourished, black and white spruce, Jack pine, balsam, and tamarack make a magnificent forest of greenery, at least in spring and summer. In the fall, when the wind is howling the return of winter, they look like an army of starved prisoners-of-war on a forced march. It's the paper birch, delicate, ethereal, elegant, that softens the sullenness of this landscape.

There are lakes of every size and shape, each with a personality of its own, rivers full of frightening, roaring rapids, and undrained boggy hollows where the biting insects like to hatch their eggs. The travel writer P.G. Downes was often asked why he returned every year to a world of rock and tundra, millions of mosquitoes, and brutal weather that can change from benign calm to a wailing gale in the blink of an eye; of snow so deep it can hide a parking lot full of snowmobiles; and temperatures that plummet to minus 60° C and, in summer, soar as high as 32° C. His answer was that the majesty of the country could only be experienced by living there.

Canadian history was supposed to have begun about fourteen thousand years ago, when aboriginal ancestors made their way on foot across an ice-free, flat plain running from Siberia to Alaska, which is now part of the Bering Sea. The area was teaming with fauna – birds, fish, big game, including caribou and mammoths – so there was a good reason to come. Ice covered much of northern Canada, but when an opening occurred between glaciers, and a corridor – the continental spine formed by the Rockies and the Sierras – appeared, the northerners went south and found a virtual Garden of Eden. Eventually these people fanned out to the Pacific and Atlantic coasts.

It's a nice-sounding theory, but one that has now been shattered. Genetic research has pushed back the time of Canada's first human residents to forty thousand years, causing anguish in academia. Among the multitude of debates that have raged since that discovery is how the Rock Cree ended up where they did.

For years scholars assumed that the Cree moved from the south and east of Canada to the northwest during the early fur trade. Once they obtained guns from the white man, they were able to conquer whatever group of aboriginals occupied the west Shield country and get their hands on the beaver, otter, lynx that were plentiful there. But recently archeologists in northern Saskatchewan and Manitoba have uncovered arrowheads of what is called the Oxbow complex, dated around 2500 B.C. The precursors of the *asinīskāwiýiniw* were hunting here four thousand years before European fur traders showed up.[2] At Frog Portage, an important juncture connecting the Churchill River system to southern routes located forty kilometres from Pelican Narrows, archeological digs have uncovered scores of prehistoric artifacts – pottery shards, knives, tools of copper, arrowheads, bone implements – dating from the Clearwater Lake phase, A.D. 770–1500, the Manitoba phase A.D. 1000, and the Laurel phase from 500 B.C. to A.D. 500. As one scholar put it, such discoveries prove "that the Cree had a very long period of cultural development . . . and that they are not easterners who have pushed to the west and northwest in response to the fur trade."[3]

What was life like for that small population that thrived in Canada's boreal forest? One thing is for sure: they mastered their environment, as harsh and difficult as it was, or none of them would be living today. The trick was to pack light and keep moving.

At the end of August, before the yellow blaze of autumn, the annual family reunion came to an end. Lodges were dismantled, the poles left for someone else's use. Tricky portages studded the route north, so loads were kept as light as possible – a small packet of medicinal plants, a few caribou skins used as blankets, some leather clothing, a weapon or two. Babies were tightly packed in papooses and positioned on the mother's back. And then birch-bark canoes, themselves amazingly lightweight, would set off. One to four families, usually headed by related males – father, uncle, brother, father-in-law – would spend the fall and winter months together.

By mid-September the rutting season had begun; the forest echoed with the plaintive bellow of moose. Rock Cree were remarkably skilled with bow and arrow, and most years there was an abundance of stew and then dried meat and pemmican for the winter. And it wasn't just food the hunters were after; the hides of big game were at their most lush in fall, ideal for fashioning clothing.

Rivers and lakes were full of whitefish, trout, walleye, and, best of all, delicious sturgeon, the grease of which was used for cooking. The fish was dried, flaked, and packed in small pouches, nutrition for hunters and fishers who didn't want to be burdened with heavy lunch buckets.

In early November the small lakes and bays froze over. With canoes immobilized and the ice still too soft to walk on, travel was impossible. But after a couple of frosts, lakes would turn into glass, and hunting would begin again in earnest. Usually by this time heavy snow had fallen, which slowed down the travel of the moose, bear, deer, and Woodland caribou, making them easier to track and slay. Beaver, fisher, otter, and muskrat not only made tasty stew but were turned into fur-lined winter moccasins and other apparel.

If the rabbits were plentiful and the hunters sensed moose or caribou in the area, if there was an adequate water supply, and lots of dry dead wood,* the families might settle into their winter camp. More likely though, they'd move, and then move again. When big game was hunted down, the entire band would relocate near the carcasses. For a people who were completely transferable, this was easier than having to haul a dead moose or caribou for several miles back to camp.

This was the busiest time of year; everyone worked from dawn to dusk. Among the many tasks required of the women was the battening down of the lodge against the ferocious cold of January and February. The Rock Cree's winter dwelling, called a *megiwap* (which became wigwam to Europeans), was built of some thirty to forty flexible poles, sixteen to twenty feet long. This structure was wrapped around with birchbark, evergreen boughs, or sometimes moose or caribou hides, chinked with mud or moss. A central hearth was made out of stone, mud, and sand; rocks were used to capture and store heat. The smoke was directed by a pole through a gap in the top of the structure, which also allowed light to flood in. Since the wigwam was cone-shaped, the heat rose, and because the opening was so narrow, it travelled downward again. "It was a lot warmer than this room," says Philip Ratt, sitting in his drafty modern house in Pelican Narrows. "The comforts of home is what your description would be after spending a night in a wigwam."

The ground was carefully covered with fresh boughs of black spruce or balsam, which were changed by the women as soon as the slightest bit of dirt was discovered, usually every day. Silky bear skins were turned into sensuous bedspreads, soft caribou robes were made into sleeping bags, pajamas were stitched together from rabbit skin. H.S.M. Kemp, a fur trader working Rock Cree territory in the 1910s, remembered:

---

* Rock Cree of Pelican Narrows never used green wood, mainly because they never stayed long enough in one place for it to dry out. Philip Ratt, one of Pelican Narrows's elders, says the practice of gathering dead wood as needed continues today, because if one stores logs outside, neighbours will feel free to come and help themselves.

Winter nights in a tepee after a hard day of travel. . . . Feet
to the fire, head on a pillow. Above the fire and the lazy-
curling smoke, a rack for your clothing or the smoking of
meat. No lights other than the light of the fire itself, soft,
throwing weird shadows on the canvas wall. An ever-
present kettle of tea, soft conversation, and that smell of
balsam. . . . You can't forget the smell of freshly broken
balsam. No smell on earth has its equal.[4]

When the temperature dropped to minus 50° C or even minus
60° C, there was little anybody could do but huddle around the fire
and listen to the old tales. "Heed your grandmother (or grandfather)," the children were told. This was how the Cree's rich, colour-
ful mythology, its history spelled out in metaphor, was passed to
each generation. *Wisahkēcāhkw*, the trickster, *mīmīkwīsiwak*, little
hairy creatures who dwell underground, *pāhkāhw*, the skeleton
spirit, were only a few of the characters that danced in the shadows
of the *megiwap*. But it was the *witigo*, a human turned cannibal,
who sent real chills down the spine. And for good reason. If the fall
hunt had failed, if it was so frigid that no creatures stirred, hunger,
or even on occasion, starvation, threatened. Perhaps a warning was
needed that the eating of human flesh was beyond the pale.

More beaver and muskrat were harvested in March or April,
until warmish weather signalled that it was time to travel back to
where the canoes had been left in the fall. It was vital to get there
before breakup. This was the most dangerous time of year; that
soft layer, "destroyed ice" as the Cree called it, was often not
spotted until it was too late. The drowning of reckless adolescent
boys was the hazard parents feared the most. Still, once there was
some unfrozen water, gill nets could be used or simply a stick,
moose sinew, and a bone hook; walleye, northern pike, lake trout
were so hungry by this time that they practically threw themselves
hermen's arms.

ımmer approached, the Rock Cree were on the move
me to the gathering spot pre-arranged the year before,

on the shores of a lake or river where cool breezes might relieve the heat and drive away the black flies and the mosquitoes. Pelican Narrows, with its sandy beach in a bay protected by large wooded islands and its nearness to two lakes, Pelican and Mirond, full of northern pike, trout, white fish, and pickerel, was one of these summer meeting places. This was the joyful, relaxing time. Family and friends, yearned for all winter, were embraced. Feasts and dances were held and gifts were often exchanged. ". . . Magnificent presents were made of pelts, wearing apparel, etc.," wrote the Oblate missionary Father Marius Rossignol, in 1939. "Naturally the visitors who took away these presents had in turn to send invitations and give presents the following year."[5] Children swam. Women dried fish and gathered their bounty – blueberries, saskatoon berries, alder berries, bearberries, Mountain cranberries, wild rosehip, Labrador tea, wild mint, rock tripe, and a variety of other medicinal plants. Men fished, hunted small game, and gambled. The festivities never ceased – drumming, dancing, singing, and above all, flirting among the young. Courting went on; marriages took place. Everybody gossiped and told stories. Then came the important discussion. Where would the best hunting grounds be located in the fall? The canoes would soon be packed up, once again headed north. This routine, repeated every year, dictated how this particular society evolved.

Even the most cynical scholar agrees that there is one outstanding trait that distinguishes the Cree: generosity. As a matter of course, a successful hunter (or sometimes the eldest woman on his behalf) would visit each household in camp, distributing meat, fish, or hides among the less lucky. As Marius Rossignol wrote in 1939, "If he [the hunter] kept everything for himself, the others would say nothing and would make no uncomplimentary remark, but they would consider him stingy and miserly, and would give him nothing when they in turn would have luck in the hunt."[6] Comments Cree writer Joseph Dion, "The Cree was always ready and willing to share his last morsel of food with his neighbour." In so harsh a land, collaboration meant survival.

Alexander Kennedy, one of those ubiquitous Hudson's Bay Company managers, worked out of Cumberland House, the first inland HBC post. In 1815, at a time when most Rock Cree had not been directly influenced by white culture, Kennedy had this observation:

With regard to the general condition of the Indians. They are happy and content, void of ambition. Their wants are few [which] a country like this easily supplys. They take no thought, or feel no care for the future depending entirely on the chase for provision. . . .7

Kennedy was probably as correct as Anglo-Saxon blinkers would allow him to be. His observations smack of a theory which, over the years, anthropologists were eager to embrace. The Cree were a happy but simple people. Their technology was primitive, their artifacts elementary, especially compared with the magnificent totem poles of the Haida and the exquisite pottery of the Navajo. But, as the anthropologist Robin Ridington has pointed out, those who accepted this comparison were guilty of "artifactual chauvinism." Material possessions, so important to the European, were a burden to a nomadic people like the Rock Cree. What was important was the knowledge of one's environment. As Ridington writes,

For such people, techniques that can be carried in the mind and implements using locally available resources are far more cost effective than artifacts carried by hand. . . . I suggest that technology should be seen as a system of knowledge rather than an inventory of objects.8

Of course, there were ways of inscribing the collective wisdom of one's clan without carrying around a totem pole. On those dark nights in winter, while girls gathered around the fire, listening to stories about the *witigo* and the *wisahkēcāhkw*, they decorated bags, belts, moccasins, coats, arm and head bands with richly intricate, emblematic designs made using porcupine quills, brilliantly coloured by berry juice, yellow, red, blue, blue-green, brown, orange. On summer afternoons, women would chew away on pieces of delicately thin birchbark. When the wafer was unfolded, a world of birds, animals, insects, flowers, and geometric designs was revealed. And then there are the pictographs still found in Rock Cree territory. Stories of the origins of the Cree, of wars, of medicine men, of bear and moose spirits, of religious parables are all painted there on rock outcrops, a people's history in symbols.

The long evolution of Rock Cree society would take a dramatic turn in the early seventeenth century. In 1612–13 Sir Thomas Button, a Welsh sea captain, and his crew wintered at the mouth of the Nelson River. The expedition's goal was twofold: to find the Northwest Passage, a shortcut to the riches of the Orient, and to rescue Henry Hudson who had disappeared in the bay named after him the year before. Sir Thomas failed on both counts and returned from whence he came. But word spread among the aboriginal population of those strange, pale creatures with hair all over their faces. Six years later, the Danish explorer Jens Munk also set out to discover the same elusive passage, but was forced to winter on Hudson Bay at the Churchill River. When spring arrived, only Munk and two crewmen were still alive; sixty-one others had died of scurvy. The debris these expeditions left behind, and their weird rituals regarding the dead, must have amazed the Cree people; talk of these discoveries would have quickly passed down the moccasin pipeline. The mere notion of the European white man must have confounded and frightened the natives. Certainly it infringed on preconceived cosmologies, the nature of one's place in the world.

In 1684 the Rock Cree and the white man finally met face to face. The Hudson's Bay Company set up York Factory on Hudson Bay at the mouth of the Hayes River, in what is now northeast Manitoba. Its purpose: to collect furs from the Indians in return for European-made merchandise. There is a standard version of this first meeting between native and white, told many times to the Oblate missionary Marius Rossignol. The Hudson Bay Company sent traders up the Churchill River to try and attract customers to York Factory.

An old lady dreamed that there would be some strangers coming. "They won't look like us," she said. "And I don't know where they will come from." Sure enough that day a couple of big boats came from the direction of the falls and when they saw smoke at the camp, they came, of course, to visit. When the Indians saw all those men with whiskers – something they had never encountered before – they were afraid and ran into the forest – all except the old lady who stayed behind. The white traders, not knowing Cree, couldn't get much information from her, but they left her with all kinds of goods. When her kinsmen finally emerged from the bush, they were astonished to find her surrounded by all these treasures.[9]

Soon they were trading furs for kettles and guns.

The journey from Pelican Narrows to York Factory would have been arduous but doable in a single summer season, if all went well. There was always a chance, though, of starvation if something untoward happened, a violent storm, a forest fire, a shortage of game. Probably only a few adventurers undertook it, and probably only once every two or three years. It was easier to trade with Indian middlemen, even when one had to pay more for a knife or auger than at the post. These brokers would likely be Assiniboine or Swampy Cree, the travelling salesmen of the period, who traded European goods from York Factory for furs trapped by Indians further in the interior. Then, in 1717, the bleak Fort Prince William was built on Hudson Bay at the mouth of the Churchill River, which made the journey more direct for the Rock Cree;

probably a trading party now went out every summer. It was during one of these expeditions that a most horrible calamity, forever branded on Pelican Narrows's memory, occurred.

On a hot summer day probably around 1730, although the exact date has not been confirmed, families from South Deer, Deschambault, Amisk, and Pelican lakes were gathered in some sixty lodges on the sandy beach of Pelican Narrows.* All the men were away on a trading trip to Fort Prince William, except for two trusted elders, who were left to help the women. One of the old men dreamed that his people were in great danger and begged them to flee into the bush. He was ignored. The next morning they woke to the singing of Sioux warriors approaching in their canoes. With guns, knives, hatchets, the Sioux slaughtered every single person, the old, the sick, the women, the babies, all except two children, whom they carried off with them, and one of the elders, who was hiding in a cave. For the rest of his life, that old man heard the echoes of howling mothers watching their children's throats being slit.

The men arrived back that same day only to discover the terrible carnage. The surviving elder told them the direction the marauders had gone, and they immediately took after them, finding the two frightened children abandoned on a reef as they went. Eventually they ambushed the Sioux and shot to death every one except the headman and a companion. "They laid a log on the shoulders of each man and tied their arms with leather thongs. 'Do not kill me,' pleaded the Headman, 'I have many goods and tools that I can give you.' The Cree replied, 'No, you will pay for this great horror you have inflicted upon us.' They began carving the Headman with their knives, continuing so until the Headman was dead. They did the same thing to his partner."

Arthur Jan, after whom Jan Lake is named, was an English immigrant and fur trader at Pelican Narrows from 1913 to 1929.

---

* There are several versions of this story. I have used oral-history accounts, particularly that of Philip Ratt, HBC documents, and the research of Ron Merasty to piece together an account which I hope is close to the truth.

He thought the story of the massacre nonsense – another example of Indian hyperbole – until an elder showed him where the bodies had been buried: on top of the hill in the middle of the settlement. When he examined the site closely, Jan saw two unusual indentations. He knew the Cree would be upset if he molested their cemetery so he waited until nobody was around. He then began digging. Only three feet down he discovered scores of bones and several skulls, large and small, as well as a crude coffin, which, he surmised, housed the remains of the elder who died during the bloodbath. "The bones were well-preserved," he later wrote, "and I took two skulls. Then I covered up the holes and by the time the Indians returned, there was nothing showing and they knew nothing of what I had done."[10]

A few kilometres from the sandy beach where the killings occurred, at the point where Pelican and Mirond lakes meet, there is a fast-flowing narrows, its width an easy bow shot across. After the massacre, Cree guards patrolled this spot, stopping travellers from coming and going, forcing them to identify themselves. If a satisfactory answer wasn't forthcoming, the sentries either killed or imprisoned the strangers. This place became known as Opawikoscikan, Narrows of Dread. The contemporary high school is called Opawikoscikan, and Opawikoscikan is what traditional Cree-speakers call the reserve – an indication that the tragedy has never left the collective memory of these Rock Cree. (Philip Ratt claims Opawikoscikan is grammatically incorrect. He says it should be Wapāwikoscikanihk.)

Over the centuries, the Narrows of Dread has continued to seek revenge on outsiders. In 1912 a Hudson's Bay Company clerk, fresh from Shropshire, England, slipped the canoe he had just purchased into the Mirond Lake waters above the rapids and jumped in. In just a few seconds he overturned, and was drowned. And in late afternoon of November 18, 1936, Shorty Russick, a free trader based in Pelican Narrows, was on his way home after collecting about five hundred pounds of prime fur in the Churchill River area. As he approached the narrows, he heard a sharp cracking noise. Suddenly his team dropped through the ice. His dogs drowned, his precious cargo was lost, but Shorty managed to crawl on his hands and knees to shore and walk the five kilometres to his post. "All we can say is he's lucky he didn't go through also," wrote the HBC post manager. "But he had no damn business travelling in the dark."

The massacre of the Cree women and children by the Sioux at Opawikoscikan reveals that as early as the eighteenth century white man's culture had left an indelible mark on Rock Cree society. The use of guns, for example. The historian J.R. Miller puts it succinctly: "Before the intervention of the European there certainly had been war, but it had been small-scale, localized, and not very destructive. The introduction of firearms changed this pattern by making warfare more devastating."[11] It was not an easy task to track down a foe and then do him in with an arrow, club, or spear. With a musket, as unreliable and inaccurate as these weapons were, a killer would have a better chance of quickly doing away with his enemy. The first recorded use of a gun by an Indian – during an Algonkian raiding party into Iroquois territory – was in 1609, so certainly both Sioux and Cree would have had the use of firearms by 1730.

Secondly, the episode illustrates the growing appetite for newly arrived European merchandise. "Do not kill me," pleaded the Headman. "I have many goods and tools that I can give you." With what glee did the Rock Cree greet the iron kettles, needles, scissors, glass beads, wool blankets, duffle packs, knives, jewellery, not to mention tobacco and rum. But how much these material things changed their society is open to debate. For the first two centuries, apparently not much; life simply became a little easier with a needle made of iron rather than bone. Hunting tools and methods were not transformed; deadfalls and snares are used in much the same way to this day. As the historian Tony Morantz points out, raw materials and tools might have changed, but the skill it took to make snowshoes, canoes, toboggans, skin and bark tents, and clothing made of hides did not. "I am not denying that the Indians used European goods – any device which was labour – and time-saving – was welcome. However it is clear that the Indians did not become slaves to a new technology; other lifestyles and interests could, and did take precedence."[12]

And finally there's the question as to why the Sioux would commit such a terrible atrocity at Pelican Narrows. It had to do with the quarrelling European nations and their Indian allies. The Cree and Assiniboine had formed a working alliance, which included the Ojibwas and Mandans. It stretched from Hudson Bay to the Rockies and pretty well controlled the English fur trade. Operating on the philosophy that my friends' enemies are my enemies, the Assiniboines' long-time foes, the Dakota Sioux, became the *bête noire* of all the alliance nations, including the Cree.

After the establishment of York Factory, antagonisms heated up. The French, who began trading furs with the Indians from the time of Champlain in the early sixteenth century, were outraged that these interlopers, the British, were cutting into *their* fur trade. And the Sioux didn't like the idea that the Cree and Assiniboine were butting into their lucrative role as middlemen. It therefore didn't take much for the French to prod the Sioux into open warfare. Simply provide plenty of guns, ammunition, and promises of lucrative trade. The York Factory journal of 1729 indicates how successful the French were.

> Poetts (Sioux) had Destroyed most of our Senipoetts (Assiniboine) by the Instigation of the French. It is much to be wished for that our masters Could prevent the frenches constant Encouraging the Above Said poetts going to war with most of the Indians that Resorts to this place.[13]

A year after this was written the Sioux massacred the Cree women and children summering at Pelican Narrows.

Over the next several decades, the fact of the white man would become even more of a reality for the Rock Cree. In 1753 Louis- Joseph La Vérendrye, the son of the famous Franco-Canadian explorer La Vérendrye, was attracted to a bustling Cree summer village near present-day The Pas. There he established Fort Paskoyac. A year later the HBC's Anthony Henday passed by this post and described it in his journals: "The house is about 26 foot long, 12 foot wide, 9 foot high to the ridge, having a sloping roof, the walls log upon log, the top covered with birch rind, it is divided into three apartments, one for trading goods, and where the Master lives; one for the men; and one for the furs &c."[14] While it wasn't exactly in the backyard of the Pelican Narrows Cree, Fort Paskoyac was only a three- or four-day canoe ride away. Almost certainly they would have traded furs there.

The HBC's reaction to audacious traders from Montreal such as La Vérendrye was not to build inland posts to attract the neighbouring native trappers, but to dispatch frontmen like Henday to persuade the Indians to travel to York Factory, even if it meant a long journey. Between 1754 and 1774 fifty-odd HBC parties were sent inland. They travelled mostly around the Saskatchewan River where the Canadian traders from Montreal were doing a thriving business. And those Indians living further north must have encountered them.

In 1771 the Montreal trader Thomas Corry set up shop at a place called Fort Bourbon on Cedar Lake, two days' journey from The Pas. He specialized in goods of real quality, English-manufactured guns that actually worked and the best brandy found in the West. He even got his hands on Brazilian tobacco, always thought to be a monopoly of the Hudson's Bay Company. The Indians, upset at the HBC's often second-rate merchandise, rushed to do business with him. He was "astride the route of the Indians from Lake Winnipegosis and Cedar River to York Factory and in the way of gathering an easy and rich harvest of furs."[15] In two years, Corry had made enough money to retire. Thereafter a crowd of Canadian peddlers swarmed upcountry into the territory north of the Saskatchewan River.

The Hudson's Bay Company's business dropped precipitously, even after higher prices were offered for pelts. The chief factor at

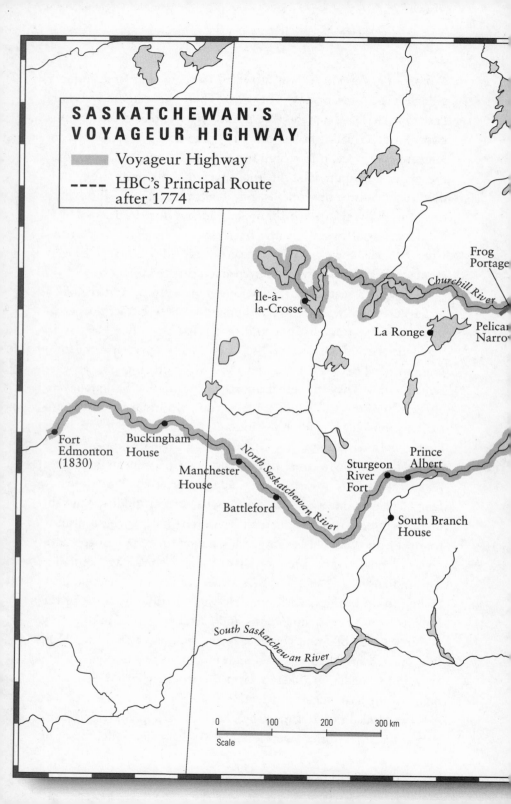

SASKATCHEWAN'S VOYAGEUR HIGHWAY

Voyageur Highway

---- HBC's Principal Route after 1774

Frog Portage

Churchill River

Île-à-la-Crosse

La Ronge

Pelica Narro

Fort Edmonton (1830)

Buckingham House

Manchester House

Battleford

North Saskatchewan River

Sturgeon River Fort

Prince Albert

South Branch House

South Saskatchewan River

0   100   200   300 km

Scale

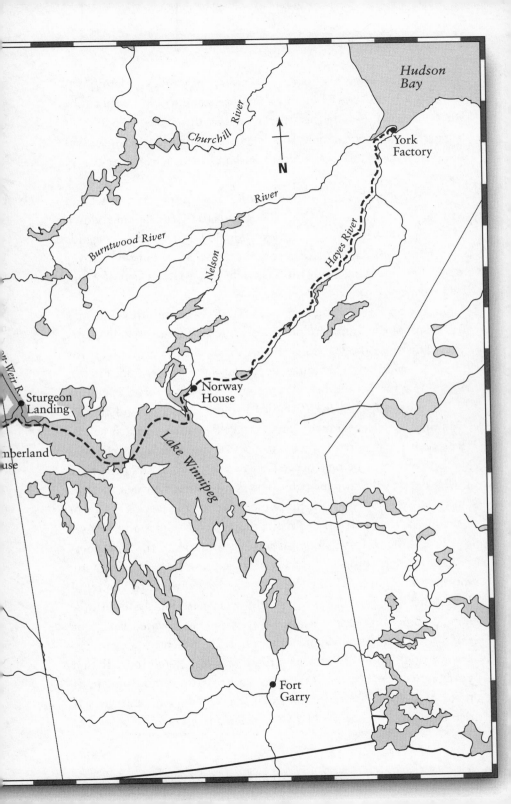

York Factory wrote his bosses in London that, unless inland posts were established, the Company's western trade would be ruined by the Canadians. Finally the HBC brass saw the light. In September 1774 their first permanent inland post, Cumberland House, was built on Pine Island in the North Saskatchewan River near Amisk (Beaver) Lake.

Starting at Pelican Narrows one can canoe southward on Mirond Lake, across the Corneille Rapids to Corneille Lake, down the Sturgeon-Weir River – a series of shallow but very tricky rapids – to the large Amisk Lake, south on the Sturgeon-Weir River again, finally ending up at the Saskatchewan River, a trip of about two days by canoe.

In the 1770s, though, it wasn't easy to trade with the Hudson's Bay Company at Cumberland House. Encircling the post, like ants after jam, were the Canadian peddlers, offering higher prices for furs. As Matthew Cocking, headman at Cumberland House, wrote, few furs would be collected at the post because, "they [the Indians] cannot pass the Circle of Pedlers that surround It, and even those that may come through the Pedlers most of them will be fleeced of great part of their Furrs." Cocking may have believed the natives were being "fleeced"; in reality the Canadians were giving better value for fur pelts. The competition between the two fur traders provided all the more incentive for the Rock Cree from Pelican Narrows territory to make the trip to Cumberland House.

Beginning in 1778 the Hudson's Bay and the North West companies, in their competition to attract Indian trappers, built many more posts inland. Pelican Narrows, located en route to Churchill River and Reindeer Lake, where furs were particularly luxurious, gained some importance as a stopover on the crowded voyageur highway. During the eighteenth and early nineteenth centuries several small outlets were set up there, but few lasted more than a year or two. Finally, in 1874, a permanent HBC establishment, at that time nothing more than a small shack, was erected at the settlement, not far from the Narrows of Dread.

Antoine Morin had been a tripper, travelling by dogsled to various winter camps and trading with the Cree; now he was in charge of the HBC post at Pelican Narrows. Fortunately for the missionary Oblates, he was a devoted Catholic. "Un métis français, le cher et excellent Antoine Morin me reçut comme l'envoyé de Dieux." ("A French Métis, the dear and excellent Antoine Morin, received me as the envoy of God.")[16] That summer the Oblate missionary Father Gasté was passing through Pelican Narrows, returning to his congregation at The Pas. He was amazed at how busy the little village on the shores of Pelican Lake was. Morin and Gasté put their heads together. Undoubtedly what was needed here was a Catholic mission, not only to save the souls of the pagan Indians but to garner valuable furs from native trappers. This would prove an unholy alliance indeed.

A pleasant spring day the following year, 1875. A little crowd of natives, many of them recently baptized into the Catholic faith, gathered in a circle on a pitch of ground overlooking the lake near the HBC post. Father Blanchet, the latest Oblate to visit Pelican Narrows, recited a benediction as he planted a cross to mark the future site of St. Gertrude's Mission.[17] The taming of *les sauvages* (savages) was underway.

Since 1840, Catholic and Anglican missionaries had been travelling from camp to camp converting the "infidels." The Reverend John Alexander Mackay, later Anglican Archdeacon of Saskatchewan, wrote in his diary of Sept. 1, 1870: "These Indians [connected to Pelican Narrows] . . . are favourably inclined to Christianity and in fact some are purportedly Christians." The reasons why Rock Cree accepted the Western religion so readily will be discussed in another chapter – horrific smallpox epidemics, shortage of game, similarities between the native religion and Christianity, all contributed – but in only forty years their rich spirituality would be driven underground and then lost. Cultural genocide is not too strong a term to describe the consequence of the campaign waged so relentlessly by the Christian missionaries.

William Merasty, a Pelican Narrows elder interviewed in the 1930s, remembered: "The first thing they did was take away our music. They hated it. The drum was the devil's instrument, they told us. I remember my father hid his under the bed, and when no priest was around, he'd pull it out and drum a bit. But after awhile he got tired of doing that. So we lost our music and when we lost our music we lost our spirit."[18]

A most effective way to destroy a person's culture is to wipe out that person's identity. Both Catholics and Protestants insisted that the natives take anglicized names before they could be baptized. Othapatchikew became John Alexander Cursitor (later Custer), Pinnases became John Bird, Tawepesim became Michael Michel, Michecappo became Duncan Cook, Wapaskokimaw became Alexander Bear. Since men were the heads of households, their family members took the last name as their own.*

Gilbert Michel is a respected elder in Pelican Narrows and the brother of Chief Ron Michel. An accident as a young man has left him confined to a wheelchair. He's hardly radical in his politics and was brought up a devout Roman Catholic – his neat little house sits directly behind St. Gertrude's Church. Yet he grows angry when the subject of missionaries is raised. "That was just wrong," he says, "for them to change our late grandfathers' names. It was the missionary and Indian Affairs that did that." When Gordon Peter is asked for his opinion, he wrinkles his nose and says maybe it wasn't such a bad thing. Before he became Peter

---

* There is a large family at Pelican Narrows that managed to keep their Indian name. The story goes that the head of the family had a spell cast on him, which prevented him from killing any game. Every time he went out, the moose or caribou would sense his whereabouts and run away. He realized he would have to do something brave and unusual to counter this hex. While standing on a hill, he saw a moose in the ravine. He found a good-sized birch, which he bent over, and just as the moose was leaving, he flipped himself into the air, over to the other hill, killing the moose with a slingshot as he flew. This daring feat was called something close to *sawaap* in Cree, and thus the large Sewap family at Pelican Narrows.

Ballantyne, his great-grandfather was called Wicikis, meaning "one who stinks."

In the spring of 1837 a family group, trapping on Acheninni Lake, stumbled across a boy of about eleven, all alone, trying to spear fish in a shallow rapids. They approached him, and the first thing everyone noticed was the dreadful smell that emanated from him. It was obvious what they would call him – Wicikis, "the stinky one." It was living with the bears – these narrows were their favourite spot for catching fish – eating suckers and anything else he could throw a rock at that gave him the disagreeable odour. It may also have been the animal hides he used as blankets. Rock Cree knew about the *moostoos*, "the buffalo," but had never seen one. Now they knew for sure that these animals smelled like the devil.

How the boy came to be by himself remains unclear. He could have got lost in the bush on the opposite side of the portage, and his family, perhaps encroaching on enemy territory, finally had to leave without him. Or perhaps they had all died of some illness, which is not improbable given the epidemics that periodically raged through the Indian territory. Whatever the case, while he was struggling for survival, he developed an ability to predict the future. Many Rock Cree still regard him as a prophet since much of what he forecast came true. "If white men come to our land," he was supposed to have said, "there will be a lot of them. Life is hard now, but it will be harder when the white man comes."

I chatted with Fred Ballantyne over a cup of coffee and a cheese sandwich in Pelican Narrows's one restaurant, called Medicine Rapids. (Not many natives patronize this place. At $8.50 for a loaded hamburger, it's too expensive.) Fred, an old-time hunter with a weathered face telling of his years in the bush, is the grandson of the original Peter Ballantyne. He recalls the old men describing how the uneducated, illiterate Wicikis "talked in the sand." He drew a checkerboard of lots, houses situated side by side, stores, churches, schools, and declared that this map was the Pelican Narrows of the future, this at a time when the community consisted of a half-dozen log huts. More famously he once held up a cup of water from Pelican Lake and said, "One day, my friends, you will have to pay for this." Every time Fred spots the bottles of Pure Springs in the Northern Store, he thinks of his grandfather's uncanny prediction. Pelican Lake is so polluted now that one can't drink the water near the shore.

Fred Ballantyne believes that it was during the time the boy spent alone – some people say days, others weeks – sleeping and dreaming that his special power evolved.

In the old Cree religion, every adolescent boy (and some girls) undertook an important coming-of-age vision quest. Sometimes the young person settled into a kind of nest far up in a secluded pine tree, sometimes a makeshift lodge beside a lakefront. There he fasted, slept, and dreamt. Eventually, as hunger pains set in, hallucinations would grab hold of the boy, and slowly from the tangle of *manitow* (spirits) who appeared before him, a dominant shape would begin to emerge. The boy would catch a glimpse of his *pawākan*. This was the spirit side of the wolf, bear, eagle, moose, beaver, just about any creature that would be his personal advocate, protecting him against physical and spiritual evil for the rest of his life. It's still a concept understood by many Rock Cree. "You use it if someone is trying to hurt you, make you sick. Yeah. You just . . . *iyako nimosom*! ['Let's go, my grandfather!'] Yeah, you say that: 'Go get him!'"[19]

Because of his prolonged time alone, says his grandson Fred, Peter Ballantyne developed a close relationship with a particularly dynamic *pawākan*, and with that his ability to predict the future.

Peter was taken in by the people who found him stranded. (There would eventually be three other sons, John, Noah, and Thomas.) At some point the family began using the anglicized last name of Parisia, adopted from the manager of a trading post in Lac La Ronge who had been born in the City of Light. Likely the Anglican minister didn't approve of hard-drinking Mr. Parisia, because he insisted the family take another name. First the label Hastings was tried, but the Indian pronunciation turned out to be "hestinks," too close for comfort to smelly Wicikis. Finally the solid Scottish name of Ballendine was chosen.

The HBC Cumberland Post records of 1819 list two brothers, William and John Ballanden from the Orkney Islands as steersmen on the York boats carrying freight on the inland waters at the time. Each of the brothers was judged a "good able man." Ballanden is a name particularly susceptible to change: Ballendine, Ballantine, Ballantyne, Ballenden, are all forms of the same Scottish surname. It may be that the "good and able" brothers, both Protestants, were considered proper role models for the natives, and their names appropriated.[*]

The Ballantynes hunted and trapped at Deschambault Lake, a large body of water shaped like an upside-down and backwards question mark, full of bays and channels. (The south section of the lake is today called Ballantyne Bay and there is a Ballantyne River.) Gordon Peter still has plenty of relatives at Deschambault, a pretty village which is now an official reserve, part of the Peter Ballantyne First Nation; his wife, Susan, was born and raised there. It's a kind of second home. For one thing, ice fishing here is considered the best anywhere.

On a sunny morning in the summer of 1876, at Fort Carlton on the North Saskatchewan River, Lieutenant-Governor Alexander Morris addressed an impressive gathering of Cree chiefs. Through an interpreter, he told the gathering: "We did not wish to interfere with their present mode of living but would assign them reserves and assist them as was being done elsewhere, in commencing to farm." The great leader Poundmaker famously replied: "This is our land, it isn't a piece of pemmican to be cut off and given in little pieces back to us." But with the buffalo gone, and starvation looming, there was nothing to do but agree to Morris's terms: a

---

[*] Ballendine did not change to Ballantyne until well into the 1920s. For clarity's sake, I have used Ballantyne throughout.

family of five would receive 640 acres of reserve land; a payment of twelve dollars would be made to every man, woman, and child to extinguish all future claims to the land; schools would be set up on reserves "whenever the Indians of the reserve shall desire it"; each Indian person would be paid five dollars per year, as well as a supply of rations; the Indians were "to pursue their avocations of fishing and hunting throughout the tract surrendered." The Indians in turn agreed to "cede, release, surrender and yield up the Government . . . all their rights, titles and privileges whatsoever, to the lands" covered by the agreement. Treaty Six was signed on August 23, 1876, by all the chiefs except the rebellious Big Bear.

The agreement was addressed to both "Plain and Wood Cree Indians" living in the vast expanse being surrendered by the Indians, from Cumberland House in the northeast to the Red Deer River in the southwest. But it would be another twenty-three years before the Rock Cree were admitted to the treaty. New settlers were itching for the fertile farmlands of the Plains Cree territory, but who wanted the scrub and granite occupied by the *asinīskāwiýiniw*?

As much as the white man had helped wipe out the buffalo, so had he mismanaged the Woodland fur-trade economy. By the mid-1870s, hard times had fallen on the Rock Cree. In 1879, Reverend Samuel Trivett wrote to Lieutenant-Governor David Laird,

> I assure you it has caused me much sorrow on visiting them [the Indians] this winter in their homes, both at Lac La Ronge, Pelican Narrows and other places to see how poverty reigns supreme. Children and parents have barely sufficient clothing to cover their bodies, not to speak of keeping them warm.[20]

An agreement with the government would at least put some hard cash into the people's hands. On February 7, a petition was sent to Laird, asking that Rock Cree be admitted to Treaty Six: ". . . we are unable to get sufficient furs to provide us with food and clothing, owing to the reduction on the price of furs, and the scarceness of the animals for which we have to depend on [for] our living."[21] It was signed by 105 trappers (some six hundred others were out hunting, but agreed with the request). Three months later came this curt reply from a bureaucrat: ". . . so far as I am aware, the Government has no intention of concluding a treaty with any northern Indians." Too bad if they are naked and starving to death.

Over the years the Anglican clergy and native leaders kept hounding the government. More petitions were sent, including one in 1886 that pointed out that these Indians "were loyal during the [Northwest] rebellion and therefore think they have a claim on the good offices of the Gov. on which they depend for a living." Officialdom remained unmoved. Finally, in February 1889, members of the James Roberts Band near Lac La Ronge and the Montreal Lake bands managed to convince the government that their hunting grounds were part of the lands ceded by the chiefs in the original Treaty Six. They, therefore, were legitimate adherents to this agreement. But the people who traded at Pelican Narrows, went to church, and spent their summers there, were considered to be outside the Treaty Six boundary. The solution seemed simple enough: join the James Roberts Band.

In 1893 Peter Ballantyne – the foundling had grown into manhood – his brother Noah, and their sons travelled to Potato Lake near La Ronge to do just that. They arrived in the pouring rain on Treaty Day. The Ballantynes waited hours in line, along with those collecting their rations and payments, and finally got their chance at the treaty commissioner. He abruptly brushed them aside. "No time to listen to that nonsense today," he insisted. A year later, this time armed with a letter from Archdeacon Rod McLennan, they argued their case again. Finally they were admitted to the James Roberts Band and received their treaty money. Interestingly, many Pelican Narrows people did not follow suit. They were not ready to subject themselves to a chief who lived 280 kilometres away and a band composed almost entirely of "strangers." What they demanded was their own political entity.

Finally, an Indian Affairs official travelled to the settlement to investigate the situation first-hand. Overnight the formation of a separate band with its own chief and two headmen (councillors) made imminent sense. It wasn't so much that the Cree had pleaded many times for this arrangement, but rather that it would save money. If the Pelican Narrows people were to remain in the James Roberts Band, the chief and government officials would have to make the long trip to their home village frequently. ". . . As the distance is so great the expenses of their trips will amount to more than the extra cost of having a Chief and Headmen at Pelican Narrows."[22] The Indian agent at Prince Albert, H. Keith, obviously had no idea of how important the new political set-up was to the Cree. In his report that year, he described, in page after page, the furnishings at Little Hills School and the cost of gilling twine at Lac La Ronge. The formation of the Peter Ballantyne Cree Nation, which was to become one of the largest and most important in Canada, was alluded to in five short sentences.

On August 24 and 25, 1900: The treaty party, which usually consisted of an Indian agent (often called a paying officer), his clerk, a doctor, a Mountie or two, and sometimes an Anglican or Roman Catholic missionary, arrived for the first time at Pelican Narrows. Every inhabitant, including the dogs, gathered to greet them as they paddled ashore. The paying officer did his business out of the Hudson's Bay post office, checking off names from a long list as he doled out twelve dollars for every man, woman, and child on a one-time only basis for relinquishing their rights to a vast tract of land, as well as the five-dollar yearly payment. The rations, a cup of flour per person, tea, salt pork, lard, bullets and shells, rabbit-snare wire, and twine used to make fish nets were distributed in an encampment outside. The Rock Cree didn't eat bannock at that time, so the flour was of little use. The hundred-pound cloth bags, though, made lovely dresses for the daughters. The five dollars in cash bought extras: buttons, beads, tobacco, printed cotton cloth at the Hudson's Bay store.

It was a happy, boisterous time. All day long there was dancing and laughter and debating. A meeting and election area was fenced off next to the HBC post. "When a man wanted to talk about this or that, he'd just get up and stand in the centre and talk," recalled John Dorion, who attended that first Treaty Day and was interviewed in 1970.[23] It was here that chief and headmen were elected. These were important positions, not only for the prestige, but also for the money – the chief received twenty-five dollars per annum and each headman fifteen. All three were given a spiffy new suit of clothes every year. The paying officer had the authority to appoint these officials himself, but he had sense enough to let the people decide. It was a close, exciting race. The command was given "For chief," and each head of a household hustled over to stand behind the person they favoured. When the dust settled, twenty-four votes went to Peter Ballantyne; eighteen to John Cursitor (Custer). As was the tradition, the band was named after the first chief; today, it is still called the Peter Ballantyne Cree Nation.

In the contest for the two headmen, Peter's brother Thomas Ballantyne won the most votes, twenty-five, and second place was a tie between yet another Ballantyne brother, Noah, and John Cursitor (Custer). John was given the position over Noah; government authorities did not want a native dynasty established.

Because of the people's peripatetic hunting life, there was no talk about what land would be set aside for the new band; it would be another thirty years before Pelican Narrows was officially named a reserve. When prospectors discovered copper and gold, when lumberjacks began chopping trees, when fishing became a lucrative business, suddenly the North was valuable. Only then would the Indians be dealt with.

In August 1904 the Indian agent Joseph Courtney visited Pelican Narrows for the first time. He was enchanted:

> The Roman Catholic church, newly finished in substantial and artistic style, built on a gentle elevation and surrounded by a few small but neatly built cottages, ensconced in the shelter of a sandy bay at the foot of a towering hill

overlooking a lake with a thousand islands, formed a delightful picture . . . numerous little gardens of potatoes and vegetables, made us question if it were possible that we were 450 miles north of the international boundary.[24]

At the turn of the century, Pelican Narrows was a bustling but still tiny village. It consisted of the Hudson's Bay Company post, made up of a store, an office, a house for the manager, and a warehouse recently expanded, the imposing Roman Catholic Church – "the walls are painted white, roof red, there is a tower and bell" – and ten log cabins, primarily for the families of Métis and half-breeds who worked for the HBC in manual jobs or as trippers. Few Cree trappers had as yet laid down roots.

At that point the Peter Ballantyne Band numbered 376 members, seventy men, eighty-three women, and 223 children and young people under the age of twenty-one. These people were still conducting life as they always had: travelling to hunting and fishing grounds, trapping in late fall and spring, and summering in wigwams at Pelican Narrows. There was a change, however, and a perceptive Indian agent noticed it: a basic skill which only a few years before no Rock Cree could survive without was being lost. "Game is becoming somewhat scarce; and even if it were more plentiful, all Indians are not skilful hunters, much less skilful moose-hunters; and it is only the cunningest and hardiest who can venture to leave the fishing waters and pushing inland depend upon their guns for a livelihood."[25] This meant that, when the fishing was poor, the natives were in trouble. The HBC post manager was succinct in his 1900 journal. March 3: "No furs arrived, Indians all starving. (No fish.)"*

Still, the Pelican Narrows Cree were surprisingly prosperous. Some of them had bank accounts – an aggregate of four thousand

---

* The HBC post managers used the term "starving" often. Since nobody ever seemed to die of lack of food, it was probably an exaggeration. They probably meant hungry.

dollars – in Winnipeg and Prince Albert.[26] What was astonishing about this was that hard cash was almost non-existent in the community. The only currency used was called Make Beaver, the value of a pelt, set down in a notebook and used to pay off debt or buy goods in the trader's store. "When they said 'once the pelt' this meant fifty cents," recalled Mary Ann Morin, in a 1984 interview. " 'Twice the pelt' was one dollar. This was the money system called Make Beaver." The Indian agent reported in 1900, "The only time these people ever see money is at treaty payments, not another look even at a dollar bill until next payments; as for silver, there is no such thing ever heard of. If one buys a plug of tobacco for 15 cents, he has to take his change of a dollar in goods he does not want."[27]

For the Cree families, the village, as well as serving as the centre of commerce, was the place of celebration, of special events, of solemn rituals. The HBC post journal for 1902 gives a taste of this panorama. "January 26: George Cursitor (Custer) came in today. Brought some fine moose meat. February 3: Thomas Ballantyne . . . brought a good lot of mink and other furs. April 21: Joe Linklater's little boy died last night. Buried today. April 24: Six deer passed in front of the post about noon. Pat Ballantyne went after them and killed the whole bunch of them. June 3: Elias Motto's girl, Harriette, died after an illness of only two days. June 25: Indian women off for rabbit hunt. July 3: Indians killing very few rabbits. August 18: the priest gave us a display of fireworks in the evening. August 25: Pierre Okikeur today married Julienne, daughter of William Nattawayuse. Dances all night and day. November 11: Philip Linklater's eldest son strayed away and got lost. His father found him five days after, stiff, cold, and face eaten by whisky-jacks. December 25: Xmas midnight mass celebrated. All Ballantynes in."

Peter Ballantyne's term as chief went well. In 1902 he told Sergeant W. Parker of the North-West Mounted Police, "There is no sickness amongst the people. All have plenty of food. We have no complaints." Says his grandson Fred Ballantyne, "In those days the chief was like a king and the headmen were like police. If one of them told you to do something, you did it. There was no money, so no corruption." And there was absolute loyalty to the Queen and the Dominion government. Says Philip Ratt, "The treaty commissioner set his own criteria [for chief]. The person had to be a respectful resident of the band, a strong family man, and a good worker. A living model to others." In a photograph taken on Treaty Day in August 1917, Peter Ballantyne is wearing a smart wool jacket with gold buttons and stripes on the collar and cuffs, a fitted wool vest, and a snazzy neck scarf. His chief's medal is proudly displayed on his chest, a Maple Leaf pin is attached to his vest. His grey hair curls at his neck and is nicely combed; he has a little moustache and beard. This could have been as much a picture of an Ukrainian homesteader as of an Indian chief.

Peter and his wife, Marie – everyone affectionately called her Oochikichum – were blessed with a large family – sons John, David, Abraham, Jacob, Cornelius, Elias, Thomas, and daughters Mary, Nancy, and Katherine. The marriage was reported to have been a happy one. Mary Ballantyne Senior died in 1901 at about sixty years of age. Four years later, Peter remarried, this time to a Barbara Bird of the James Roberts Band. But only a few months later, in the early fall of 1905, she too passed away. Peter was a sadder and quieter man in the years that were left to him.

August 4, 1914: The wind raged from the southwest driving forward sheets of black rain. Nobody ventured into a canoe, so the Hudson's Bay post at Pelican Narrows was quiet. The manager thought the weather was weird; the lake was boiling, not something that was often seen in August, and there were big pellets of hail that damaged his carrot and tomato crop. He would learn only weeks later, by mail, that the First World War had been declared on that day. Pelican Narrows was so completely cut off from the outside world – no roads, no telegraphs, no radios, mail that took as long as a month or two to be delivered – that Europe might as well not have existed. By treaty the Indians could not be conscripted, so they were not worried about that. Life simply went on as usual. The temperature fell to minus 52° F in February. The trader "Elias the Jew" arrived with three loads of goods. Mrs. Ballantyne (women's first names were never given), wife of Peter's brother Noah, died. Noah Ballantyne remarried. Reverend Edwards arrived from Stanley Mission to give services in the Anglican Church. Abraham Ballantyne came in with two hundred rats (muskrats). The priest left for his usual fall fishing trip at Medicine Rapids. Throughout the entire four years, the post manager did not mention the terrible war raging overseas once.

Nonetheless there were consequences. The London fur market temporarily closed. The HBC governor ordered its employees in Canada not to buy any pelts during the winter and spring of 1914. "Things were pretty grim at that point," said William Merasty, "most of the men stopped trapping and went hunting so they could feed their families." Fortunately, fur auction houses sprang up in the United States and Canada, real competition for the HBC in London. By 1917, fur prices had picked up again. During the Roaring Twenties, mink caps, red fox coats, mink cuffs became all the rage across North America and Europe. For the Pelican Narrows Rock Cree it was something of a golden age. Three trading posts – the Hudson's Bay Company; the Revillon Frères, a Paris-based firm; and independent trader Arthur Jan – all catered to trappers. If you didn't get the price you wanted at the HBC, you went to the French outfit, or Arthur Jan's house. One thousand dollars, formerly an unheard of sum, could be earned per year if one was a conscientious and clever trapper.

But trapping wasn't the only good fortune that smiled on Pelican Narrows during those years. A rich zinc and copper ore body was discovered that would become the foundation of the present-day Hudson Bay Mining and Smelting Company. Then in 1915 came a gold strike at the south end of Amisk (Beaver) Lake. Suddenly, "there were more prospectors than mosquitoes," as one native put it. On hunting and trapping trips the Rock Cree kept their eye out for precious minerals, although they weren't always sure of what they were looking for. Hundreds of samples were brought in to be examined by the trader Arthur Jan who was also a keen prospector. Usually these were ordinary worthless rock, but now and then something looked promising, and a party would travel to the site. These were strenuous trips by canoe which often took more than a month. On one such occasion, Alphonse Bighetty of Pukatawagan brought in a sample rich with bornite (copper), which he had found on the north arm of Granville Lake. After a long and arduous journey, Bighetty, Jan, and an experienced prospector, Bob Kerr, arrived at the spot where Alphonse had come across the mineral. But as Arthur Jan later wrote, "the old chap had already chipped out all there was of the ore except a few small fragments . . . Kerr said it was probably deposited there in the glacial period and if there was a body of the ore, it would likely sit in the middle of Granville Lake."

The scent of gold spilt over into the 1930s. When the rest of the province was suffering horribly from drought and the Great Depression, four charter airlines were flying prospectors across the north, and at the same time hauling fur pelts out. Radio finally came to Pelican Narrows in 1936, as did outboard motors, cylinder phonographs, high-powered rifles, and canvas-covered canoes. Like everyone else, the natives loved radio programs. Arthur Jan remembers seeing Albert Ballantyne and David Custer, headphones on, arguing over whether the song they were listening to was "Annie Laurie" or "The Last Rose of Summer." "It showed how poor the reception was," said Jan.

Nineteen-thirty had been a year of celebration for another reason. Part of Pelican Narrows was finally decreed Reserve 184B by a Canadian government Order-in-Council.

In 1911 Chief Peter Ballantyne had first requested that the band be allotted its 128 acres per person spelled out in Treaty Six. It would take nineteen years to accomplish this, partly because the populace had settled in different spots over a huge area, and all insisted that their community must become a reserve. Eight families of Ballantynes, including the chief, wanted the largest portion of the reserve to be located near their camps at Sandy Narrows, just south of Pelican Narrows, where, they claimed, the best trout and whitefish in the whole territory was found. The Cursitor (Custer) clan insisted that land on the Sturgeon-Weir River near Amisk Lake was better suited; headman John Custer had planted a vegetable garden there for many years, and had even kept cows and a horse. Cornelius Whitebear, the chief who followed Peter Ballantyne, wanted acreage on the west side of Deschambault Lake where there was soil suitable for growing hay. Everybody assumed there'd be a reserve at Pelican Narrows, where the missions and trading posts were situated, but they thought – mistakenly – that its population would never be large because it would never play an important role. There were only fourteen houses, mostly log cabins. In 1922 the Dominion land surveyor arrived, and he certainly agreed with the assessment that Pelican Narrows was not exactly prime real estate:

> the south part of the settlement around the houses and improvements is fairly well cleared, and consists of rocky ridges running in a north-easterly direction with rather swampy gullies between them. The remaining part of the settlement consists mostly of rocky ridges with a thin covering of soil in places and well wooded with aspen, birch, spruce, and Jack pine . . . It is not a very suitable location for a settlement. I would consider the land in itself worth very little, the better areas might be worth 50¢ an acre.[28]

In the end the simplest thing to do was create seven families under one roof: Sturgeon-Weir, Amisk Lake, Birch Portage, Pelican Narrows (lots four and six), Sandy Narrows, Woody Lake, and Mirond Lake became separate reserves, but all part of the Peter Ballantyne Cree Nation.

Over the years Pelican Narrows bucked the odds and blossomed into a bustling place where both whites and natives wanted to live. Indian agent W.R. Taylor described the settlement in 1927:

"I visited a number of the houses and gardens at this place and found the houses clean and the gardens looking nice, that is the potatoes."[29]

Even as white society with its surveyors, pilots, prospectors, and radio technicians infringed on the Cree, the rhythm of hunting, fishing, trapping had not changed much. But a government edict handed down in this interwar period was to transform their lives and the nature of Pelican Narrows village itself.

In 1920 the federal government's Indian Act was amended to make attendance at school compulsory for every native between the ages of seven and fifteen and residential schools were built to accommodate the new law. Suddenly the Rock Cree, who considered their children their most precious possession, were forced to wave goodbye to their sons and daughters in mid-August, knowing they would not see them again until late June the following year – a tragedy that all but destroyed the community. Ida Swan, an attractive schoolteacher in her mid-fifties, who lives in one of the nicest houses on the reserve, believes the residential school experience has undermined the generosity and co-operation that was at the heart of Cree society. "I think the old people still have it. If you help the old people, some way or another they'll find a way to help you. It's my generation. We were sent to residential school and all that got killed off. And we in turn have passed it on to our own children." J.B. Custer attended Guy Residential School for years: "We can't erase what has happened to us during childhood. It will stay with us at all times. Sometimes I have a silent cry."

This pattern would repeat itself through generations until the 1950s, when a full-time day school was finally opened on the reserve. Parents were then forced to settle permanently at Pelican Narrows, because the government threatened to cut off their family allowance cheque if their kids weren't in school. There was no consideration given to alternative ways of providing education, the building of smaller schools near winter hunting grounds, for example, and no imagination used to create a different type of teaching, tailoring correspondence courses so that students could still join their parents on the trapline. "The government said, we won't build a school out there. You gotta go to school here," says Gerry Morin, the provincial court judge and Michael Bomek's nemesis. "Who made that decision? Do you think the people did? No. And the chickens came home to roost." The Rock Cree way of life was profoundly altered. The father would now have to tend to the trapline by himself or with other men, and his wife would stay in the settlement with the children.

"People used to come and go," recalls Ida Swan. "There used to be log houses in Pelican. You just moved in, wherever one was available." "There was a little bit of housing assistance," remembers Philip Ratt, "a few windows, a door and roofing material, some nails, just enough to build a log cabin." In 1926 the Anglican diocese of Saskatchewan had reported that 142 Treaty Indians and eight whites lived in the little village of Pelican Narrows; in 1961 the total number of people had risen to 628. Forty years later the population of the reserve had grown by 18 per cent to 2,800. Sixty per cent are under the age of twenty-one.

Gordon Peter was born in 1958, and his early childhood wasn't much different than his great-grandfather's, the old chief Peter Ballantyne. He spent most of it on his father's trapline. It was a happy time. "I would go with my late mom, and aunties, and grandmother to gather some moss from muskeg, and snare rabbits, and find medicine plants. They had a lot of places where they grew their vegetables, mostly potatoes. The only time we had money was when my father killed something like a beaver and sold it to the Hudson's Bay Company. He and my uncles hunted for food – moose, caribou, beaver, muskrat. I remember the cache, the storage, was about three feet high. They kept the fresh meat on top, the dried meat next, and a little lower the fish. They used to punch a hole through the fins and hang them upside down to drain all the blood away. They tasted better that way."

By the time Gordon Peter turned six, the Chachakew Roman Catholic Day School had been built at Pelican Narrows, so he was fortunately saved from the devastating experience of being sent away from home to residential school. Still, his first encounter with the white race wasn't exactly pleasant. "The nuns were really mean," he says. "I still remember standing in the corner with my nose against the wall. They put gum on my nose, because I was caught chewing. And when the lay teachers came along they were worse. They used the strap more often."

By that time the Ballantyne family had acquired a permanent home in Pelican Narrows, a one-room log cabin, sixteen feet by twenty feet. It was not much different than the tents or rough shacks they used in the bush. It was all right, says Gordon Peter, when only he, his parents, and his two brothers lived there, but more children kept coming along, ten in all. By the 1970s Roderick Ballantyne was having trouble feeding and sheltering his brood, all going to school in Pelican Narrows. And he was not the only one.

In 1967 only three people in Pelican Narrows had steady, year-round jobs: two caretakers and a clerk in the store; the rest were still hunting their food and trapping as they always had. The fur trappers grossed on average $586 a year. The total income of all six hundred people living in the community was $86,700 – in other words $145 per person per year.³⁰ "Pelican Narrows was one of the poorest places on earth," wrote a researcher, white of course, not realizing that the bush economy was still in operation.

The community was still isolated. Mail was flown in once a week. A SaskPower generator provided electricity every now and then. Television would not arrive for another few years. There was no telephone, only telegraph, and the Department of Natural Resources radio connected Pelican Narrows to the outside world. The houses looked ramshackle, especially the tottering, old out-houses, but they were simply convenient log cabins that had sprung up like mushrooms.

Celena Bone's parents died in the early 1940s while she was only a baby. She was looked after by her paternal grandparents who lived in Pelican Narrows until she was five. Then she was shipped off to residential school at Sturgeon Landing. Since she was considered an orphan, she spent most of her girlhood being cared for by nuns. She considers this a blessing – eventually she would become a nurse, and she avoided the difficulties of growing up on the reserve. She says, "My friends describe their life as a child in Pelican as hard work, especially in the winter. There was no electricity, and no running water. They had to cut a hole in the ice to get water – those pails were really heavy and they had to carry them quite a ways to their house. If it was wash day, there was extra water to haul. They had to chop wood, and saw wood. Their father or eldest brother were out trapping and somebody had to maintain the house and keep it warm."

"It was beautiful then," says Susan Custer, former chief of the Peter Ballantyne Band. "You didn't see garbage lying around like you do now." And Suzette Ratt: "This reserve used to be so pretty. There were so many trees. And people were friendly, they liked to visit." "It was very quiet," comments Gilbert Michel. "In those day we had lots of recreation, soccer and softball. All men and some of the women played." "You knew the people and grew up with them," says Gilbert's half-brother Napoleon Michel. "You accepted them as your brothers and sisters." "There used to be lots of birds and animals," adds eighty-year-old Mary Custer. "Now there's too many people and too many buildings."

By the 1960s, the white world was sneaking up on Pelican Narrows. The Jan Lake Recreation Area, only an hour and a half away by motorboat, was setting down roots. Eventually it would turn into a holiday mecca for whites acting out their dream of the True North. For a while it provided the opportunities it was supposed to for the natives of Pelican Narrows. Jobs were to be had in the construction of the outfitters' lodges and private cottages. Fishing guides were hired, as well as cabin cleaners and maintenance workers in the beautiful government-owned campsite. But, as the years passed, the original proprietors, most of whom had grown up in the north and had had some appreciation of Cree history and culture, sold out to entrepreneurs. Intolerance and impatience became a motif. It was simply easier to hire apple-cheeked teenagers to motor people to fishing holes marked on a map than to put up with the eccentric timetable of a weathered old native guide who actually knew where the pickerel were to be found. In time, the two communities would grow completely apart, two worlds, two cultures. Laurie Ballantyne, Gordon Peter's sister, says, "It was never like that when we were growing up. I don't know why they [the lodge owners] would be like that now. You can't even walk in there now and be left alone just to look around. They'll stand there and watch your every move. I don't even like going there any more."

In 1968 Pelican Narrows's isolation came to an abrupt end; an access road, Highway 135, was built connecting the community with the main Highway 106, most often called Hanson Lake Road. Flin Flon was now an easy eighty kilometres away, Prince Albert was reachable in three hours. (Highway 135 may be the worst road serving a community the size of Pelican Narrows in Saskatchewan. Still unpaved, full of sharp curves, blind corners, steep hills, narrow lanes, it's a nightmare to drive, especially at night. Crosses dotting the roadside attest to a number of fatal accidents.) Many of the elders of the community had opposed it. "The old men were really wise," says Fred Ballantyne. "They don't want no road. They told us not to. No, never. Like my dad, David Ballantyne, and Solomon Custer, and all the old fellows. They were really holy people. They knew what trouble would come."

In the wake of the bulldozers and steamrollers came bootleggers, drug pushers, and the army of social workers needed to help clean up the mess. "When I was growing up," says Cindy Ballantyne, a single mother of five children and a cousin of Gordon Peter's, "there was hardly any drinking, no drugs, no gangs, not much violence, few suicides. Now look at it."

BENNETT HALKETT

He took his father's trapline
a 48 mile square of woods and lakes.

A winter's yield of furs was good
enough to feed a family of six.

Then the pulp mill came to Prince Albert:
chainsaws screamed and trees collapsed.

Bulldozers ripped roads through trees
So trucks could rumble their loads away

and lakes became targets for campgrounds
and cabins with more roads. The animals

alarmed with this intrusion moved
farther into the forest away from the furore.

Finally the government claimed his trapline
made him another victim of our northern vision.

Now Halkett sips his beer slowly and reflects
while the worm of anger gnaws inside him:

I fought for this country during the war
Now why would they want to do this to me?

Glen Sorestad
Jan Lake Poems

2

niso

THEY DO BUSINESS

ATĀWEWAK

Gordon Peter was ten years old in 1968 when he went out on the trapline for the first time. He wanted to get right in there, but his father insisted, "Watch what I'm doing first, and learn." Finally, after he mastered the art of snaring rabbits, he was given his own beaver traps. One day he and his dad set out to check their lines at Marshall River some twenty kilometres from Pelican Narrows. On their arrival they headed off in different directions. Peter was late getting back to the snowmobile – the light was fading – so he didn't see the creature right away, in fact he had stowed his ammunition in his backpack and was about to place it and his rifle on the box sleigh. There, sitting in the driver's seat, as though it were waiting impatiently to get back to town, was a very large coyote, its black fur glistening in the late afternoon sun. Gordon Peter let out a screech and jumped about ten feet. His father came roaring out of the bush, laughing his head off. Roderick had shot the coyote and had sat it up straight, waiting for Gordon Peter.

For years father and son have laughed at this story. Today, though, Roderick sits playing solitaire and hardly nods when his son walks in. He lives in a plain little bungalow with yellow siding and brown wood trim. Like most Pelican Narrows buildings, it has suffered its share of graffiti and broken windows, but Roderick always makes sure this damage is repaired. The interior is immaculately clean and it's prettily decorated. There are three bedrooms: one for his daughter, Laurie, one for the baby of the family, George, and one for Roderick himself.

On this particular day he is not feeling himself. He's been ill lately, partly a result of too many drinking binges combined with old age. He's seventy-one. George tries to cheer him by unveiling a large portrait of suffering Jesus that he has had framed, and Roderick does brighten when he sees it. But it's the time of year that really gets to the old trooper. It's a glorious autumn day, the yellows and reds are stunning, the first breath of winter is in the wind, exactly the season he used to relish. For sixty-five years, from the time he was a small boy, to 1992, when his beloved wife and helpmate, Sarah, died suddenly of a heart attack, Roderick Ballantyne trapped furs for a living. "It was like an obsession," says Gordon Peter of his dad. "The more he did it, the more he wanted to do it. But after my mother's death, he lost heart." Roderick's children believe he has never stopped mourning Sarah. Booze and his religion are his true comforts now.

In the old "Catholic" part of the reserve, where houses are perched at every angle, Fred Ballantyne lives with his wife, Margaret, and their grandson. "Trapping is my life," he says and, at age seventy-four, he still goes out in the fall. "When I am out in the bush, I have a bible written in Cree syllabics. I can read that. And I sing hymns – as loud as I can."

His childhood was spent in the bush with six families living together in one cabin on the shores of north Wood Lake. The wives stayed in the camp minding the kids, cooking, cleaning, and stretching the pelts. Fred, his father, his uncle, and his brother, would check the traps, lay the bait, readjust the trap spring, bag the beaver or fox or mink. They'd cover twenty to twenty-five kilometres a day on snowshoe; then they'd sleep in the bush, on evergreen branches woven together to make a mattress, canvas covering them. Next day they'd work the line the other way and end up again at the six-family cabin. There was nothing to do at night unless the neighbouring trapper with the little radio and huge battery invited them over. One of Fred's fondest memories is listening to the Joe Louis–Max Schmeling fight from Madison Square Garden.

In the "suburbs," not far from Opawikoscikan (Narrows of Dread), Philip Ratt and his wife, Suzette, live with a great-grandson in a neat-as-a-pin house. Their view is glorious: Macaroni Bay spreads out before them, rimmed with trees of every colour. But their house is small, too cold in the winter, and mildew is spreading. Philip has a serious heart condition, and a doctor has told him that he should not be living in such an environment. It's the band council's prerogative to allocate new houses, and so far nothing has been slated for him. It's surprising, given how much the man has done for his community. For years he was an energetic spokesperson for the fur industry. He started the Treaty Trapping Association, he was a member of the Assembly of First Nations' Harvesters committee. He held a seat on the Fur Institute of Canada board, worked for the Saskatchewan Federation of Indian Nations, and, in 1996, when the European Union threatened to ban Canadian fur products, he was a part of the delegation who travelled to Brussels to talk the politicians out of it. He is very sharp, with a mind that remembers details, dates, and names, and he is a fearless, articulate debater. Because of his censorious manner and his uncompromising fury over issues he feels are destroying his family and community, booze, for example, he is not the most popular man on the reserve, but he is one of the most respected.

These three old trappers have much in common. All are directly related to the first chief: Roderick and Fred are grandsons of Peter Ballantyne; Philip is a great-grandson. All are fine-boned, wiry, and neatly dressed – Fred has a certain flare, with his longer hair and a rakish muskrat hat (partly chewed by his dog). Collectively they know every secret there is to know about the fur-trapping trade. But what value is this, they say, when no one can make a living at it any more?

They no longer have to haul water – running water arrived twelve years ago – or chop wood, and their houses are now heated by electricity or propane. They won't starve to death if moose, fish, or rabbits are in short supply; they buy food at the local grocery store with their government pension cheques. And yet all three believe that, difficult as it was, their trapping in the bush made for a better life than the one their children are living today.

Aboriginal people were, of course, snaring and trapping millennia before the European fur trade snaked across this country. But they had a different attitude towards fur-bearing animals than that of the French or the British. There was no commercial trade; the creatures they caught, they ate and made into coats, blankets, and other useful items. As one scholar put it, "Production and consumption were perfectly balanced," creating "a harmonious economy."[1]

Number one among the fur bearers was that industrious, flat-tailed, big-toothed rodent, the beaver. Because its habitat is so wet and cold, it is protected by two coats of fur, the glossy, long-haired outer layer and a thick under-fur made up of strands that are spiked at the end. The winter attire of the northern Cree was made from several beaver pelts stitched together with leather thongs. Eventually the outer layer of the fur coat would rub away leaving only the soft inner fur. These garments were called *castor gras* or "greasy beaver" by the French, and were particularly attractive to European merchants, for they made ideal felt, the material in the stylish top hat – "The Wellington," "The D'Orsay," "The Regent," "The Paris Beau" – that was so popular with the British upper class in the eighteenth and early nineteenth centuries. Indians were taken aback when they discovered how much the Europeans coveted their shabby old coats. That these foolish foreigners would trade any number of wonderful objects – mirrors, knives, muskets – for worn beaver pelts was amazing indeed.

Still, aboriginal peoples must have had some idea of the value of animal pelts. The first documented trade in beaver occurred in the summer of 1534 when Jacques Cartier encountered fifty Micmacs having a picnic on a beach in Baie de Chaleur. "They made frequent signs to us to come on shore, holding up some furs on a stick," the explorer wrote in his log. The Indians eagerly traded the robes, the *castor gras*, right off their backs for beads and other shiny objects.

There is no question that for the next two centuries, native trappers and middlemen controlled the fur trade as much as, if not more than French or British entrepreneurs. As the historian Paul C. Thistle writes,

> Far from Indian dependence on the trade, it was European dependence on Indians which characterized the early contact stage. The Europeans relied on the Cree not only for guidance, transportation and translation services inland but also for marriage partners, a supply of labour and food for the Hudson's Bay posts.[2]

And, of course, if there had been no Indian trappers, there would have been no fur trade at all, something that many of the white merchants seemed to forget in their interminable bad-mouthing of their customers.

The actual form of the trading ceremony – the gala performance upon arriving at a post, the pipe-smoking, the oratory, and the gift-giving – was based on centuries of Indian religious and peace-making rituals. As the historian Gerald Friesen puts it, "Trade was not merely an economic event but a gift exchange ceremony and a time of celebration."[3] To give a valuable possession was a token of friendship and loyalty. Indians were generous, presenting the best of their furs to the white traders. And the Europeans quickly learned that if they didn't carefully observe these rites – if the most exotic and valued goods, lace, embroidery silk, and "garterings," were not included among the gifts – there would be no business.

Early on it became obvious that the native trapper was not willing to take chances. Only if he was grubstaked – with supplies of ammunition, tea, axes handed out before the season began – would a Cree take time out from his hunting and fishing to engage in commercial trapping. The understanding was that the proceeds from the next pelt harvest would cover the cost of these provisions; whatever was left over would be used to buy European merchandise. This worked fine unless the competition showed up offering brandy, better quality kettles, and more credit. Then a trip to a rival post would be tempting, never mind how much money was owing elsewhere.

Post bosses kept careful records of who owed how much; the amount of credit a trapper would get depended on how reliable he had been in paying his debt in the past. The Cumberland House journal of 1819 lists sixty-two Rock Cree trappers doing business with the HBC post. Each was given a crude credit-rating. "Apitowiscum, 'a good hunter, generally pays,' Kew-ka-chiwan, 'a quiet fellow generally comes near [paying] his debt.' We-chin, 'lame but tolerably thrifty.'" The post manager could find himself in trouble if he allowed too much credit. "Be very careful about your debts," wrote an HBC boss, Horace Belanger, to the Pelican Narrows post in 1886. "They were far too heavy last spring."

What infuriated the white traders was the nonchalant attitude many Indians took towards their debt, the fancy European merchandise, and the fur trade in general. They were always berating the native trappers, calling them "leasy indolent fellows" for not spending enough time and energy collecting fur pelts. It didn't seem to faze the Indians. "The trader remained at the rim of the native universe," writes historian Gerald Friesen, "a supplier of arms and luxuries and a few technologically advanced items. The native agenda continued to centre around the quest for food, the seasonal cycle of movement, the usual process of birth, maturing and aging of every individual and family." Hunting for moose or grouse, fishing, singing, dancing, and storytelling were more essential to the Rock Cree than trapping for the HBC or any other fur trader.

For a century and a half, from Cartier's original bartering session in 1534 to arrival of the British in 1670, the French had the fur trade in the Canadian West to themselves. These were adventurous merchants, who developed canoe routes from the St. Lawrence basin to southern James Bay and into the Great Lakes with the help of those rugged individuals, the *coureurs de bois*, "forest runners," the unlicensed, vagabond traders from New France whose job was to do business with the Indians in the interior, thereby cutting out the native middlemen. Since *coureurs de bois* were mostly of the plebeian class, they had an affinity with the native and came to know, admire, and copy Indian ways. They married Indian women, producing offspring who eventually formed the Métis nation. They were "natural diplomats," good at promoting French interests by distributing gifts and honours. Yet, despite their enterprising nature, they had not reached as far as Rock Cree country before the Hudson's Bay Company arrived on the scene.

Actually it was two of their number who paved the way for the British enterprise. Frustrated with regulations that snarled the fur trade in New France, Pierre-Esprit Radisson and Médard Chouart, Sieur Des Groseilliers (Mr. Radishes and Mr. Gooseberries, to generations of Canadian schoolkids) defected to the English in 1668, taking their knowledge of canoe routes, the intricacies of trading furs, and the peculiarities of Indian nations with them. A trading expedition to Hudson and James bays was funded by wealthy investors and when the ship *Nonsuch* returned with her hold full of valuable furs, certain British businessmen, including the king's eccentric cousin, Prince Rupert, realized they might have a gold mine on their hands. On May 2, 1670, King Charles II granted the prince and nineteen fellow "adventurers" a Royal Charter, giving them exclusive trading rights to Hudson Bay and its drainage basin, an incredibly huge area which became known as Rupert's Land. The Hudson's Bay Company sprang into being, and within a decade, three trading posts were established on the east side of Hudson's Bay. In 1684 York Factory was set up on the west side, and fur bartered for European goods became part of the Rock Cree's landscape. It would be a full century later, however, before the inland fort, Cumberland House, was finally built, and fur trading became more convenient. It couldn't have happened at a worse time. The fur trade by that time was violent, unethical, depraved – all a result of cutthroat competition.

Even though the HBC had been granted a monopoly to trade in Rupert's Land, the French never stopped harassing the Brits. York Factory was captured in 1697 and operated as a French post until the 1713 Treaty of Utrecht (putting an end to the War of Spanish Succession) gave monopoly trading in Hudson Bay back to the British. But the fur trade was just too lucrative for the French traders to comply. By the 1750s they had advanced up the Saskatchewan River and its tributaries. With the fall of Montreal to the British in 1760, however, most scurried back to their home-land rather than live under British rule. Their place was taken by Scottish, English, and American traders, working in small, loose partnerships, later stitched together as the Montreal-based North West Company, who were at least as aggressive as the French. Relying on the famous *voyageurs* who manned the canoes, these Canadian "Pedlers," as they were called by the British, didn't hesitate to move into HBC territory, eventually reaching Great Slave Lake in what would become the North-West Territories.

When, in 1783–84, the North West Company was reorganized, it became an even more formidable force. Over the next forty-seven years, the competition between the two trading giants, HBC and North West, was homicidal. "The NWest are some of the damnedest Rascals that God ever created. They stop at nothing. House breaking, robbing, murder, it is all the same to them. Their morals are deformed to a degree that shocks us," wrote the HBC manager of the Pelican Narrows post in 1818. And his competitors, the Pedlers, felt the same way about the British. Caught in the middle, and suffering the most from this strife were, of course, the people who lived on the battleground – the Indians.

The Montreal-based traders who were the first to arrive in Rock Cree country were knowledgeable about the fur business. Louis Primeau, nicknamed Nick'a'thu'tin ("Windbound") by the Indians, had manned inland posts for French traders for years. In 1759, with the British victory at the Plains of Abraham, Primeau chose to stay in bush country, adopting an Indian lifestyle. He worked for the Hudson's Bay Company for a few years, but in 1772 he quit that company and teamed up with the Frobisher brothers.

Joseph, Benjamin, and Thomas Frobisher arrived from England just in time to fill the vacuum left by the French traders. They worked well as a team: Benjamin directed the business in Montreal, while Joseph and Thomas took to the forest. By 1772 they were doing business with First Nations people on the North Saskatchewan River. They were always on the lookout for savvy investors, and found one in Alexander Henry. A long-time trader, Henry knew native languages and ways, having spent time as a prisoner of war in an Indian camp.

In 1773–74, Joseph Frobisher, Louis Primeau, and seventeen voyageurs wintered at Pine Island, near what later that year would become the HBC's Cumberland House. In the spring, as soon as the ice was clear, they travelled up the Sturgeon-Weir River, past Pelican Narrows, 140 kilometres west to Frog Portage.

I flew into this spot with my friends from Jan Lake, Tina Pomeroy, co-pilot, and Dr. Harvey Christiansen, pilot of a 1957 de Havilland Beaver. A pretty, wooded spot with a sandy beach, Frog Portage belies its importance. It crosses a height of land connecting the Sturgeon-Weir River system to the mighty Churchill, and for centuries was the north and south conduit most often employed by natives. It's still used, but today the wooden railway carries not birchbark canoes, but sixteen-foot aluminum boats.

motor, and gear are placed on a small but heavy flatbed and pushed along the old wooden railway. So isolated is this place that coming across a stone cairn with a modern-day plaque was something of a shock. It explained the origins of the portage's name. The Cree were fond of belittling the trapping skills of the Dene and other enemy tribes, especially in preparing, stretching, and drying beaver skins. To show their disdain, they stretched the skin of frogs and hung them up on a tree at the portage. All during our visit I could hear echoes of time past – the lip, lip of paddles, the rhythmic beating of drums, the laughter around a bonfire. Doc Harvey laughed at my fancifulness, and claimed I was "going native." Four days later his Beaver crashed and he perished.

During their first visit to Frog Portage, Frobisher and Primeau engaged in an astonishingly profitable trade with Athabaskan Indians – Slaves, Dogribs, Hares, Yellowknives, and Chipewyans (Dene). And there was an added bonus. The Chipewyans had been on their way to trade at Fort Churchill – the detested Hudson's Bay Company had been thwarted! Joseph Frobisher and Louis Primeau returned to Grand Portage, the huge trade depot on Lake Superior, their canoes loaded with precious furs. This, of course, whetted everybody's appetite for more.

The next fall Joseph Frobisher and his brother Thomas returned to Frog Portage with six canoes and a huge load of rum, guns, tobacco, cloth, knives, and blankets prepared to do a mighty business once again. They built the first inland post in the area, unimaginatively called Fort de Traite (Fort Trade). The trouble was that most of the natives had moved north for the caribou hunt. With no one to supply them with provisions, the Frobishers almost starved to death that winter. Joseph later revealed that one of his men was so famished he had resorted to cannibalism, probably eating one of the crew who had succumbed to starvation. When the local Rock Cree returned in early spring and heard of the breach of their most serious taboo, they shot the man "for eating human flesh." Philip Ratt told me they probably didn't want a *witigo* wandering in their neighbourhood.

This misfortune certainly did not dampen the enthusiasm of the Montreal Pedlers. A huge contingent of traders set out again in June 1775 for the northwest with 130 men and twenty canoes, packed with every kind of merchandise to trade with the Indians.

On October 8, 1775, they reached Fort Paskoyac (The Pas) and encountered a village of Woodland Cree consisting of thirty families lodged "in tents of a circular form, and composed of dressed ox-skins, [moose or caribou hide] stretched upon poles twelve feet in length, and leaning against a stake driven into the ground in the centre." Their chief was Chatique (Pelican), "a man of more than six feet in height, somewhat corpulent, and of a very doubtful physiognomy." He invited the Canadians to his wigwam, where they immediately found themselves surrounded by armed guards. Alexander Henry would later write in his memoirs:

> Chatique presently rose up, and told us that he was glad to see us arrive; that the young men of the village, as well as himself, had long been in want of many things of which we were possessed in abundance; that we must be well aware of his power to prevent our going further; that if we passed now, he could put us all to death on our return; and that under these circumstances, he expected us to be exceedingly liberal in our presents.[4]

The chief then presented an inventory of what he wanted: three casks of gunpowder, four bags of shot and ball, two bales of tobacco, three kegs of rum, three guns, as well as knives and flints.

> He went on to say, that he had before now been acquainted with white men, and knew that they promised more than they performed; that with the number of men which he had, he could take the whole of our property, without our consent; and that therefore his demands ought to be regarded as very reasonable; that he was a peaceable man, and one that contented himself with moderate views, in

order to avoid quarrels; – finally, that he desired us to signify our assent to his proposition, before we quitted our places.[5]

Although the trading party outnumbered the Indian warriors, most of the Canadians were not heavily armed. Alexander Henry promptly turned over the desired merchandise. As the historian Paul C. Thistle writes, "This incident shows clearly that the Western Woods Cree were in control of the trading relationship."[6]

While most of the other traders in the group headed for the parkland or prairies, the Frobishers and Henry, with ten canoes and forty men, pointed north. Freeze up arrived early that year, so the Montrealers were forced to winter on the west side of Amisk Lake where they built a palisade and trading post.[*] This time, with temperature dropping to minus 32° C they almost froze to death. They survived only because of native generosity: "Indians brought beaver and bear's meat and some skins." And the Canadians began building a thriving export-import business with their friends.

The Frobisher-Henry exploits were the major reason the HBC, still snoozing on the shores of Hudson Bay, was nudged into setting up that first inland post, Cumberland House, in September 1774. At first relations were cordial between the HBC and the Nor'Westers. But this camaraderie would quickly vanish.

That winter Matthew Cocking sent the HBC veteran Robert Longmoor to the Churchill River above Frog Portage with some trading goods, chiefly tobacco, in an attempt to intercept and then steer Chipewyans and other natives to Cumberland House or York Factory. If this didn't work, wrote Cocking, "it will at least increase the Pedlers Expences by causing the Natives to rise in their demands upon them." It was the beginning of an increasingly nasty battle between the HBC and the North West Company in Pelican Narrows country that would go on for years and feature insults,

---

[*] The remains of the Frobisher-Henry Fort was discovered during the 1950s. It is renowned as a historical sight, nationally and internationally.

theft, harassment, blackmail, beatings, and even murder. Cocking relates a typical scene from this never-ending drama that occurred that winter at Frog Portage:

> In the Evening and during a great part of the Night Robert Longmoor observed the Pedlers men to be very busy in Carrying into their House all the Indian Furrs they could find, this they did whilst the Indians were Drunk, lifting up the Eves of the Tent Cloths & taking the Bundles out, the Indians not having courage to resist.[7]

Brandy and rum became potent weapons, and the Cree suffered from the violence and chaos that ensued. "The Indians cannot pass a place where Liquor is without stopping and when they are intoxicated few of them have discretion to keep their furs," wrote Matthew Cocking in May 1776. With so much alcohol stashed away, the Canadian Pedlers could, and often did, take advantage of the native population. As Cocking reported, "the Pedlers have traded their Goods at an exorbitant rate . . . The Natives have received little or nothing for their Furrs, and some of them have been beaten and otherwise maltreated when at the Pedlers settlement."[8] The Indians retaliated. In the spring of 1777, at least three Canadians were murdered by outraged Cree who had been cheated in one way or another.

But the indigenous population wasn't exactly enthralled with the Brits either. As Cocking admitted, "I believe the chief reason of our Men not being well with the Natives is their not being affable and otherwise endeavouring to make themselves agreeable, seeming frequently displeased and unwilling to render little Assistance in their way."[9] One wonders if Cocking ever blamed himself for his servants' condescension, given the contempt he himself felt towards the Indians. "The Natives in general are a dastardly People, and some of them from the Badness of their own minds become fearful of others"[10] and "The Indians are certainly great Lyers, having been often known to carry false reports between People of different

Interests"[11] and "I am positive the Indians will never trouble themselves with any Laborious work."[12] The natives retaliated against the haughty, blockheaded Brits by refusing to trade their furs at Cumberland House.

The war between the North West Company and the Hudson's Bay Company grew even more heated. By 1802, an HBC boss reported that there was "no trade and the Country all over is in a ferment of murder and robbery so that men were not in safety to stirr out." The culmination of this violence was reached in 1818 at Pelican Narrows.

The Nor'Westers were the first to build, in 1779, a trading post at the village exactly where the present-day Northern Store stands.[13] The surveyor Philip Turnor arrived at Pelican Narrows that year. There, he wrote, "we found three tents of Indians waiting for Mr. Small [a partner in the North West Company] with provision and to take debt . . . this lake called Sa-suck-kew or Pillicon lake."[14] In those years trading posts came and went according to the amount of business each competitor could suck out of the native population. The North West's closed down at Pelican Narrows in 1792, but a year later the Hudson's Bay Company opened a store there, although the exact location is unclear. It lasted until 1799 under the stewardship of Thomas Linklater, of Indian and English background – to this day Linklater remains a prominent family name in Pelican Narrows. It failed because of stiff competition – the Nor'Westers had once again set up business in the neighbourhood.

This hip-hopping of competitive posts, makeshift affairs all, continued. The North West Company built in Pelican Narrows in 1809, and the HBC opened a post there in 1810, which lasted a year under the management of Charles George and was one of the few times the Bay servants went after the Nor'Westers, "damned Rascals all." By 1817, the posts of the two rivals sat side by side near the sandy beach of Pelican Narrows, all the better to spy on each other.

In the winter of 1817–1818, the Nor'Westers had convinced most of the natives to take debt with them – supplies were charged on the understanding that they would trade their furs with the North West merchants the next year. The manager of the HBC post, John Pocock Holmes, complained bitterly. "I am afraid I shall not be so successful as last year, Connolley [William Connolley, a North West partner] having seized 11 Indians, forced them to take debt from him that traded with me last year. I have only four Indians that I can expect anything from."[15]

Holmes wrote this journal entry on his way to Pelican Narrows. When he got there, he realized he had been over-optimistic. There was not a single native to be found anywhere – not a soul at Pelican, Mirond, or Deschambault lakes. The North West's men, all heavily armed, had travelled from camp to camp, rounding up every Indian family they could find and forcing them at gunpoint to travel 150 kilometres to Lac La Ronge. There, the Nor'Westers were "living" with the indebted Indians, that is, keeping them prisoner until they had traded their furs with them. "My boat is in such a rotten state or I should proceed immediately to Lac La Ronge," wrote the HBC's Holmes, but one wonders whether even if he had owned the spiffiest new rig, he would have had the courage to face one hundred armed men.

On December 29, 1818, Holmes and two of his men, Charles Lucier and Jerome Blanchette, were returning to Pelican Narrows from Christmas celebrations at Cumberland House when they came across a group of Indians, three of whom "belonged" to the HBC, that is that they were indebted to that company, and one whom the Nor'Westers claimed as their own. This latter fellow told the group that when he had planned to deal with the HBC, Benjamin Frobisher had caught up to him, "pillaged him of his Fur & beat him."[16]

The following January, in 1819, Charles Lucier ran into a group of eleven Indian trappers, including Moose Hunter Snake and his three sons. (This Kinepik'ut'niw, Snake Person, was likely the head of the family that adopted the foundling Chief Peter Ballantyne.) A North West Company partner, Thomas McMurray, was travelling with the group, to ensure that the Indians who were in his debt would sell their furs to him. The HBC's Charles Lucier, "like an ignorant blockhead made the NWest man drink and traded all his furs from him and debauched his wife from him also," wrote Matthew Cocking. ". . . I told the men before they went away not to pillage or do any mischief but Lucier having had his wife debauched last fall at Cumberland by Connolley he was determined to retaliate the first opportunity."[17]

Four days later, Cocking again attempted to pry "one of his Indians" from the grip of the Nor'Westers. The North West partner, Archibald McLeod, told his rival to butt out. Cocking reported, "I being disappointed I laid hold of the Indians, immediately someone [a North West man] came behind my back and gave me two or three heavy blows on my back and head before I had any time to turn around. However as soon as I turned around I gave him a blow with my right hand on his left eye which swelled up immediately and with my left [punched him in the] stomach which laid him nearly breathless on the snow."

In February 1819, a Pelican Narrows Cree, known as Che-ki-pick ("Near The Water") was selected by the NWC to be made an example of when he attempted to trade with the HBC. One story has him being chained, gagged, and dragged off to Grand Portage, where, the Nor'Westers informed him, he would be hanged. Holmes, however, writes that Che-ki-pick and his three sons were seized by Benjamin Frobisher, the younger, and taken to the North West's Lac La Ronge post.

Che-ki-pick and the other Pelican Narrow natives were finally freed in the late spring of 1819 after five North West partners, including Benjamin Frobisher and William Connolley, headed back to Grand Portage. On June 18, the Nor'Westers were captured by Hudson's Bay Company men at Grand Rapids on the Saskatchewan River. Charged with a variety of thefts (although not kidnapping), they were to be imprisoned at York Factory. On the way Frobisher escaped. He got lost trying to find the North West post at Moose River and starved to death.

Facing such competition, the fur traders kept urging: "Trap more, trap more," never mind that this went against everybody's interest, native and white alike. In the past, conservation had always been part of trapping – at least for the sedentary beaver and muskrat. The Oblate priest Marius Rossignol lived for over forty years in Rock Cree territory. He wrote:

> I have often heard them relate how they had a young beaver at the very muzzle of their gun but had not shot it, and this in order not to bring about the extermination of the race.
>
> As regards, however, the other fur bearing animals, there was no reason to spare them, since their tendency to wander led them to pass from one locality to another and to go far. But the hunting for them ceased as soon as the fur lost its value, that is, when the hair shed or when the interior of the pelt turned black.[18]

Pressed on by the Europeans and Canadians, however, the Indians ignored their own conservation practices and began seriously to over-trap.

The rival traders might have eventually killed each other off if an extraordinary announcement hadn't arrived from the HBC's head office in 1821. The two antagonists were to become cousins; the HBC and the North West Company were to amalgamate. The British parliament granted exclusive trade in Rupert's Land to the HBC as well as to certain partners of the NWC for a period of twenty years. While the new act was an attempt to placate both sides, it was obvious the Nor'Westers had lost. The new coalition would carry the name and logo of the Hudson's Bay Company; the North West Company was soon forgotten.

The competitive era, which had lasted for forty-seven years, did enormous damage to the Woodland Cree. Their over-trapping, promoted by the white fur traders, meant that the supply of fur-bearing animals, beaver in particular, was depleted south and east of the Churchill River. "Furs are much scarcer than was anticipated. Lynx (or beaver or otter) have almost disappeared," wrote an HBC employee in 1896.[19] It was a lament repeated for many, many years.

There had been so many white traders to provision – the North West Company operation at Pelican Narrows had included three clerks, two guides, three interpreters, and thirty-six labourers; the HBC post had employed thirteen "servants"[20] – that game animals, particularly moose, were suddenly in short supply. As an HBC journal recorded in September 1899: "Lots of Indians here waiting for the Indian agent and they are all hard up for grub. Fish is scarce. Moose probably will be too." The Cree were forced to turn to local trading posts, such as Pelican Narrows, which were beginning to stock food goods shipped from Europe and eastern North America. Flour and bacon, for example, replaced pemmican; bannock made of flour, lard, and baking powder became, for the first time, a staple of the native population. Now, the symmetrical self-sufficiency of the Woodland Cree – their perfect balance of production and consumption, their "harmonious economy" – was being tragically undermined.

George Simpson, the HBC governor who was placed in charge of the Canadian operation, was determined to make it "a profitable, fur-gathering machine."[21] He ordered that gifts, really bonuses for good work, that had grown ever more extravagant during the competitive period, be largely eliminated. "This ruinous practice has been discontinued and nothing beyond Tobacco and Ammunition in some parts and a few trifles such as Firesteels, Needles, Vermillion, etc., have been given and occasionally a dress to a Chief or Indian of considerable influence."[22] Credit to native trappers was to be cut significantly and high-quality trade goods, in particular Brazilian tobacco, much loved by the Indians, were to be replaced with cheaper varieties. "The consumption of woolens, I am concerned to say, is increasing very much throughout the country among the natives, this is a very heavy article for which they cannot afford to pay . . ." At least one person understood how the HBC was twisting the screws on the Woodland Cree tighter every year. In 1910 a senior bureaucrat working for the Department of Indian Affairs wrote:

> These [HBC] officers are in some cases humane men but in other cases they are cruel and despotic and think no more of the life of an Indian than they do of the life of a dog, and all of them, even the best, when it comes to the question of trade, are very exacting. . . . The profit begins by holding the Indians in a sort of slavery; paying them as small a price as possible for the furs collected and selling them goods at exorbitant rates.[23]

Of course, the Canadian government did nothing about this "slavery."

Under Simpson's regime, many trading posts were closed, including the Pelican Narrows operation. The HBC had intended to build a substantial log structure there in 1822, but after merging with the NWC, these plans were dropped. The North West Company's outlet was, of course, no longer in operation, which meant that for the next fifty years, trappers in the Pelican Narrows district had to travel hundreds of kilometres, to places such as Île-à-la-Crosse or Cumberland House, to trade their furs or pick up emergency rations.

Replacing freight canoes with York boats was another of Simpson's cost-cutting measures that profoundly affected the Rock Cree. Hardly a new innovation – the first arrived at Cumberland House in 1797 – these flat-bottomed wooden vessels, operated by ten to twelve men, carried three times the payload of a *canot du nord* (freight canoe). As well, they didn't smash up so readily on ice and survived stormy seas better. Most of the boatmen were Métis or Indians, sometimes trappers looking for extra income in the summer months, sometimes full-time freighters. The trader

H.S.M. Kemp described them this way, ". . . in unison they stood, dipped, gave a mighty pull, and, at the end of the stroke, dropped back against the thwarts. The motion was slow but rhythmic. Dip, and pull . . . Dip, and pull . . . The galley and the slaves. It needed but the rattle of fetters to make the picture complete."[24]

Boating was horribly low-paid even into the twentieth century. In 1918 John Dorion of Pelican Narrows made the top salary of $2.50 a day as a tripman on a York boat when an average salary in the outside world was thirty-eight dollars for a six-day week. And often wages were taken, not in cash, but in goods at the HBC store, sometimes as advances. In 1876 a dozen tripmen from Pelican Narrows are listed in the HBC account books as having taken goods in lieu of wages. Pinnases (after baptism John Bird) received the following: tea, a handkerchief, flannel, ribbon, a blanket, two deerskins, soap, a Hal shirt, a yacht shirt, and print cloth. This meant that, with so much debt on the books, little cash was forthcoming after weeks of hard work.

And it was brutal work. The heavy, clumsy York boats did not navigate rapids very well and had to be dragged overland at every portage, along with the cargo. The freighters wore what were called portage straps, or tumplines, wide headbands joined to two strips of leather about ten feet long and one inch wide. These were tied around articles of freight, then hoisted up, making sure the weight was evenly distributed between a man's back and his shoulders. "At that time no paper boxes, just wooden boxes . . . some of them were that thick, heavy stuff, loaded with axe heads and the like," recalled Solomon Custer, a tripman himself. "They were about 140 pounds. . . . Those round barrels, you know, they put sugar and rum. Oh boy, that's a tough one to carry."[25] Accidents or sickness were common. The Methodist minister John Semmens wrote, "One of my party after seeing the men carry two hundred pounds across these swamps remarked that it was no wonder that so many widows were found at all the pay stations when the husbands were compelled to work so distressingly hard."[26] The boatmen were given some food – flour, bacon, lard, tea, sugar, jam or syrup, salt – but usually these provisions lasted less than a week, while a journey could be as long as twenty days or more. The rest of the time they had to fish or hunt for their supper once they had stopped for lunch or in the evening.

Still, there was a certain cachet, a prestige, in being a tripman. As the trader Harold Kemp related: "They were a gaudy lot – shirts of black sateen and flowery scarves, wide Stetson hats and ornate moccasins. They'd stop a mile or so short of their destination and change from their working clothes. No self-respecting York boatman would arrive in a settlement looking like a tramp."[27]

The HBC manager chose the *okimā*, the chief or boss of the trip. If this man was too hard on his paddlers, a spontaneous strike might flash, and often he would find himself in a fistfight. Furthermore, if agreed-upon commitments were not lived up to, the tripmen would rebel. In August 1892 the supervisor at Cumberland House wrote George Halcrow, manager of the Pelican Narrows post: "Terrible growling occurred after the boats arrived about you not having given enough away . . . & also about your allowing nothing for the families of the tripmen when they were absent at D4 [District Four] . . . Altogether the matter appears ugly."[28] In this case Joseph Linklater of Pelican Narrows operated his own York boat. He threatened not only to quit freighting for the HBC but to sell his furs to independent traders in Prince Albert. The Company coughed up $120 in back-fees, ten times what they originally intended to pay him.

After 1870, more and more independent traders moved into the Northwest. The threat of these belligerent, shrewd competitors arriving on the scene was one reason that, in 1874, the HBC finally built a permanent post at Pelican Narrows. But the HBC's competition there came from elsewhere, indeed from a most unlikely source – the local Oblate missionary.

There was never much love lost between the Roman Catholic orders and the Hudson's Bay Company. For one thing, most of the HBC "servants" were dyed-in-the-wool Protestants and didn't appreciate the influence the missionaries held over *their* customers.

Eventually though, the Oblates and the HBC negotiated an agreement: the Catholics would be allowed freedom to set up missions in the Northwest as long as their clergy didn't engage in trade or purchase furs from Indians. The Company made a point of saying it would enforce this edict.

As the Oblates pushed further into the interior of Canada, they needed some way to pay the natives for provisions or services such as guiding and translating. This currency came to be called *butin* and consisted not of cash, but tea, tobacco, sugar, ammunition, and cloth. "Stores" were set up in most missions to accommodate this merchandise, but soon the natives were trading furs for food and other things they needed, most often on credit; the "store" also became a "bank." This provided a tricky dilemma for the missionaries. What to do about their agreement with the HBC? And, of course, the Oblates had taken a strict oath of poverty; no profit was to be reaped from the dealing of *butin*. What a scandal that would be.

Father Étienne Bonnald, a thin, aristocratic-looking man, thought that looking after his flock's temporal welfare was just as important as administering to their spiritual needs; if "his" Indians were hungry, he was obliged to feed them. He had taken up his post at Pelican Narrows in 1876, at age twenty-eight. He was shocked when the HBC, forever economizing, eliminated gifts and credits to the Pelican Narrows Cree and over time he grew more and more infuriated with the Company's parsimony. In 1891 the manager at the Pelican Narrows post, George Halcrow, a particularly mean-spirited man, reported to his superiors that a forest fire had devastated the area, so that both the fur catch and the hunt for moose had been poor. The Cree were in dire need. That didn't stop him from making the following suggestion: "The custom of giving 'gratis' should be limited to a certain amount, as at present the Indian who begs the most gets the most for nothing. One skin to be given to each Indian who traded ten would suffice."[29] As Father Bonnald was aware, this would do little to fill the stomachs of hungry children. It was incidents like this that finally pushed the priest into taking matters into his own hands. He became a full-fledged fur trader.

Twelve years after he arrived in Pelican Narrows, Étienne Bonnald was running a complex business, buying and selling pelts, complete with trippers who, in the winter, would dogsled to the various winter camps to collect furs from the Cree in return for goods. When the Oblate superiors received complaints, the Father replied that the HBC was waging a campaign against his good name because of his popularity among the Cree. In response, George Deschambeault, the Pelican Narrows HBC post manager, decided to keep track of the priest's activities. "June 23, 1888: Rev'd Père Bonald arrived this morning. He brought many furs." "Nov. 27, 1888: Bonald arrived with wolverines, minks, rats." "Jan. 9, 1889: One of the priest's men killed a silver fox but we cannot get it from the cuss." When Deschambeault complained about Father Bonnald's activities to his district manager, Horace Belanger at Cumberland House, his reply was a sharp slap on the wrist. "Referring to the unpleasant rumours and tales between you & Père Bonald . . . I want to say for your own sake – talk less about this. You will give less chance of being blamed."[30] After that reprimand, Deschambeault dropped the matter. Later he quit the HBC, going into business for himself as an independent trader.

But Bonnald kept increasing his traffic until the HBC could ignore him no longer. Ironically, the man who was sent in to deal with the entrepreneurial priest was the same Horace Belanger who had castigated George Deschambeault seven years before. Immediately on his arrival at Pelican Narrows, in the summer of 1896, Belanger called on Father Bonnald. While sipping his tea, the priest insisted that he no longer had any interest in trading furs. Belanger was totally taken in by the charming curé – for about three days – until "Père's men were seen at it again." A couple of months later, Belanger sent Bonnald a letter.

It is with great sadness that I write these few lines. I had hoped that nothing would come between us, that is any misunderstanding. First of all, I'd like to remind you of the promises that you made me. During my first visit, you said that you would no longer trade and that you were happy that I came. You also said you traded because the Company wouldn't give any advances [to the natives] . . . I believed you because I thought that you were a man of your word. But now I see that I was wrong.[31]

This stinging note occasioned another meeting during which Father Bonnald again promised not to interfere with HBC business. That December the district manager wrote to Belanger: "I was pleased to learn that you have had an understanding with the Rev father but whether he will keep his promise or not remains to be seen." It soon became obvious that the Reverend Father had no intention of giving up his lucrative trade. In January 1897, Belanger once again wrote Bonnald:

A while ago, you asked me in a letter to see you as a priest and friend. But it is with great sadness that I cannot do so. . . . You lied to me and even tried to cheat me by sending me a fox fur that was worth nothing. I firmly believe that you lied to me many, many times. But what surprises me more is the damage that you tried and undoubtedly managed to inflict on my character by spreading the rumours you heard about me at Cumberland [House].[32]

Despite the venomous tone, Horace Belanger continued to try and persuade the priest to get out of the fur business. On two occasions he invited Bonnald over for dinner after Sunday mass. This cordiality quickly vanished and the war of the pelts was on. "May 29, 1897: Cornelius Bear came in, brot a few furs for the Priest." "October 9: William Natawayan came in last night but did not come near us. He is a Priest's Man and he Killed a Brown Bear. I am told he went off back this morning and on his way he shot a moose . . . but none came here." "November 28: he [Pierre

Peter Ballantyne, chief from 1900 until his death in 1917, and headman Thomas Ballantyne. This picture was taken just a few months before Chief Ballantyne died.

Cornelius Whitebear, the second chief of the Peter Ballantyne Cree nation, with two other chiefs. (Saskatchewan Archives Board, RA-8956)

Pelican Narrows, c. 1921. (Saskatchewan Archives Board, RA-4213)

Noah Ballantyne, the brother of Chief Peter. The picture was taken during a Treaty Party visit in 1921. (Saskatchewan Archives Board, RA-1014-6)

Ovide Charlebois, Oblate successor to Étienne Bonnald at Pelican Narrows. He went on to become the bishop of Keewatin.

It was the women's job to skin the moose. The hide made dandy blankets. (Saskatchewan Archives Board, RA-15681)

Canoes were used for all transport until they were replaced by motorboats in the 1930s. (Saskatchewan Archives Board, RB-857)

A portrait taken of Philip Ratt's grandfather, his wife, and a daughter.

Children were precious to the Woodland Cree and seldom punished.
(Saskatchewan Archives Board, RB-1449, RA-6961)

The infamous Guy Residential School, better known to students as "The Prison." (Saskatchewan Archives Board, RB-255)

The native children at residential schools often had their clothing burned and their hair cut short supposedly because of lice. The school uniforms were without any distinguishing feature. (Saskatchewan Archives Board, RA-6929)

Bear] has sold all his furs to the Priest's traders and the Priest's men are bragging."

By the late fall of 1897 Belanger had admitted defeat and was replaced in his job as HBC manager at Pelican Narrows by William Whiteway. In his journal of 1898 Whiteway seemed to be as much obsessed with Father Bonnald as his predecessor had been. He wrote: "Nov. 18, 1898: 'the Red weather' priest is going off to visit the . . . Indians at Thomas Ballantyne's. Mr. Clarke [an HBC tripper] is going after them to see what fur they might have." "Nov. 22: the Priest sent his man off to follow Mr. Clarke to Antoine Bear's. The Priest is bound to follow the Companys men. Well I shall wake him up & annoy him."[33]

Finally in March of the following year, Father Bonnald received a letter from the commission overseeing the agreement between the Oblates and the Hudson's Bay Company, forbidding him to engage in the fur trade. The Bay people breathed a sigh of relief. At last the wayward priest was out of business. But only three days later the HBC journal reported: "Pierre Bear came in this evening. He brought in a fisher. I am told the Priest got that for sure." Father Bonnald had no intention of obeying the order. Nor did he comply with instructions the following May when he was asked to come to Prince Albert, and was told by his superiors in no uncertain terms to stop interfering with the Hudson's Bay Company. A few days after he arrived back in Pelican Narrows, the HBC journal noted: "the Priest sent two men today to Pukatawagan. He sent goods to trade."

That August William Whiteway was replaced by Angus McLean who had a reputation as a tough character who would surely curb the priest. Nevertheless he was warned by the district manager, "Don't let Bonnald get the better of you in any way. Have no dealings with him of any kind." But McLean must have talked to Father Bonnald, for he became convinced that the priest had obtained permission from the highest authorities to engage in the fur trade and he wrote the district manager, J.W. McDougall, telling him so. On September 6, 1899, McDougall replied from

Prince Albert that no such permission had been granted. If Father Bonnald was caught again dealing in furs, McDougall instructed, McLean was to swear an information before a Justice of the Peace and the priest would be charged. That threat finally worked – for above all, the Oblates did not want a scandal. In March 1900 Bonnald and his men sold five lots of furs at Prince Albert for the goodly sum of $1,331. In May 1900 the Oblates announced that Father Bonnald, for reasons of health, was leaving Pelican Narrows.

Once again the Cree were caught in the middle of warring factions. If Athenas Head, Bonnald's tripper, showed up at your camp, you knew he represented the authority of not only the priest, but also the Church. If Mr. Clarke arrived – and often both factions came at the same time – he carried the power of the mighty Hudson's Bay Company. How to keep both happy required the patience of Job. The Bear and Nateweyes families were particularly strong Bonnald supporters. What happened to these people after the priest's enterprise crumbled is not known, but HBC "servants" were sometimes known to be vindictive. From 1900 onwards the names Bear and Nateweyes show up much less often in HBC journals then they had before Bonnald was transferred.

Père Bonnald was not the only competition the Hudson's Bay Company was facing. Independent traders were closing in on the Pelican Narrows region. The district manager, McDougall, wrote in 1896: "Cursitor's [Custer's] camp where the Ballantynes are, watch closely to send [trippers] to them at short intervals as these are the only ones the opposition know of."[34] The now independent trader George Deschambeault engaged two experienced trippers, Antoine Morin and John McAulay. "These men might get among your Indians and others unawares and if so they would have a chance of making a haul," the district manager wrote to Angus McLean at Pelican Narrows. Thus the battle of the trippers began.

In his book, *Northern Trader*, Harold Kemp described an independent tripper trying to outwit his opponents. He had received a tip that there was a good bunch of marten and mink at Little Deer Lake, eighty kilometres to the north of La Ronge. "You wait until nightfall. Under cover of darkness you load your toboggan with a line of trade goods, strip the bells from your dog harnesses and, like the Arabs, silently steal away. You pray, meanwhile, that your opposition is doing the same thing – heading for the mythical fur down the Churchill while you are heading for the certain fur on Little Deer Lake."[35]

Fortunately for the HBC, it had one advantage over the itinerant peddlers – the trading post itself. Kemp described the La Ronge post as it was in 1908, but it could just as well have been the one at Pelican Narrows.

> Here are old and rusted guns, boiling kettles and frying pans; dog harnesses, dog whips and snow shoes. Hanging from the rafters, out of reach of the mice, you'll find tents and rabbit-skin blankets. In one corner is a massive fur press used periodically to bale fur for shipment; in another corner, an ornate and high-headed toboggan, its rawhide sides emblazoned with the crest of the Company. And over all there is the tangy, woody smell . . . the smell of the North itself.[36]

It was here the Indian trappers, the Ballantynes, the Sewaps, the Bears, the Daylights, the Morins, the Custers, the Dorions, the Nateweyes, the Cooks, the Linklaters, the McCallums, would sit around a warm fire, nonchalantly accept the manager's tobacco, drink tea, and tell tales. As Pelican Narrows manager Angus McLean recorded in 1899: "Peter Daylight (Michel) sitting in the office telling yarns to the Indians. Some good ones at that."

Now and then the patriarch, Peter Ballantyne, would come in from the family's camp at Deschambault Lake (at what would later be named Ballantyne Bay) and be treated with deference even by the HBC clerks, who called him Chief and offered him the most comfortable chair. But the ones who came to the Pelican Narrows post most often were Peter's brothers, John, Thomas, and Noah. As the HBC journal noted: "Jan. 15, 1906: Thomas Ballantyne in and brought very few furs. He was out to see the Henry Cursitor (Custer) crowd who are doing nothing." In fact the Ballantyne brothers, and others of their generation, were not champion trappers. It was not their first priority; hunting or fishing food for their family was. The HBC people considered that as "doing nothing."

In 1907 the Hudson's Bay monopoly came to an end when the Revillon Frères of Paris set up a post in Pelican Narrows. Revillon (famous still today for Revlon cosmetics) entered the North American fur market in 1899 in Edmonton and went on to operate forty-seven posts throughout Canada. No matter where they established themselves, they gave the HBC a run for its money, and Pelican Narrows was no exception. Their post was a neat, square wooden structure painted white with red trim, with large windows and a false front proudly displaying the elegantly lettered sign *Revillon Frères*. The Indians called it "Frenchie's Place." A year after Revillon Frères arrived, the Bay's manager complained, "no fur coming in. This is the dullest year that I ever put in. No fur at all or else the traders are getting it all." Buying furs was not a simple matter, by any means. Alex Robertson, the long-time proprietor of Robertson Trading Company in La Ronge, explains the skill that was involved: "If someone brought in 50 mink, they'd say for fun, 'I bet you can't tell when I caught them!' So I'd look at a pelt and tell them what day it was caught on. And weasels, you could grade those with your eyes blindfolded – by feel. Weasels are normally white but if there is one brown hair you can tell by the feel. Every animal has its idiosyncrasies. You grade them like you were reading them. In many cases you can tell exactly where the trapper got the fur."

It was in 1914 that Arthur Jan set up as an independent trader in Pelican Narrows, building a four-room house, one of the most attractive buildings in the village (until it burnt down in the late 1990s), a store, a warehouse, and a fish house, all made of logs. Jan had worked for a haberdasher in London, England, before he decided to try his luck on the Canadian prairies. Farming, he quickly discovered, was for him loathsome. As soon as he got his patent for his homestead, he sold it, and moved up north. For a while he worked for Revillon Frères as a freighter on a scow which floated from Prince Albert to Pelican Narrows. In 1911 and 1912, he trapped and traded on Reindeer Lake, famous for its enormous lake trout. "The largest I caught was 52 pounds, but I have heard of others to top that," he wrote.[37] By 1913 he had set up shop at Pelican Narrows. He had learned Cree and this gave him a big advantage over those HBC "servants" who didn't know a word of the language.

Arthur Jan bragged about his ability to get along with the Indians. Yet in his memoirs he doesn't call a single native person by his given name, not even his regular customers. And he is always patronizing towards them. The following is Jan's account of one of the Woodland Cree's most distinguished and revered medicine men:

> There were Indians I came across who were pretty smart in some ways. One very old Indian who was past his working years used to come over to see me every time he heard that I was starting off on a trip. His story was always the same: that he would set up his bag of tricks and guarantee me against rain in the Summer and snow in the Winter. That meant I had to hand out a plug of smoking tobacco . . . as I was on the trail a great deal of the time, he had plenty of free-smoking.[38]

Philip Ratt remembered how much his father and uncles disliked Arthur Jan. "I guess Jan, when he operated the store, he came up with a theory that the only way to deal with an Indian is to keep him in debt. When you give him credit, you are assured he'll be your steady customer. Most of the trappers didn't like him much."

For many of the white traders, prejudice remained deeply lodged in their souls well into the twentieth century. Doug and Elvena Pearson are one of the few mixed-race couples in Pelican

Narrows. In 1970 he was the manager of the HBC post on the reserve when he fell in love with a local, Elvena Linklater, and proposed. "They [the HBC bosses] told me that if I married an Indian woman or a half-breed woman, they'd give me little hell-holes [to manage] in Canada for the rest of my life. It was their policy. They didn't want their staff being married to a Native. They thought they were gods, those district managers." Doug and Elvena married anyway. They have prospered in Pelican Narrows. Among the businesses they are or have been involved in: a laundromat (closed when the band bought everyone washers and dryers), a variety store, gravel trucks and construction machinery. They own one of the most handsome houses there. Elvena is an outspoken political activist, the insult levelled at her by the Hudson's Bay Company still a harsh memory.

By the time Arthur Jan was doing business, most of that first generation of Cree who had been baptized and taken Christian names were either retired or had passed away. All four Ballantyne brothers, Peter, John, Noah, and Thomas, had obeyed the biblical command "go forth and multiply." Chief Peter Ballantyne and his wife, Marie, had ten children; the youngest was named Thomas after his uncle, but, perhaps to avoid confusion or because he was the baby of the family, he was called Chalecheech*, a nickname which stuck his whole life. Chalecheech was Roderick's father, and Gordon Peter's grandfather.

His life was spent on the trapline. As a young man he travelled long distances by dogsled to where beaver, mink, and other fur-bearers were still obtainable. On February 3, 1914, the HBC journal at Pelican Narrows recorded the temperature that morning as minus 44° C. "This will probably have been the coldest day of the whole winter. Chalecheech arrived from the Churchill River." Even though he grew more hard of hearing each year until he was finally deaf, nothing prevented him from trying to make a good living for his family.

---

* There seems not to be any meaning to the word.

In 1917 Thomas Chalecheech Ballantyne married Marie McCallum, who was sixteen at the time. Eventually they would have five daughters and three sons; Roderick was the second youngest. The centre of their fur-trapping business was located at Wunehikun Bay at the north end of Mirond Lake, about fifteen kilometres from Pelican Narrows. The camp consisted of a main cabin made of logs and roofed with poles and earth, and smaller buildings – latrines, storage sheds, dog kennels, drying racks for moose and other meat. Marie stayed at the cabin, teaching her children, weeding her vegetable garden and shooting or snaring the small animals – rabbits and prairie chickens, ducks, geese, and wild grouse – she found in the area. She fished both for her family's food and for the dogs. And she prepared the pelts for trade. A friend of the Ballantynes', Catherine Linklater, in an 1988 interview, described the stretching of beaver skins thus: "skin the beaver and put the skin in the ice; clean and scrape the fat off; nail the skin to the [stretcher] board; take the stretched pelts off and dry them overnight; start again." Catherine Linklater claimed that a skilled woman could stretch about twenty beaver skins a day. And some of the women were pretty good hunters as well. Eighty-year-old Mary Custer says that when she was young she and her siblings were skeptical that their mother could bag a moose. "So one time we saw one at a lake, so we chased that moose to a little curve in the lake. Mom took a canoe and went off alone. She killed that moose, brought it back. She always had moose meat at the cabin."

Thomas Chalecheech Ballantyne ranged further afield, north of the Churchill River, trapping foxes, mink, and the occasional otter. In the spring he'd search far and wide for muskrats. Rats paid okay; they took the place of beavers, which were all but extinct at the time. Chalecheech had two places where he liked to sell his furs, depending on who would give him the best price: the Hudson's Bay store in Pelican Narrows and the independent trader Jack Henderson of Deschambault Lake, much favoured by the Woodland Cree. "It was pretty well the only source of income at the time," says Roderick. "My dad had to be a good trapper."

Chalecheech and Marie also had a cabin in Pelican Narrows, which they considered their home base. "They used it basically as a shelter," remembers Gordon Peter. "It was a very nice, comfy little place, sixteen by twenty feet." It was close to St. Gertrude's Roman Catholic Church, important since both were devout. Roderick says his parents were good people who wouldn't touch alcohol. "We were taught really well, how to hunt and trap. And we were well-disciplined." "And that's the way my dad tried to bring his kids up," Gordon Peter added.

The Pelican Narrows elder, Gilbert Linklater, relates an incident that reveals a lot about Chalecheech Ballantyne's character. When Gilbert was young, his father, trapping in the late fall, fell through the ice into the freezing cold water. He developed arthritis in his legs, and could hardly walk. "We were sitting around at eleven o'clock in the morning. There was a knock at the door, and Chalecheech walked in. He had been shopping and was pulling a sleigh laden with groceries, including tobacco. He said to my dad, 'Partner,' – they used to call each other that – 'I heard you were ill, couldn't work, so I'm here to help.' We were very honoured for what that old man did for us, because my dad couldn't support us that winter." Gordon Peter says that such kindness was not only typical of his grandfather but it was the norm among trappers. "They respected each other and they cared for each other."

There was a strict code of ethics, which was seldom violated. As Father Rossignol wrote, "He [the trapper] marked the [beaver] lodge by planting a stick or post, and his mark was respected by everybody. Later, after a month or a year or longer, whenever in fact he wished, he could come to kill the beaver therein and he would find them still there."[39] It was not uncommon for someone to leave a bundle of furs hanging from a tree, with a note to a trader explaining which account to enter it in. No other trapper would dream of taking it. "You'd leave a knapsack in your boat, won't take it, leave some gas, won't take it. Leave your jacket, won't take it. But now you could trust nobody," insists Fred Ballantyne.

Bragging was also frowned on. Henry Dorion in a 1970 interview, illustrates how modesty was the norm. "One time I had 109 beaver. I was making more than $2,000, and a lot of people told me, 'You're a good man, because you know how to trap.' 'No, no, that's not right,' I'd say back. 'If you got a good area, you'll get the same thing that I get, but if you've got a bad area, you'll get nothing.' "40

As the outside world crept closer, the men of Pelican Narrows became interested in making a living by means other than the traditional trapping and fishing. Unfortunately their introduction to Western-style capitalism proved a catastrophe.

In 1910 David Collins, a Cree working his trapline, discovered the zinc and copper ore body, perhaps the richest in Canada, that would become the foundation of the Hudson Bay Mining and Smelting Company at what is now Flin Flon, Manitoba. Since Collins knew little English, and even less about the process of registering a claim, he approached Thomas Creighton, after whom the Saskatchewan town next door to Flin Flon is named. Creighton brought three more partners – all white – aboard at the same time, promising Collins, "For sure you'll be paid, if we find anything." Yet when the claim was staked five years later, the names of the four white men appeared on the registry form; David Collins's was not among them. "He was an Indian so he didn't count for nothing," said John Dorion in a 1970 interview. "They all got rich and he got five bucks."41 Dorion is not entirely correct: what the white prospectors gave David Collins, "as a kind gesture," was some tea, ten pounds of flour, some lard, sugar, and a couple of biscuits.

It took a long time, thirteen years, to work out the snags of extracting and refining, but the first shipment of purified ore from Flin Flon's Hudson Bay Mining and Smelting was finally dispatched in 1928. Although it was situated on land that Rock Cree had trapped for centuries, the huge mine would have almost nothing to do with long-time residents. Few Indians were involved in its construction, and few were hired for its operations, a trend which continued over the years. In 1973, for example, of the 2,800 employees, 16 (or .6 per cent) were native.[42] And it has not improved much in the twenty-first century. The excuse given is that natives find working underground abhorrent, and the punch clock a trial. There is some truth to this, but many other similar operations managed, through education and training, to engage many more aboriginals. In fact 86 per cent of northern mineral-sector employees in Saskatchewan are native. Gordon Peter says he'd sure grab one of those high-paying jobs if it was ever offered.

If HB Mining and Smelting was a non-event for the Cree, the development of the hydro needed to run the operation was a disaster for them. When, in 1927, engineers discovered that the rapids at the Twin Island Falls, near the Indian-Métis community of Sandy Bay on the Churchill River, seventy kilometres north of Pelican Narrows, could be transformed into a hydroelectric dam, permits and licences were handed out by the Saskatchewan government fast and furiously. On one application to the province's Water Branch, under the category "Population Numbers," was written a single word: *None*. Never mind that this had been Rock Cree territory for millennia, that it was prime trapping and fishing ground – the sturgeon were especially plentiful – and there was a Hudson Bay post situated there. The first notice proposing the dam, to be built by a subsidiary of Hudson Bay Mining and Smelting, was published in the *Regina Leader* on June 20, 1928. The licence was issued three months later.

Sandy Bay was considered a satellite of the more populated Pelican Narrows, and Cree there, including the Ballantynes, rushed to get jobs while the dam was being constructed. The company would hire them only if they gave up their treaty rights – they were told it made for easier bookkeeping – and many did. For the first time Pelican Narrows experienced an exodus of people. "Really, in those days," says Philip Ratt, "there was no benefit in being in treaty. We didn't have the housing, the welfare benefits, we have now. So a lot of people from Pelican Narrows left. Sandy Bay was where many went."

Angus Bear was one of the first hired, as a guide for contractors and surveyors. He recalled: ". . . They paid me a dollar an hour. I was alone with no one to help me – it was a nineteen-foot canoe with an 835 motor with three propellers. . . . I walked every portage three times. [Angus Bear was about five-foot-three-inches tall and approximately 135 pounds.] Twice they (the bosses) helped me along. They each carried a little. But they didn't bother with the heavy loads. . . . At the time I quit travelling back and forth, my pay scale was abruptly cut back to 50 cents an hour!"[43]

It was only the beginning in a long, dreary tale of discrimination and exploitation. From 1930 to 1935, Cree workers were paid not in cash, but in groceries, at a rate of thirty cents an hour, ten to twelve hours a day, with no overtime. "Baloney, mainly baloney. Sometimes bacon. That's how we were paid," remembered one worker.[44] The trader Arthur Jan, who operated a concession at the construction site, came up with a money-saving scheme: pay the Indians with the meat left over from the white workers' sandwiches. And apparently the company did just that. There were two separate grocery stores: one for whites, which was well-stocked, and one for Indians, with just the basics. At their store, the natives were told to place their order at a back window and pick it up later; the whites were allowed to inspect their roast beef before they bought. Attractive, well-built houses with picket fences were constructed for white employees; Cree were given a bit of lumber, usually scrap wood from the construction, but only if they agreed to build their cabins in Sandy Bay (a good distance from the all-white enclave, Island Falls). There were separate schools for Indians and whites. As a survey of northern schools reported in 1944: "Island Falls: The pupils have the convenience of a modern school. Indirect lighting is provided, bubbler fountains, hot and cold showers are available, with a full line of modern equipment. Sandy Bay: A rough crude log building serves as a schoolhouse. Little equipment is provided except the usual government grant of library books."[45] The Indians were not allowed entry to the recreation hall in the white settlement. "I remember once in the 1930s," recalled Philip Nateweyes, "one Christmas the company sent for a movie show for the Christmas party. The kids were so excited. Tom Ballantyne [Chalecheech] travelled miles to pick up the package and miles back in a snowstorm. But they wouldn't let him or his kid into the recreation hall to watch the movie."[46]

But as bad as it was, it wasn't the degrading discrimination that made the Rock Cree community so bitter. When the dam was completed in 1930, acres of the best fur-trapping and hunting land, reserve land, were flooded, without permission from the aboriginal people. "The government never told one Native person they were going to flood. They didn't tell us. Nobody knew," recalled Angus Bear in 1984. After the deluge, the water used by the Sandy Bay community became polluted; the mud sturgeon as a species was all but wiped out; nine houses with fishing and trapping equipment were destroyed, and many more gardens disappeared; boats were damaged by floating logs; ducks, geese, birds of all kinds chose a different migration path. "We have not been able to make a decent living since the devastation," insisted Angus Bear. "A sturgeon was made extinct and the fish never really came back at all. Trapping was never really restored."[47] The people of Sandy Bay are still angry, are still fighting for compensation.

November 5, 1938, was a clear, cold day. The HBC post manager, W.W. Lowrie, was glad to see Tom Ballantyne, "Chalecheech" as he called him. He was such a likeable man, soft-spoken and good-humoured. As usual he had brought in some fine furs – red fox, cross fox, and ermine. And this, said Chalecheech, as he opened another packet, is from my son, Roderick. Lowrie entered into his account book exactly what the skunk and rabbits were worth. At the time Roderick was six years old.

Even at such a young age he was always with his dad on the trapline. Chalecheech and Marie had sacrificed their other children to residential schools where they hadn't been fed properly and had become ill. This was not going to happen to this boy, who seemed such a kindred spirit with his father. They even looked alike, "two peas in a pod," Marie used to say. "Every time my father went someplace I had to go with him. We were always so close, always together." Roderick did not attend a day of school in his life.

When he was twenty-two, his family thought him old enough and smart enough to set out on his own. His experience was similar to many young Rock Cree in the early fifties: he worked at Pukatawagan (a Rock Cree community on the Churchill River) as a labourer on the rail line that was being constructed from The Pas to Churchill; he cut timber to make railroad ties at Cranberry Portage, Manitoba; then on to Flin Flon to work in a sawmill; then back to Cranberry to another sawmill. These were jobs of hard labour and he was paid eighty-five cents an hour. Nine months after he started out on his adventure, elder brother Peter caught up to him and told him his family wanted him home. It was back to the trapline.

With the outbreak of the Second World War fur traders held their breath. What effect would the European conflagration have on fur prices in Canada's Northwest? In January the bad news arrived. Most traders lost between two and four dollars a pelt on mink, even more on muskrat. By the end of the war the fur industry was in disarray.

It wasn't only the bedrock prices; fur-bearing animals had never been so scarce around the Pelican Narrows area. But it wasn't the Cree who were over-trapping. In the Dirty Thirties, scores of unemployed southerners came north. "The only place to make a living was in the north, to go trapping. So a lot of townspeople trapped out at Big Sandy Lake and that area, and a lot of them perished because they couldn't do it, they couldn't survive in the bush," says Philip Ratt.

Sometimes, eccentric loners, the infamous mad trappers, lived like hermits in the bush. For the Indians, they were a breed of white man apart, creatures as strange as the *witigo*. Others were *kimotisk* – thieves who paid no attention to the native trapper ethic of not touching anything on another person's trapline. Animals that had been caught and the traps themselves, various items from cabins were all fair game. One old trapper even had his Cree bible stolen. Fortunately, the independent and HBC traders supported their regular customers and refused to provision the *kimotisk*. Most became so isolated that they were forced to move on, probably to wreak havoc elsewhere.

For the Cree, the worst thing the white trappers did was use strychnine. "It isn't what these trappers get that we complain of," said a chief at La Ronge, "but what their poison kills and they don't get. These animals go away and die, and other animals come along and eat of these dead carcasses and also go away and die." William Graham, the Indian Commissioner reported, "This complaint is made year after year, and no doubt, is one cause of the disappearing of the fur-bearing animals."[48] The poisoning continued.

When the socialist Co-operative Commonwealth Federation (CCF) was elected in Saskatchewan in 1944, a priority of the new government was to save the fur trapper's livelihood. Two radical schemes were implemented: one a failure, the other a success.

It was felt that the Hudson's Bay Company and other traders were making huge profits at the expense of the native trappers; low-as-possible prices for furs, high-as-possible prices for goods had always been their modus operandi. To counter this the Saskatchewan Fur Marketing Service was set up, and it became mandatory that beaver and muskrat be sold through it. As these were the most valuable pelts, an angry HBC promptly cut back on credit it would hand out to trappers. Many independent traders simply went out of business. As Sydney Keighley wrote, "bootlegging of furs out of the province became prevalent, ensuring that the province lost not only the profits it hoped to make by controlling the trade, but also the royalties that had previously been a nice addition to the province's coffers."[49] In 1957, at the insistence of practically everyone in the fur industry, the mandatory rule was dropped; eventually the Fur Marketing Service itself disappeared.

The Fur Conservation Program was far more successful, although not any more popular, at least at first. Until that time, exclusive use of a trapping area was unknown; whoever put down a trapline first was allowed to work that territory. It was a system that worked well until the "town" people, with little sense of the trapper's code of ethics, invaded. Then it became necessary to protect the few animals that were left. Saskatchewan's northland was divided into seventy conservation blocks in which only the people who lived there were allowed to trap. Each licensed trapper was assigned a large area that was his alone to work. Roderick Ballantyne proudly shows his licence which lists Block N34, zone 5; Frederick Ballantyne's is Block N34, zone 2; Philip Ratt's is Block N34, zone 3. "Before the zoning scheme," says Philip, "people moved from one area to another, so they didn't care. They killed off all the animals because, if it wasn't good enough the next year, they didn't have to come back. Now we have to look after our own conservation."

Also, a quota was placed on beaver. Each trapper could sell only a certain number of pelts a year to the Fur Marketing Service. "This was unpopular but it had to be done," says Phil Ratt. As well, some 1,800 of these rodents were transported from the southern part of the province to the north. They flourished. The average annual harvest of beavers in the years 1914 to 1952 was 5,310; from 1959 to 1960 that figure was 56,106.[50]

While fur-bearing animals became more plentiful, the value of their pelts staggered downwards. Not only that, fur ranchers had arrived on the scene, creating cutthroat competition. Says Alex Robertson, the long-time trader out of La Ronge, "You can raise fur in mink ranches. You can raise foxes, you can raise lynx. Russia raises marten, which is called sable, on their ranches and they're ten times better than the wild. They're fed properly, they're watered properly, they're killed at the proper time." But ranchers too have to contend with adversity, sickness which could wipe out an entire farm in weeks, the caprice of fashion, and the ups and downs of the fur market. In 1963 fur prices were down 50 per cent from what they had been in the late 1940s. Says Robertson, "In the years of 1965 and '66 fashion changed. All the mink ranchers who were making big, big money found out that they couldn't sell their skins. The whole fur business collapsed." That didn't deter single-minded trappers such as Philip Ratt; it only made them work harder. "I wanted to be in the top five trappers in town, and I wanted to make up for my size. 'He's a small guy,' they'd say, 'but he's able to do a man's work.'"

In October he'd begin collecting his supplies. Since he had two households to support, his own in the bush and his family's in Pelican Narrows, he had to be judicious in his selections. And, of course, it depended on how much credit the trader would give him. "You'd get the basics – flour, margarine, tea, and sugar. If you had these, your survival was assured. You could make bannock. If you could afford a few more extras you'd get beans and rice and dried foods – prunes, apples, milk. If you were really living high you'd have canned goods – corned beef, and vegetables. You snared rabbits for stew and the wives made pemmican – dried moose meat mixed with the fat of the kidneys, with a touch of salt or a little bit of sugar. You'd make meatballs out of that, and they were good. And, of course, you had to have lots of dried fish for the dogs and as bait."

Philip trapped north of Pelican Narrows near Sandy Bay. He would stay in the bush by himself for two or three weeks at a time, and work from 9 a.m. to 7 p.m. He'd take tea breaks, but only once a day, any more he considered a waste of time. And time was important to him. "I was always slender and light on my feet. I used three or four dogs and they just pulled me like nothing." If there was a storm, he would break a trail by snowshoeing for two or three nights, and then use his dog team to pick up the pelts. "I was always the first one in making a trail for the dogs." Only on Sunday would he relax a little, sleep in, clean his cabin, replenish his woodpile, indulge in the *Reader's Digest*, listen to the radio if he had a generator with him. In 1983 the Colin Thatcher saga, the case of a Saskatchewan politician who was found guilty of murdering his wife, made headlines across the country. Philip could hardly wait to get the daily news about the case. It made him feel part of the world.

Most natives trap with two or three others, usually relatives, but Philip liked working by himself. "I was lucky to do so. I could practise conservation the way I wanted to." But since he was alone, he always worried about accidents. "If you were careful with your guns, no trouble at all, but the axe and the knife were unpredictable. Even if you were a good woodsman, it [the axe or knife] could strike off and cut you in the face or somewhere else."

Philip had several close calls, but the one he still has nightmares about occurred one spring at about breakup time. The ice was clear of snow, but then a storm had dumped another foot on the lake. A couple of days later, Philip was driving his dog team when he noticed some ducks swimming about in open water around a reef. The dogs took off after them. Philip hollered for them to go to the left, but the lead dog wouldn't listen. Philip jumped off the toboggan and, grabbing a head-rope, started running along the side of the sled. Finally the dogs took a sharp left turn, but the toboggan went flying into the hole, catching Philip's legs as it did so. He too landed in the freezing water. "Boy, was it cold," he says. The ice at the opening kept breaking into crystals, squeezing Philip downward. "It was like being pinched," he recalled. "The more I broke, the tighter it got." He smashed more than fifty feet of ice and then, because of the effort, began seeing sparks. "I figured, well, I can't make it." Finally, he just let himself go. As he descended into the water, his feet touched something. "Then I had the wakeup call, get out of here." He was able to use a log lying on the bottom of the lake as a lever to push himself up. Eventually, he was able to crawl out and reach shore. "It was a very close call," he says.

Don Bird is a prosecutor for the Saskatchewan Department of Justice. He is also a Rock Cree who grew up on the trapline near La Ronge. He says of the 1950s, most of the 1960s, and early 1970s, "There was almost too much employment. I can remember my uncle having to hide from his boss – he was guiding tourists out of La Ronge – just to get a day off. You have to remember, back then commercial fishing was a thriving industry. Trapping was a very successful business. . . . Fur prices were adequate. Fish prices were good. There was a sense of accomplishment and we were very independent. Many people were happy."

Rod Ballantyne agrees. It was a good time, he says, even though he had to take lots of different jobs to provide for his growing family. After fur trapping ended in the spring, he worked in commercial fishing or on construction of homes being built for white folk on Amisk Lake. But the job he enjoyed the most was guiding. "I really liked guiding," says Roderick. "I went out with white people and learned their language from them. I learned how to read a little, because I never went to school." For twenty-two years, he and his family came to Jan Lake Recreation Area for the summer.

Henry Custer, now seventy-one, laughs when he thinks about his twenty-three years as a guide. "I guess my photograph is all over the United States now. All over the place." Not only did the Indian guides find the best fishing hole, they made a superb shore lunch, and told tall tales. There was a mystique surrounding them, as Glen Sorestad, Saskatchewan's poet laureate, imparts so nicely in the poem "Jan Lake" from his book *Jan Lake Poems*:

> George, our silent Cree guide
> cuts the outboard motor
> as we troll slowly past a rocky point
> wordlessly allows the boat
> to drift towards the shoreline.
> I think:
> *George is hungry, so it's lunchtime.*
> *George thinks it's time to stretch our legs.*
> *George needs to take a piss.*
>
> We drift towards a clump of willow
> jutting like an afterthought from the rock
> and George seems intent on something.
> I look eagerly but see nothing at all.
> The boat touches the rocks of the point

and at last we see the three large eggs
camouflaged in their feathery nest.
We stare in silence.

Loon, George says softly
and starts the motor again.

The outfitters were paid only ten dollars a day, but good
guides such as Roderick often earned thirty or forty dollars extra
on tips. Then there was the five cents made on each fish filleted.
Roderick's wife, Sarah, also made money, by cleaning cabins.
Roderick liked to drink a beer and play pool at the Miniquay Hotel
at night, but, he insists, he never drank when he was out with
fishermen. Henry Custer agrees. "I didn't bother with it [alcohol]. I
didn't even drink when I was out on the lake. My job came first."
Both Roderick and Henry worked for an outfitter, Garnet Martin,
who liked Indian people, and, for the most part, the tourists were
respectful and kind towards them. There were occasions though
when racial hatred came boiling to the surface. "The Americans
weren't like that," recalls Henry Custer, "but our Canadian people,
some of them were real bastards, especially the farmers. If you're a
farmer, I don't like you."

One afternoon a tourist discovered that his money was missing
and pointed his finger at the first Indian he spotted walking down
the road. "There's the bastard," he yelled, grabbing at a terrified
Roderick Ballantyne. The RCMP were called, and they obviously
believed the white man. "Where is the money?" they kept asking
Roderick, not giving him a chance to explain. Garnet Martin's
son, Dennis, quickly stepped in, and told the cops, "I bet he didn't
do anything 'cause he went out early in the morning. Anyway he's
not the kind of person to steal. Even if he found one nail on the
road, he would give it to me." The police left shortly afterwards.
The tourist never apologized.

For the first ten years the Ballantynes lived in a tent for the
summer in the guide's circle with other families, then the Martins

found them a little trailer with a propane stove and running water. "They treated us real good," says Roderick.

The kids of the guides grew up playing with the children of the outfitters and the cottagers. Gordon Peter, who loved his summers at Jan Lake, says that, while they might have fought now and then, as kids do, it was never about race. His only bad experience again involved some white anglers. "There were some drunk guys shouting names at me and my brother Oscar. I went to tell Dennis Martin, but he had already overheard them. He was so angry he called them into his office, and said, 'I don't want you talking to anybody around here like that. I want you out of here.' The next morning they left."

In the late 1970s the thriving economy of the Rock Cree collapsed. First, very stringent quotas were slapped on the number of fish that could be caught; in lakes designated for recreation, commercial fishing was cut back to almost nothing. Gilbert Michel insists: "The government was more interested in making the tourists happy. They didn't care about Indian fishermen. Didn't give a damn."

Then the fur industry went belly up. The trouble began in 1975 with the publication of *Animal Liberation* by the American philosopher Peter Singer. Soon Brigitte Bardot was bewailing the fate of baby seals and Lily Tomlin was crying over trapped muskrat. The anti-fur movement was about to destroy the livelihood of the native trappers. Phil Ratt remembers the 1978 World Fur Fair in Montreal. He was shocked to find that, outside the train station, protestors had gathered, screaming anti-fur slogans. "They had a coffin and there was a young lady in there with only a couple of flowers covering her tits and crotch. That's all she wore. There was a sign near the coffin that said, 'I'd rather be naked than wear furs.' I was amazed."

Says trader Alex Robertson, "Trapping methods have improved tremendously. Most animals today are caught in snares and connibear traps so they're killed instantly. They [the trappers] do it because of the mercy idea, but also so there's no damage on the fur. There's been a fur trade since history started, it could very easily be the oldest industry in the world today. Then you have some dummy that doesn't know a marten from a hole in the ground telling these old trappers how cruel they are."

Fur prices plummeted. A lynx pelt that had been worth $1,000 in 1972 was worth $150 in 1982. "All of a sudden all these guys were caught," laments Don Bird. "It had taken a lifetime to build up their skills to be good fishermen and trappers and the rug was pulled right out from under them. For a lot of them it was a time of real despair. The anti-fur lobby have no idea what they did. Absolutely none. They created a lot of hurt."

"Those people, the Greenpeace, they don't understand," adds Fred Ballantyne. "God gave us those animals to eat and to take their furs."

The Canadian government did so little to counter the international attack against trappers, that many Cree still believe the politicians were in league with the anti-fur movement. John Merasty, who works for the band council in Pelican Narrows, comments, "See, the government wanted to develop forestry, mining, and hydro. People were on the land [with their traplines]. The best way to get rid of them was to depress the fur prices. It worked. You go out on the land now and there's not a soul in sight. . . . Three hundred years of trapping down the drain. That's when poverty came to Pelican Narrows."

Fred Ballantyne looks over the ice-covered Pelican Lake, shimmering in the weak winter sun, and he says, "It used to be so good out in the bush. We were so healthy. But now there's too many bad things – drugs, alcohol, gambling, bingo. And the young guys, nobody wants to trap any more. There's no TV or DVD machines in the bush." Not one of Gordon Peter's three boys has ever put his toe down on a trapline; neither their father or their grandfather have shown them what the good old way of life was like. Why bother, they ask, if you can't make a living off of it?

XXX

VESPERS

Against the light's fading
the spruce line the lake
with darkness, inky extensions
of earth's Cimmerian core.

Spectre birch slink away
into boreal night
and spruce reach
their ragged arms up
to bring down the light.

Glen Sorestad
Jan Lake Poems

XXXXXXXXXXXXXXXXXXXXXXXXXXXXXXXXXXXXXXXXXXXXXXXXXXXXXXXXXXXXX c   b

U   q

3

nisto

ONE PREACHES, ONE PRAYS

PĪYAK AYAMEKIMĀW, KOTAK OTAYAMIYĀW

Gordon Peter, his wife, Susan, and a cousin, Cindy Ballantyne, are fishing in the late summer afternoon on the second day of the derby. Gordon Peter recalls the extraordinary event that happened. "Susan shouted, 'What's that thing?' So I looked, and it was hovering between the two islands not far from the Anglican church. That thing was just hovering with no sound. It was white, oval-shaped, about forty to fifty feet long. As we looked at it it got rounder and smaller and changed colour to black. Then it expanded, then it grew smaller, expanded a second time, and then suddenly disappeared."

When Gordon Peter returned home, he discovered that his old acquaintance from Jan Lake, Dr. Harvey Christiansen had died that day. The news made him think about the yellow Beaver he had spotted. It had taken off after gassing up and flown over the Ballantynes' boat. Gordon Peter had been surprised that he had heard no sound coming from the engine. Not long afterwards the plane crashed into a lake about forty kilometres away. Dr. Christiansen had perished at almost exactly the same moment the

Ballantynes, and many others, had watched the white oval hovering on the horizon.

Ask anyone living at Pelican Narrows what religious denomination they are, and they'll emphatically reply either Anglican or Catholic. Around his neck Gordon Peter wears a large medallion of Madonna and Child, made of some shiny, reflective material, and there are pictures of Jesus and Mary on the walls of his house. Yet, like everyone else on the reserve, he goes to church only occasionally, and, when he does, he attends the Anglican service, although he considers himself a devout Roman Catholic. While he and Susan were married in an Anglican service at Deschambault, they were not upset when their daughter Vanessa had two sons out of wedlock. Indeed, Gordon Peter was overjoyed at the arrival of more babies in his house and accepted the responsibility for their care without question. There was some talk that Vanessa might marry the father of Andrew and Arwin, but he once hit Vanessa while he was drunk, she had him charged with assault, and that was the end of that. Vanessa's situation is certainly not unique. While there are plenty of funerals performed in the reserve churches these days, there are few weddings. The majority of births are to unwed mothers, and this is considered neither unnatural nor lamentable. And there are other basic tenets that are ignored – the prohibitions on birth control and premarital sex, for example. It's as though Christianity has decomposed here until it's simply a façade, propped up only for appearance' sake.

As for the old Cree religion, the religion of the forest, only a few elders have an understanding of what it is all about. Fred Ballantyne certainly knows how important *pawātamowin* (dreams) are or the damage a *witigo* can cause, and has managed to blend these ideas with his Catholic religion. And there are a few others who are trying to reconnect with the past, both with actual practices and, more importantly, with the old-time value system. But many on the reserve have declared the old beliefs utter nonsense. Philip Ratt goes so far as to say that religious practice didn't exist until Christian missionaries showed up. His ancestors, he believes, were all truly heathens. And yet even he concedes that living in the boreal forest, it's almost impossible *not* to encounter otherworldly phenomena.

Early morning. The round silver moon is still shining as bright as white ice. Clouds hang layered like deep snowbanks in the sky. Suddenly the white mass turns into a grizzled monster. It opens its mouth and swallows the moon.

The puce-green neon bumps and grinds along the horizon; the spirit of the aurora borealis is having fun. Suddenly a streak of red plummets downward; the drop of blood reaches the horizon and the magic show disappears.

Strange footprints in the snow that lead nowhere. A heavenly scent emanating from a foul-looking dung heap. Bizarre noises, not the howl of wolves, coyotes, lynx, wolverines, but something else, a whiny, piercing wail. Anything seems possible in this dense, capricious wilderness. The ever-rational Philip Ratt admits even he sometimes heard voices as he worked his trapline. "I'd be walking home at night through a forest that had been inhabited by people long, long ago. I'd get the creeps, like someone was watching me." George Nelson, a perceptive fur trader whose journals, written in the early nineteenth century, have long proved a bonanza for scholars studying Cree belief, wrote that, "I am as positive and as firmly persuaded of the truth of the assertion that they have dealings with some supernatural spirit, as I am convinced that I live and breathe in air."[1]

The world of the pre-contact Cree was full of mythical beings, and their oral literature reflected this. Among the many characters who danced on the Rock Cree's metaphysical stage:

The *mēmēkwēsiw* lived in rock caves near fast-flowing rapids. The American writer P.G. Downes was told that these creatures were "a strange and elf-like people with flat faces and just two holes for a nose. If one comes upon them unexpectedly, they are inclined to bend over and hide their faces with their hands."[2] They had supernatural abilities, but seemed only to have used them to play pranks on animals and humans.

The *pāhkahkos* were flying skeletons who "preyed upon bad hunters – men who wounded animals and let them escape or killed them unnecessarily." The Cree writer Joseph Dion described the creature thus: "He was . . . a ghost of a mischievous nature who had long bony fingers which he could use with dexterity and he carried a small gun of sorts."³ An attack by a *pāhkahkos* often led to paralysis.

The wonderful *wīsahkēcāhk*, the trickster/transformer, is a central character in Cree oral literature. Both a joker and a teacher, both a tragic and a comic figure, friendly and unfriendly, clever and dumb, always hungry, and desperate for sex, he is totally unpredictable. And in out-fooling just about everybody and everything, he becomes a hero.

The terrifying *witigo* was once a human, who, perhaps driven insane by hunger, has eaten human flesh. His appetite for cannibalism grows as he ranges the land, looking for man meals. He is black as coal, has blood made of ice, and a face with no lips, since he has already eaten them away. (And he could just as well be a she.)

The historian Gerald Friesen writes, "Indian religious beliefs emphasized the importance of reconciliation with the supernatural and usually found their expression in metaphors drawn from the natural environment."⁴ Certainly it was from nature that the Rock Cree world view was constructed. Central and most important to their cosmology was the belief that animals were either created before, or at the same time as, man. "At first humans and animals were identical, superimposed on each other in some nebulous human/animal form," writes the scholar Calvin Martin, giving his interpretation of the Woodland religion. "Only subsequently did the two become differentiated, or polarized, in their outward, physical nature."⁵ From time immemorial, then, Cree belief centred around this deep bond between humans and animals. This is no human-centric world; both are equal. There is sympathy, courtesy, even love, between the two. Unlike man, animals live in a non-linear, supra-physical world. They exist as spirits "who don fleshy robes from time to time for human benefit. The fox that one kills today is not the real animal. The real fox himself, his spirit or shadow or soul, is alive, watching the hunter."[6] The fox "gives" himself because of his love for humankind. And the hunter must reciprocate.

Robert Brightman is an American anthropologist who lived with the Rock Cree at Pukatawagan, some 220 kilometres from Pelican Narrows, in the 1970s. He writes that the Cree hunter shows his gratitude to his prey in many different ways. Whispering endearments as traps are set and singing songs accompanied by drums and rattles just before the hunt – "This is the hole which is the home of the muskrat. I am going to live with the muskrat. This is the lodge which is the home of the beaver. I am going to live with the beaver" – were meant to comfort and appease the animal so that it would voluntarily sacrifice itself.[7] An efficient kill was absolutely essential, as one hunter points out. "Kill them quickly! You can't let them suffer! Kill 'em quick! You got to give them the same respect you give yourself."[8] Once the game animal has been taken, rituals of gratitude become even more important. The animals must be butchered carefully, so the vertebrae isn't broken, and in as clean an environment as possible. There is to be no waste, no wanton killing. When a hunter returns to camp, he must do so quietly, displaying little excitement and certainly not boasting about his catch; the people waiting for their share of meat must also act in a dignified and solemn manner, a show of respect to the dead animal.

The quarry is taken into the hunter's dwelling, where it is placed at the back with the head facing forward. The meat is then distributed to everyone in camp, depending on their age and their relationship to the hunter.[9] The flesh must not be stored for too long a period – thus the eat-all feasts that followed a successful hunt. The bones and other inedible parts were made into useful objects or decorated and put on display. And the skulls and carcasses of large animals were placed in trees so that no dog or other animal would molest them. In the woods around many homes at Pelican Narrows these skeletons can still be found. "They tie up the bone and hang them, and they say the animals turn back again after they're gone. They turn back to life and start scattering again. They go back to life."[10] And therefore can be hunted again.

A Rock Cree was not stuck in the material world; he had access to the supernatural and all the spirits who roamed there through his *pawātamowin*, his dreams. "They [hunters] have certain kinds of dreams," said Solomon Custer in a 1970 interview.[11] "They know if [in their dreams] they have fur in their traps, they will kill a moose the following day. Sometimes after his dream the man just can't sleep, he stays awake late at night and he knows he will have good hunting luck the next day." Added Morris Bear, "They used to have a leader who had a stronger power than the rest of those people. They used to have one leader that was in front hunting all the time. Yeah, his dreams were stronger than the rest."[12]

There was no standard dream among the Rock Cree – nothing like Freud's naked-among-strangers fantasy; interpretations were unique to each individual. Solomon Merasty, interviewed in 1936, contended that, if one man dreamed of a naked woman, he was assured of getting the largest moose. Peter Ballantyne, grandson of the chief, brother to Roderick, interviewed in 1970, said he would dream of good fishing, then the next day his shoulder would start twitching and he knew to get at it.

Philip Morin tells of a dream once visited on his brother-in-law Morris Bear. "In the morning he got up and he [Morris Bear] said, 'I saw two white ladies coming here, and they served me dinner.' They were the same size, he said, nice-looking white ladies. 'Maybe we'll have some luck today.' We started hunting around two that day, and the wind started to blow right away. We saw a couple of moose going up the hill, and we run after them, and Morris Bear said, 'They must be here.' He's a really good hunter, that old boy. Anyway we ran over, and he said, 'There they are!' On top of the hill stood two big milk cows. 'That's the two ladies I dreamed about last night,' he said."

Dreams were also important for women. Mary Custer, and her husband, Henry, live in a tiny house on the "outskirts" of Pelican

Narrows Reserve. Although she is eighty years old, she still laments the fact that she bore only one child. "I should have had more kids, but there was some kind of curse. I kept dreaming that my babies were hairy all over. And I lost them, one after another. Finally I went to a medicine man to heal this curse, and I had my one baby.

"I used to believe in dreams when I was young, but nowadays I don't like my dreams, and I pray a lot for those dreams to go away. But, yeah, I used to believe in them a whole lot."

It was in his dreams that the Rock Cree encountered his *pawātākan*, that guardian spirit that he had first caught a glimpse of when, as an adolescent, he had undertaken his vision quest. A timber wolf, or wolverine, an eagle or owl, a lynx or fox, a sturgeon, or otter, the wind, just about anything was a candidate for this role. The relationship was supposed to be one of respect and love, although sometimes, like everything else in the Rock Cree's life, the *pawātākan* could be "unpredictable, demanding and dangerous."[13] The essential point was that the strength of his *pawātākan* determined a man's success in the physical world and his survival against the wicked. Naturally, it was the spirit guardians of a medicine man or shaman who were often the strongest, and the most difficult to contend with. Cree oral literature abounds with stories of wrongdoing performed by *pawātākan* on behalf of a human. John Dorion, in 1970, recounted the story of how a hunter went out looking for moose and saw a fat lady walking in the bush, "just like one of those little Jack pines. Then he saw a partridge, and he shot the partridge, you know, and he got it. Branches fell off but no feathers, just spruce boughs, you know those? Just those fell out but no feathers."[14] The hunter tried again and again, bear, partridge, rabbits, moose, squirrels. He caught nothing. Finally he remembered a ferocious argument he had had, under the influence of homebrew, over a woman. Now the hunter discovered that his protagonist had stronger *pawātākan* than he did. Not only he, but his entire family, was in danger of starving to death.

The most famous story of a vengeful spirit is told by Ratt's father, Albert Ratt, who in 2004 was ninety-six yea involves two shaman, medicine men who have strong *pawamiwin*, spiritual powers: John Alexander Custer better known as Othapatchikew, the force for good, and Pikekun, the instrument of evil. Pikekun was a shaman who used his powers to blackmail and terrify people. His favourite trick was to demand plug tobacco for his pipe from anyone he met. If they refused, he'd sent bad medicine, or even a *witigo* to kill them. Several people died of fright simply because he threatened to hex them.

Othapatchikew landed at Pikekun's camp one day. Immediately, Pikekun went down to greet him, saying, *"How, Othapatchikeses, petwa'en."* ("Okay, Little Othapatchikew, give me a smoke.") In using the diminutive, Pikekun tried to insult his guest. Othapatchikew replied in front of everyone that Pikekun was not getting anything from him. Pikekun became extremely angry and promised Othapatchikew that he would pay for this insolence.

The next winter during the moose hunt, Othapatchikew became unwell, and drank some medicine which only made him feel dizzy. One time he was crossing a small muskeg. Suddenly a light flashed in front of his eyes. He heard a loud racket, and saw a huge eagle coming straight for him. Just in time he fired his gun. The eagle let out a human cry and flew away in distress.

The next spring Othapatchikew travelled to Nelson House, to sell his furs and once there inquired about the health of Pikekun. He was then told what he expected to hear: the very moment he had shot the eagle, Pikekun had clutched his heart and fell to the ground; he had been slowly dying ever since.

Albert Ratt says that the ability to perform *pawamiwin* died out because shaman abused their power. By the time Christian missionaries had arrived, many Rock Cree had lost faith in their diviners.

The Cree religious rituals were not elaborate – a lone trapper tossing tobacco on the lake ice in the hope of an early spring thaw or checking the burnt bones of animals to determine how good a hunt would be. This is one reason many Pelican Narrows Cree do not consider their ancestors' spiritualism as a "true religion." But there was one observance that brought people – that is men – together in dramatic ceremony and that was the strange "shaking tent," or "prediction," performance.

Six poles are lashed together to form a barrel-like structure which is then covered by moose hides (or later canvas). There is drumming and everyone is singing, calling to the *pawātākan* to come. The shaman enters alone; the male elders of the tribe remain seated outside, listening. As he shakes his rattle, the shaman begins to croon to the spirits. Soon the tent begins to shake and then shake harder, as more and more guardian spirits cram in. There is shouting and laughter from the audience outside the tent.

In a 1970 interview Peter Ballantyne (grandson of the chief) described what went on in the tent: "Jackfish *pawātākan* doesn't speak but the rest of the *pawātākan* all speak. The beaver, the bear, the wind. All the *pawātākan* come in the tent, standing around, making noises, not Cree. This man [the shaman] goes in the centre and all the *pawātākan* gather around him. He asks them questions and the men outside ask them questions: What about tomorrow's hunt, good or bad? What medicine for rotten feet? Where is the body of my wife's auntie's drowned cousin? The *pawātākan* make more noises and the shaman understands and tells the people."[15]

The *pawātākan* liked to laugh; the funniest, often scatological, jokes were told by them. They liked tobacco even more, and, all during the performance, the spectators would push pouches under the tent. Sometimes homebrew was included, but the shaman always claimed he never touched a drop; the *pawātākan* drank it all. By the time the ceremony was over and the crowd could peer into the tent, the brew and tobacco had disappeared. Sometimes the shaman would have himself tied up Houdini-like. Naturally he was found free as a bird after the *pawātākan* had left.

In 1951 the American anthropologist Eleanor Leacock came across a shaking-tent rite of the Montagnais-Naskapi just as it was concluding and people were leaving. "Hearing them murmur and laugh about what the various gods had said . . . it struck her how similar they sounded to people coming out of a rural theatre and repeating the interesting and enjoyable parts of the film they had just seen."[16]

Directing this mélange of animal spirits and humans was a supreme being, or *Kisēmanitow*. He is the creator of all things and, according to George Nelson, the Rock Cree perceived him as, "uncommonly good and kind. . . . This one they love, they love him a great deal, and are no means afraid of him, because he always addresses them, 'My Little Children, etc.,' and all the rest of his character is a piece with this."[17] In an allegoric prayer given by Pontiac, chief of the Ottawa nation (Algonkian speakers of the Eastern Woodland), the Great Spirit is talking to a young brave: "I am the Maker of heaven and earth, the trees, lakes, rivers, and all things else. I am the Maker of mankind; and because I love you, you must do my will. The land on which you live I have made for you, and not for others. Why do you suffer the white men to dwell among you?"

The Cree parallel to that prayer was in the form of a lecture by the elders to the children: "Here, you young people, destroy nothing. Take good care of everything and do not waste anything, because it is God who is the master. Do not insult the wind, God has made it. Do not have contempt for water, God has created it. Accept rain without murmuring, for God sends it to us. Do not abuse the trees or anything else, because God has provided these things for our use."[18]

When the missionaries arrived in the nineteenth century, the Cree were able to intertwine many Christian beliefs with their own. The concept of a supreme being; the idea of intermediaries, ("Haw! You [*pawātākan*] have now reached our Father's house," goes one Cree prayer); the guardian spirit that was, in effect, a guardian angel (*pawātākan* could fly); the *witigo* as devil; an adherence to a philosophy that emphasized generosity as much as the Golden Rule – all these things were not incompatible with European beliefs. Too bad these men of God thought it necessary, as part of their proselytizing, to denigrate and demolish aboriginal culture.

The first missionaries to devote themselves to the west Woodland Cree were Jesuits who set up shop on the west side of James Bay at what would become Fort Albany. They lasted for seven years, from 1686 to 1693, before they finally admitted defeat, lamenting that it was impossible to convert these Indians, because they wandered all over the place. It would be another 130 years before the experiment was tried again, this time by a Church of England clergyman who was stationed at York Factory. By 1840, the Anglicans had established a mission inland at Cumberland House, and by 1846 at La Ronge. Under the tutelage of missionaries in both these places, the Ballantyne family were baptized in the Church of England, probably sometime in the early 1850s.

The Anglican presence was regarded as a challenge, if not a threat, to Roman Catholic ambitions. Joseph-Norbert Provencher, the Bishop of St. Boniface at Red River (presently Winnipeg) decided something must be done and he appealed to a French missionary order to bring The Word to the vast Northwest.

The Oblates of Mary Immaculate were founded in 1816 in southern France by Father Eugène de Mazenod, later Bishop of Marseilles. "The evangelization of the poor" was a touchstone of the Oblates'; they too took vows of poverty. And they were strong proponents of Ultramontanism.

This was a religious movement that had begun in Europe during the French Revolution. It appealed to those craving a world devoid of "free-thinkers," liberals, socialists, and anarchists, where the hierarchy of society was firmly set and the lower classes (including aboriginals) showed deference and knew their place. The order looked "across the mountain" to Rome and the Pope for stability. This nostalgia for a lost order eventually hardened into an ultra-Catholic dogmatism that insisted on the supremacy of the Church over the civil state and would brook no dallying with modern thought or, for that matter, any ideas that did not originate with, or were not approved by, the Pope. It turned into a cult of the passionately devout, and the dangerously closed-minded.[19]

Bishop Ignace Bourget of Montreal was a strong proponent of Ultramontanism and he was the first Canadian clergyman to contact Bishop Mazenod. In 1841 he requested that any available Oblate missionaries be sent to him. Four priests and two brothers arrived in Montreal the next year. "You are charged with the establishment of the community in those vast territories, for Montreal is perhaps only the gateway to the conquest of souls in many lands," wrote Bourget. "Conquest" became a keynote of their evangelizing.

Four years later, in 1845, responding to the pleading of Bishop Provencher, two Oblate missionaries travelled to Red River. In 1846 Oblates reached Île-à-la-Crosse by canoe, and from there spread like weeds, north, east, and west, setting up a mission at Pelican Narrows in 1876. When they left France, wrote Father Garry LaBoucane, the Oblates had a "sense of freedom and exploration, a sense of renewal, of heroism, of adventure." Yes, and a full-blown belief that their religion, culture, science, art, was far superior to anything offered by *les sauvages*. ("Brutes" or "savages," as the Oblates insisted on calling the Rock Cree. The correct French word is *Indien*.)

Twenty-five years after the Oblate missionaries arrived at Pelican Narrows almost the entire population had been baptized, most in the Roman Catholic faith. Why did the Rock Cree succumb so readily to the Christian message? The reasons were many and complex. The terrible toll taken by the epidemics, which had killed so many – smallpox in 1781–82, whooping cough and measles in 1820, measles in 1846 – may have resulted in a loss of faith in the Indian medicine man. The shortage of game, especially beaver, after 1800 may have persuaded many Indians to no longer put faith in their *pawātākan*. And the Cree must have been overwhelmed by white mastery: their technology – their ability to predict such fearsome events as eclipses, and chart directions with a gadget called a compass – their ability to read and write, their amazing true-to-life paintings that decorated the churches, their superior weapons, their absolute belief that their world was so much more advanced than the Indian's.

It was a vicious circle. The more the Rock Cree got caught in the maw of the fur trade's materialism, the more they came to believe that the white man represented authority. The fur trader, the clergyman, the Indian agent, the educator, the doctor, all became *okimā*, boss men. In a short time, so much that the Cree had believed was meaningful in their culture was deemed improper and inferior. Their way of dressing, their hairstyle, their religion, their art, their names, their ancestors, their medicine, their law, their music, their marriage traditions, their sexual habits, their child-rearing methods – all of these were challenged and then stamped with the mark of the devil.

The Oblates were particularly enraged at Indian music; the drum and rattle symbolized to them everything "primitive" about the *sauvage*. The musical instruments were thrown in lakes, axed, or burnt. Their songs were labelled "the voice of the devil." Soon the heart of their spirituality, their music, was destroyed.

Oblates learned the Cree language, but only so they could preach at the heathens, not listen to them. So rigid was their belief that Christianity was the only possible path to salvation, most (there were exceptions) did not move one inch towards genuinely understanding Indian spirituality. The difference between a shaman who may or may not perform evil acts and a medicine man was of no interest to the priests, so they attacked both. Grand Chief George Manuel, a Shuswap from British Columbia, once wrote, "My grandfather was an Indian doctor and a respected leader of his people, and during the last 10 years of life, I saw a proud man stripped of his dignity and pride. I saw his face as the priest told our people that if they listened to him, or sought his advice, they would burn in hell."[20]

The Oblates often wrote about how shocked they were when they encountered "the depravity" of the savage. They were talking about sex, of course. The puritanical, misogynist attitudes of the priests were as far away from the Cree's acceptance of the sexual act as natural and pleasurable as choral music was from drum beats. And then there was polygamy, a tradition of the Woodland

Cree. Wapaskokimaw had five wives, and Othapatchikew had two, but as shamans, they had great stature in their society. American scholar Harriet J. Kupferer, believes polygamy didn't occur very often, "as it would have taken a very successful hunter to provide for more than one spouse and her children."[21] But when the wife's sister became a widow, it would have been the duty of the husband to marry her also. "That's the way it had to be," says journalist Ron Merasty. "Otherwise the widow and children would have perished." Certainly it was a practice that was a total anathema to the Christian missionaries.

As a prerequisite for baptism, the Oblates insisted that families with more than one wife be split apart. Philip Morin's grandfather had five wives, and to obey "God's regulations" he had to sever his ties with four of them. In a 1970 interview, Philip revealed what his grandfather told him. "They use those spoons (rattles), you know, they turn their back, the man facing towards one way, and the woman, the other. The man says, 'Well, I'm leaving you now.' And the woman answers, 'It's alright if you leave me.' And then they start to walk away. After they got a little further, they turn around, and this man says, 'One more thing, I want you to understand, them kids of ours, what we've got, three or four, I leave all to you, so they could look after you.'"[22]

Philip Morin makes it sound easy, and so do the writings of the Oblates and scholars, when, in fact, it caused great pain. Says Julie Caribou, a student at First Nations University in Regina: "Think how you'd feel. The man had to choose the wife he liked best, and naturally the others were very jealous, very upset. I'm sure there was a lot of shouting and arguments and tears. My great-grandmother was one of those kicked out and my mom and aunts still talk about it."

Of course, not everyone succumbed to Christian teachings. Oblate missionary Marius Rossignol, who lived among the Rock Cree for over four decades of which eleven years were spent at Pelican Narrows, wrote the following story about an old man, Namegus ("Trout"), who remained a devoted pagan until his death.

When his wife wanted to become a Christian and be baptized, he did not forbid her, just made fun of her. As she came back from the [baptismal] ceremony, he asked her what her new name was and invited her to eat, offering her a piece of dried meat, the hardest he could find, and saying to her: "Let's see if your teeth will cut better now that your name is Nancy."[23]

Despite the odd holdout, by 1900 most of the Rock Cree had become Christians, and devoted ones at that. Joseph Courtney, the Indian agent for Pelican Narrows, reported in 1904: "In Peter Ballantyne's band the Roman Catholics predominate. They all attend their religious services with great regularity. Their morals are comparatively good, and no intemperance has been so far reliably reported." But many clergymen – at least the honest ones – began to doubt whether their congregants really understood Christianity and how deeply the faith was felt. P.G. Downes relays a poignant story told to him by the Oblate missionary to the Dene, Joseph Egenolf:

There was a little girl in my [catechism] class. She looked very bright – most Indian children do. Every day I took special care of this little one. I went over the questions and answers with her alone. You know, there is a part in our catechism where the question is asked, "What is the most beautiful thing God created?" The answer is "Man and all the angels." But do you think I could teach this simple thing, that this little mind could learn? Every time I asked: "What is the most beautiful thing God created?" She would look up at me and say: "*Idthen!*" – "the caribou!"

The old priest rocked in his chair for a while. He buried his lined face in his hands. He was thinking. "You know," he burst out . . . "sometimes when I feel weak, I say to myself, 'Thirty-four years here I have perhaps done nothing.'"[24]

No matter how hard the clergy tried to instill their ideas of heaven and hell, the *witigo*, the cannibalistic human, remained far more frightening than the Christian devil.

May 6, 1907, a clear, bright day. Several canoes land at Pelican Narrows. It seems the entire Ballantyne family, led by Chief Peter, has arrived. The Hudson's Bay post manager knows immediately that something is wrong – there is terror on every face. In one canoe sits a woman in her forties. Her long hair is dishevelled, her clothing is twisted every which way, and her eyes are sparking madness. This is the wife of Robbie Ballantyne, one of Chief Peter's grandsons. She is turning into a *witigo*, they know that for sure. "They were all crazed with fear," the HBC manager reported, "and seemed to wish to rid themselves of the poor woman by dumping her on the populace here. She is in serious condition because her people have terrified her so. She'll surely die if she goes back with them." At that time the Ballantyne family had been Christians for at least forty years and Peter was a lay reader.

In the 1930s, while he was out trapping, Fred Ballantyne's father, David, a devout Catholic, was stalked by a *witigo*. "My dad had a .22 in his hand, but if you shoot the *witigo*, the bullets bounce back, because under his skin is ice. You have to know where to shoot him, but my dad said, 'I don't want to hurt him, he's a person (who is cannibalistic).'" Instead Fred's father held up his rosary beads, which he always wore around his neck, and the monster was too unnerved to attack. "*Witigos* don't like rosary beads," says Fred who often gives the Sunday sermon at St. Gertrude's Catholic Church.

Of course, there were those that completely embraced Christianity. The cultural amnesia that resulted could sometimes have dire consequences. P.G. Downes tells the story of a Pelican Narrows man and his son who set out in a boat in the late 1920s, confident that their new outboard engine could handle anything. They had gone only a few yards when the engine conked out. The man grabbed his son and the two kneeled down and began praying, only to be swept over the edge of a falls to their death. The unfortunate man had, wrote Downes, "put his faith in the white man's god instead of his forefather's paddle."²⁵

Étienne Bonnald, Oblate missionary and sometime fur trader, arrived at Pelican Narrows, in the spring of 1877. Luckily, the Hudson's Bay post manager, Antoine Morin, was a Catholic, and provided him with the best room in his small house. There the priest spent the summer teaching and preaching and getting to know "*mes sauvages.*" In the fall he returned to The Pas, but the next spring he was back building a church, "a poor little thing," three by four metres square. It was called St. Gertrude's. Later, in the summer, Charles Thomas's barge arrived laden with building material and two passengers, Brother Labelle and Brother Némos. The three Oblates built a residence, a little larger than the church but by not much, consisting of a chapel and bedroom. By 1878, Father Bonnald had settled in for an indefinite stay.²⁶

He was twenty-eight years old, wiry, small-boned, and handsome in a refined way. He had grown up in the picturesque villages of Auroux, Lambert, and Behiezt, in southern France, holidaying in the ancient town of Mussac. In his letters he mentions a mother and a sister (who became a nun), but never a father. It may be that that parent was dead, since an uncle seems to have had the greatest influence on him. In 1884 Bonnald wrote, "I still have the letter that he [the uncle] sent me from Maussac in December 1866. In this letter, he gave me permission to follow my religious calling, and asked me to always remember him to God, especially after his death."²⁷

After Bonnald was ordained, he was sent to Saint Albert near Edmonton, headquarters of the Oblates in the Northwest. From there he travelled to Reindeer Lake's Mission de Saint-Pierre du Lac Caribou, where he studied Cree and Dene. His first major posting was to Pelican Narrows, and he would remain at the mission for twenty-three years, converting the ancestors of many of the people who live there now. (It helped that he sometimes handed out cheaper goods at his "store" than the HBC did at theirs.)

When Bonnald first arrived, he followed the practice of many missions by hiring Métis labour, *engagés*, who did much of the manual work; collecting enough firewood for the winter was in itself a huge job, as was catching the thousand or so fish it took to feed the dogs each winter. He decided, however, that individual workers were too expensive and married couples cost two or three times more because of the room and board that had to be provided. He fired his aboriginal servants and, instead, adopted an Indian boy.

Seven-year-old Cyrille Castel arrived at St. Gertrude's Mission, not long after Bonnald. Eight years later, the priest would write: "Cyrille works for us, he catches fish, cuts and hauls wood and comes with me during my trips." By 1883 Father Bonnald had acquired another orphan, Elie. "He's very nice and does a good job assisting me during mass. He lights our fire, goes to fetch water and stays with us."[28] There's a hint here of slave labour, but the priest seemed to genuinely care for his charges. He built for Cyrille "a beautiful wooden house where he stays with his mother and one of his aunts." And Cyrille seemed fond of the priest. In an 1884 letter Bonnald describes a poignant scene. On returning from one of his many trips (Pukatawagan also relied on his services), the dog team stopped at the island near Pelican Narrows. Cyrille was waiting there for the priest with a cup of tea. They chatted happily, exchanging news and gossip. Then the young man tucked the elder under two blankets of hare skin, and accompanied him home.[29]

Bonnald also seemed to have real affection for his parishioners and was appreciative of what they gave up for him. He wrote, "This morning after mass, a savage brought me several pounds of wild meat pâté which was delicious with the fruits from last fall. The savage had to deprive himself so that he could have the pleasure of presenting me with this portion which he kept for me for so long."[30] But he often grew frustrated with his "*sauvages*." One day during catechism class, he asked, "Children, where does God live?" "He lives on an island in the lake," several replied. "And who created the fishes?" he asked again. One little boy spoke before the others, "My mother." "I am not impressed at the religious knowledge of our children," the priest wrote.

Bonnald was the first Oblate in Canada's Northwest to insist that his congregation pay an annual levy. About half did so, and the money was distributed to the poor of the parish. In his sermons and readings he was always dwelling on charity as the great good. (As if the Cree did not already know this.) This may be a hint as to why he decided to compete with the HBC as a fur trader. He was truly disgusted at the parsimoniousness of the company.

By the time he was ordered to leave Pelican Narrows, he was fifty years old. The reason given was ill-health, but he was soon preaching at a mission that was as isolated as Pelican Narrows, and he lived until he was eighty. His uprooting must have sent a message to other Oblates: don't fool with the mighty Hudson's Bay Company.

Étienne Bonnald was not the least interested in traditional Cree religion or customs, or with contemporary issues – the dealings with the Canadian government over reserve land, for example. Yet he did not malign or denigrate the aboriginal people in his writings. The same could not be said of all Oblate missionaries.

Ovide Charlebois was born in 1862 to a farming family in Oka, Quebec. Although not a good student, he was very pious. In 1882 he entered the Oblate novitiate, and was consecrated a priest three years later. When Bonnald left St. Gertrude's Mission in 1900, Charlebois was named as his successor. He would stay there only a few years, but his influence on the Catholics in the settlement remained strong. He climbed the Oblate's hierarchical ladder and by 1910 he would be Bishop of Keewatin.

In 1902 a pretty new church, painted white with a bright red roof, was constructed in Pelican Narrows with labour volunteered by Cree parishioners. There was an imposing bell, shiny new lights, and a lovely statue of Our Lady of Lourdes. Charlebois believed that his congregants would be delighted. Indeed, they might have admired the new church, but they didn't like him at all. They were particularly outraged when he lay poison along his trapline in the hope of a quick kill. Several dogs, including one of his own, died.

He was a cold, stern man, who appreciated nothing about Cree culture – except perhaps kindnesses towards himself. The Indians, he wrote, were "ignorant," "lazy," "hypocritical," "coarse." And most revealing: "The true missionary life is a continual death to self, death to daintiness, death to sensuality, death to self-will, death to the whole being, but not to the soul."[31] And that, of course, is why he and so many other missionaries invaded Indian country. They would become sacrificial lambs, and as such, were assured of eternal salvation.

Since my last retreat my mind has dwelt upon one thought. It is to become a martyr. That is no small ambition, is it? You will at once ask me, who will be the executioners? That is very simple, they will be the mosquitoes; they will be my Pierriche;[*] they will be the children of my catechism class; they will be my faults, my temptations, my pains, my privations, and all the rest of it. I do not seek a little martyrdom lasting for a few hours, but a life-long martyrdom. . . . So I will think of myself as being burned at the stake at a slow fire that will keep me alive for a long while.[32]

Pelican Narrows was actually a Roman Catholic island in a sea of Anglicans. The closest settlements, Stanley Mission, La Ronge, Cumberland House had long been Church of England strongholds. Many Pelican Narrows Indians, including the Ballantyne family,

---

[*] The meaning of this is not known. It may refer to one of the many orphan children whom Charlebois collected and deposited in residential schools as he made his way across the Northwest.

had been baptized at one of these places and remained practising Anglicans. At first services were held in the Hudson's Bay Company's office, but eventually a small shack was constructed. Reverend James Settee from La Ronge visited Pelican Narrows twice a year. The natives felt comfortable with him, for he was one of the first Indians to be ordained in the Church of England.

Visiting Anglican priests were supposed to come four times a year for services, but that often didn't happen. "Last year our people at this place did not have a visit from a Missionary or Mission Agent of any kind for nearly the whole year. The wonder is that they remain faithful," reported the Synod Journal of 1908. For years the Anglican leaders kept promising to build a church at Pelican Narrows, and finally in 1911 it happened. "The Indians gave of their offerings and also turned out with a will to prepare the timber for the building," informed the journal. But it would not be until 1961 that an Anglican clergyman would actually live at Pelican Narrows. The Anglicans then, by their absence, were a benign force compared to the Catholics, although their attitude towards the natives was no less patronizing and paternalistic. In a 1906 report, the Reverend Thompson Ferrier made it clear he had never bothered to study Cree culture. Indians were to him "dirty, lousy, greasy aborigine." He wrote,

No pen has yet ever adequately portrayed the heroic, self-sacrificing efforts of those who have laboured among the dusky brothers of the forests and plains. We believe nothing but the constraining love of Christ could induce any one to undertake a work which in almost every respect must be void of congeniality. . . . About 11,000 in our Dominion are still pagans; they worship the Great Manitou and sacrifice to the great White God. They are ruled by cunning medicine men and are the prey of superstitious fears. Shall these go down to darkness and to death, unillumined by the blessed light of the Gospel of Salvation?[33]

By the mid-nineteenth century, the Catholics and Protestants invading the Northwest loathed each other. In 1879 the Anglican missionary Samuel Trivett wrote: "I verily believe that the Romish religion . . . is as bad or worse than the idolatry of the Brohmins or superstition of Mohamed."[34] And the Catholics were just as bad. As the Oblate J.M. Pénard, the biographer of Bishop Charlebois, informed his readers, "The Protestants . . . have neither certain dogmas, nor a solidly founded scheme of morality. Their whole preaching takes the form of senseless commonplaces, or furious and lying attacks on the Catholic faith."[35]

Converting the heathen became a bitter contest. An Oblate document dated 1911 carefully catalogues all the Protestants, both adults and children, who have been converted to Catholicism in Pelican Narrows, including the dates of their baptisms. Listed are forty-seven names, a large number given that the Anglican population at the time was only about three hundred. "I send this report with great joy," writes the author, who is not named.

Just before Chief Peter Ballantyne died in 1917, he too turned from the Church of England to the Church of Rome. This conversion was celebrated by the Oblates as a significant victory over the Anglicans, but Fred Ballantyne has another interpretation. "He [Chief Peter] got sick and he worries and there was no Anglican minister here at Pelican Narrows. Only the Catholic priest was here. The Catholics and Protestants and the other ones [Evangelicals] were pretty near the same. Just little things were not the same. So it didn't matter to the Chief which priest came."

John Merasty points to his great-grandfather as an illustration of how the Woods Cree accepted both denominations. "My great-grandfather was a pretty religious man. The Catholics and Anglicans have different songs they sing in Church, but that old man could sing both." The Indians might not have understood the theological differences between the two sects of Christianity, but the acrimony and deviousness for which Catholic and Anglican priests were responsible seeped deep into the community.

The core of Pelican Narrows, the original village, is shaped like a lopsided lobster. A short claw protrudes a little ways into Pelican Lake, and on it sits the Catholic church. At the end of the longer claw, jutting further out into the lake, is situated the Anglican church. Smack in the middle rises a steep hill. It is here where the graves of the 1730 massacre victims were found, and it is this rocky ridge that has divided the community for decades. On the west, the little houses of the Roman Catholics are scattered, on the east the equally modest homes of the Protestants were built. Depending on your affiliation, the good guys were on one side, the bad on the other. "You wouldn't dare go for a walk on the opposite side," Philip Ratt remembers. "You might not come out alive."

When denominational day schools were built in the late 1950s, the situation heated up even more. The kids would stand on their side of the hill and throw rocks at each other. "I used to go over to the Protestant side, they'd beat the hell out of me, and when those other guys came, if we could catch them, we'd beat the hell out of them," remembers Gilbert Linklater. Gordon Peter laughs, "It was all-out war."

"We were together at one time before the black robes came in," says artisan J.B. Custer. "It was one big, strong circle, spiritual, emotional, physical, mental, all intact. Now we're like a pie. The Anglicans are one slice, the Catholics another, the Evangelicals a third."

"It's still there, you know," adds Ida Swan, a teacher. "The animosity is still there. Most of the leaders are Catholic, and most of the good jobs go to them, because there are more of them."

The Catholics had the upper hand because their clerics, sometimes two or three at a time, lived in the community and their power was enormous. Étienne Bonnald, for example, often held cash the Pelican Narrows Cree gave him for safekeeping. In the fall of 1898 several Indians approached the HBC manager and complained that Bonnald had refused to give it back to them. They insisted they were not indebted to the priest or his "store." The HBC had them sign orders (with an X) before witnesses and present them to the priest. "Hand the money over to the owners to spend as they wish," wrote the HBC manager. Over the years there were many accusations of this nature against Bonnald.

The cleric who had the most influence over Pelican Narrows residents, simply because he served the longest, was Nicholas Guilloux. He was born in a small village in Brittany in 1879 and was ordained a priest in 1903. Three years later he began a sojourn at Pelican Narrows that would last forty-two years. He was very much part of the lives of his parishioners. At the government's bequest, he handed out medicines and rations to widows and the disabled; he acted as a translator and negotiator between the federal government and the Cree leadership during the negotiations over reserve land; and he decided who was ill enough to be sent to the hospital. He adhered to a strict moral code and he expected his parishioners to do the same. Self-discipline was his major theme. Remembers Gilbert Michel, "He was a tough guy, Nicholas Guilloux. Oh yeah, he was tough."

P.G. Downes was in Pelican Narrows in the summer of 1939. He was good friends with the Hudson's Bay Company post manager and visited his home often. One night Father Guilloux came over for a game of bridge. He and the schoolteacher, an Anglican, teamed up with the HBC manager and his wife. "It was very amusing," wrote Downes, "the Roman and Anglican Churches at peace with each other and presenting a united front against the fur trade. The old priest, who had been at Pelican as long as anyone could remember, went into gales of laughter at his own description of the Indian who hanged himself from the bed post while in the hospital."[36]

There was progress in the air at Pelican Narrows during the 1930s. There were two fur traders: the Hudson's Bay Company and Shorty Russick, who was also starting up the commercial fishery that would bring a bit of prosperity to the settlement. One or two other businesses were established by white entrepreneurs. Geologists, surveyors, and forestry officials flew in and out. The first native activists showed up and gave rousing speeches to "the brothers." And social life in Pelican Narrows flourished.

In the winter the entire white community skied down the village's steep hill, and in the summer played tennis on a well-kept court behind the Hudson's Bay Company store. There were tea parties and bridge games. Every July 1 a sports day was organized with foot races and canoe – the natives won almost every competition. In the evening, there was the highlight: a softball game between Pelican Narrows and Island Falls. The priest was involved in all this action. The HBC manager had a wicked way with his pen as his journals for the years 1938 and 1939 attest:

April 13, 1938: Mon Père round today on one of his infrequent but lengthy visits. One has to be a good listener when he's around. Topic today was gardens.

July 1, 1938: Reverend Ahab Spence [Anglican] came in from Stanley and there was a bell-ringing competition between him and Father Guilloux.

August 22, 1938: Father Guilloux, the self-appointed transportation committee of one here at Pelican, has decided that the plane is not coming so Johnny Merasty has the "contract" to deliver the children to Sturgeon Landing [school]. He has a big boat and an eight H.P. engine.

September 23, 1938: The priest arrived back after ten days at Sturgeon Landing. He says somebody broke into his warehouse, but as apparently nothing was stolen and the lock was not broken we fail to see how it is possible.

December 8, 1938: Father Guilloux rushed off to the Churchill River to baptize a baby that is expected to die shortly.

January 6, 1939: The Father is raising Cain with many people here, and things are warm!!

January 12, 1939: The Priest was down this afternoon. He is going to get his bell, book, and candle after Arrow Airways for not bringing in his mail.

January 19, 1939: The Holy Father doled out a bale of old clothes to the natives. He favoured the Catholics, of course, but he also gave to the Protestants and atheists.

January 20, 1939: Had target practice over at the R.C. Mission. The Father bought an air rifle, and has targets all over his office. He is practising up for a big squirrel hunt in the near future.

February 6, 1939: Father Guilloux headed a deputation asking that we run Buster Flett [a rabble-rouser] out of town to the mutual safety of the community. We declined.

February 16, 1939: Entertained Father Guilloux, or rather he entertained us, in the office.

May 6, 1939: Cursiter brought news that Dorion's wife is very sick and Dorion has left the [fur] trade and is awaiting the Priest at Manawan.

May 7, 1939: Apparently the Priest did not think the case of Dorion's wife sufficiently important to call him from his garden. We hope that Dorion goes back to his trade.

June 9, 1939: Both churches making good competition with their bells ringing.37

Many in the Catholic community admired Father Guilloux. He could speak Cree "perfectly," and lived as part of the community, not outside it. Remembers Philip Ratt, "I admired the guy because of the way he looked after his living. He lived off the land. He didn't hunt, but he gardened and he produced a good crop every year. And he burned wood. He employed a few people to get seasoned wood for him. Compared to the priests that came after him, I think he was just a wonderful man." Fred Ballantyne and Roderick Ballantyne felt the same way. In 1949 Nicholas Guilloux was transferred from Pelican Narrows to the Île-à-la-Crosse Mission where he worked until his death in 1961 at age eighty-two.

Over the next few years several priests arrived in and departed from Pelican. Finally, in 1959, Gérard Beaudet, an Oblate from Victoriaville, Quebec, settled on the reserve. He had served in Île-à-la-Crosse from 1949 to 1955, and there had developed a passion for the Cree language. At Pelican Narrows, with the help of Solomon Merasty, he translated the New Testament and a hymn book into Cree syllabics. He also compiled a Cree-English dictionary, written in his precise, elegant script. But he was not liked by everybody. Philip Ratt remembers his first sermon. "He said, 'If anybody wants money, you don't come to me. I'm the priest here. If you need financial help you go to the Indian agent living next door to me.' He made his point, but it put people off."

Others liked him a lot, including Gordon Peter. "The Church flourished while Father Beaudet was here," he says. "There were church services every day. He used to put on Sunday schools, Bible studies, and he led Sunday services at Jan Lake in the summertime. He was the first person who organized bingo games for charity, but there was no prize money, only miscellaneous items like blankets, pillows, dishes, pots and pans, which the nuns had got through donations from various places while on trips out of town." Rummage sales were organized – one dollar got a bundle of clothes. "Some of them were very nice and very fit to wear." But what ultimately epitomized the priest's goodness for Gordon Peter was his friendship and kindness to Moonie, his beloved younger brother.

Melvin Ballantyne was referred to as "Mr. Encyclopedia," because he had a brain that remembered details and he was interested in everything. He liked to organize sporting events for the kids on the reserve, soccer, baseball, and almost everyone liked him. He was nicknamed Moonie, because he was such a day-dreamer in school. He was a church-going man, attending mass every Sunday with his friend Tony Sewap, and he developed a friendship with Father Beaudet. "Moonie liked buying stuff from Father Beaudet," says Gordon Peter, "religious items like medallions, hymn books, and bibles, along with portraits of Jesus. Father Beaudet used to call Moonie, 'My number-one customer.'"

Moonie wasn't married and he lived in a house once occupied by his father, Roderick. One day in the winter of 1996, Moonie told his younger siblings, whom he had always looked after when his father was indisposed, that he was leaving soon and wouldn't be coming back for a while. There was someone who had it in for him, he claimed.

Early in the morning, a week later, Gordon Peter was awakened by a banging just below his windows. "Somebody was yelling, 'Wake up, Peter, your dad's house is on fire!'" He jumped out of bed, dressed, but by the time he ran the half-block, the fire was already out of control. "I could see my two brothers, Philip and Anson, crying, so I knew someone had been in the house." It was Moonie, dead at age thirty-two. "I felt that I just lost a piece of my soul because me and Moonie were so close." Father Beaudet had given a copy of his Cree translation of the New Testament to Moonie as a special gift. This little book was the only thing that Gordon Peter found of his brother's. "I will always cherish it," he says.

Before taking up his duties at St. Gertrude's Mission, Gérard Beaudet had been principal of the now-notorious Guy Indian Residential School. Why he stayed in his job there for only four years when the other principals had remained for decades is not known. But in 1959, he arrived in Pelican Narrows. Fred Ballantyne often volunteered to work around the church grounds and got to know him well. "He was a good, good guy," he says. He encouraged the two religious communities to work together. He organized children's activities and the choir never sounded so good. Then the Catholic world fell apart.

Gilbert Michel was home watching television one night in 1986 when a neighbour dropped in with disquieting news: Gilbert's eight-year-old daughter had confided to her that the priest had sexually molested her. That evening, several parents gathered in the Michels' front room: their daughters, including one that was in her teens, claimed the same thing had happened to them. The mother of one girl talked about how she nagged at her daughter to go to confession, and had been angry when the girl refused. Finally the youngster did as she was told, only to return in tears. "The Father had done it again," she insisted. "He's done it again." Although several families were involved, it was Gilbert who wrote the letter to the Catholic authorities. His brother, Ron Michel, then and now the chief of Peter Ballantyne Cree Nation, did not doubt the girls' accusations for one minute. He phoned the bishop, thinking he could bring the two sides together, but the decision had already been made. Within two weeks Gérard Beaudet was gone from Pelican Narrows.

Once again the community was divided. Many Catholics simply did not believe what the young girls claimed. How could someone as pleasant and dedicated as Father Beaudet do such a thing? Says Gordon Peter, "One thing I learned from my parents, they used to tell me never say a bad thing about a priest no matter what you hear about him. 'That's judging,' they said, 'and who are you to judge?'" After Father Beaudet left, the Michels were ostracized. "I had arrows in my back," says Gilbert. "No one would talk to my wife and I, few people visited us – and it went on for years."

But some people believed that the priest should have been charged. "Other priests have been, why not him?" asks Philip Ratt. In fact, Beaudet said that he was ready to face criminal charges. Fred Ballantyne remembers, "He told me it was a bad story from that little girl. He told me he was going to have to go to court. 'I'm not afraid,' he said. 'I'd go to court.' But he went somewhere else."

After Father Beaudet's departure, Father Steve arrived. He was another brand of Oblate priest altogether, a white man more Indian than the Indians. Instead of a cassock and surplice, he donned suede jackets decorated with beaded Cree motifs. His songs of praise sounded more like powwow chants than hymns. In the confessional he placed a blanket with Indian designs and carried out smudging ceremonies. Almost the entire Pelican Narrows community was outraged. "He turned me off," says Suzette Ratt. "I stopped going to church." And so did many other people. For one thing these were the customs of the southern Plains Cree, not the Rock Cree. Father Steve was at Pelican Narrows for three years before he left for an African mission. After that no priest replaced him.

January 2004: It's cold, and about forty people, including a gaggle of children, mostly with their grandmothers, are gathered this Sunday in St. Gertrude's Catholic Church. It's been years since a full-time priest has been stationed here, so the congregation is used to performing the service themselves. Judith Bear, who is white and married to a native schoolteacher, leads the service; Bella Michel, the wife of Gilbert, performs the blessing of the Host; Donna Highway reads the gospel; and John Merasty gives the sermon in English. One of the five hymns is sung in Cree, the rest in English. There's an old organ in one corner, brought years ago from Quebec. Napoleon Michel used to play all the time, but he has arthritis, and now it's too painful. These days, only occasionally, will someone try their hand at it. This plain, utilitarian church could be found anywhere; there is no visual evidence that this is a Cree community. An effigy that stands in the corner depicts children kneeling before Our Lady of Lourdes. They are so white they could be Norwegians. The service is over in forty-five minutes and the congregation quickly disperses.

At the much prettier St. Bartholomew's Anglican Church, the service is being conducted by the Reverend Angus Sewap, who lives with his wife in the rectory next door. His is an interesting background: he worked for the provincial government cleaning up the camping grounds at Jan Lake; then he moved to Prince Albert, so that his wife could receive treatment for a severe drinking problem; afterwards he returned to Pelican Narrows, where he set up a taxi business. Over time he says he had astonishing dreams in which he saw Christ's face and even walked beside Him. He had always been devoted to the Anglican faith, and these visions spurred him on to become a lay reader, a catechist, a deacon, a priest, and a canon. For all that, he is not a paid cleric. He receives $250 a month as a stipend, and he must do other work to support his family. Despite his presence, only about sixteen people are in attendance this Sunday, including the christening party for Rev. Sewap's grandson. There is no choir, no Sunday school, no ladies' auxiliary, no Boy Scouts. "I try to call meetings of my wardens, but nobody ever comes," Angus Sewap says.

"Religion is dying here," insists John Merasty, who that Sunday gave the sermon for the Catholic service. "God is not dead, but religion is dying. Hardly anybody goes to church." Gordon Peter agrees. He and Susan used to attend St. Gertrude's every Sunday, but ten years ago they stopped. Without a priest it seemed a senseless exercise. Gordon Peter likes the Anglican church better, and will drop in on services every now and then, but Susan seldom goes with him. He'd like his five children to study Christian teachings and read the bible, as he did as a boy. But all they want to do is sleep on Sunday morning. "I don't know what they believe in," he says. In the Rock Cree's long history, Christianity might be nothing more than a blink of an eye.

REEFS

Below placid surfaces lie
fists of rock.   Unseen

they lie like anger, ready
to destroy the unwary.

Indian guides have learned
avoidance of these reefs.   We

call this history and try
to read their internal maps,

but like our vision our words
too fail in the silence.

Glen Sorestad
Jan Lake Poems

CH   M

ᒐ   L

4

ONE LECTURES, THE OTHER LISTENS

PĪYAK PĪKISKWĒ, KOTAK NITOHTAM

Gordon Peter's house overlooks an expanse of Macaroni Bay. There's an island in view (called The Island), where sled dogs used to roam in the summertime, and where the man who looked after the dogs was scared out of his wits when the fur trader Louis Morin turned *witigo*.

Gordon Peter's is a typical, standard-plan reserve home: 768 square feet, plus a porch/utility room added on as an entrance, an open-plan living room and kitchen on one side, and three small bedrooms on the other. Nine people live here – Gordon Peter and Susan, their five children, and two grandsons. While usually clean and neat, it bears the bruises of so many people coming and going. Paint has been scuffed, the cupboard doors have been torn off by kids, and there are a few holes in the walls. But there are two television sets attached to a satellite dish, a washer and dryer, and an ancient fax machine.

On the kitchen wall hang two mortarboards and many credentials nicely framed. These are not Ph.D.s: grandson Andrew's graduation certificate from nursery school is on display, as is Susan's Certificate of Merit for a basic literacy course she took. Centre stage is the Grade 12 diploma of the Ballantynes' eldest son, Peter Junior. When he graduated from high school two years ago, there was a family celebration that lasted three days.

Despite this success, Gordon Peter worries about his children. What will they do to earn their livelihood? Like most young people on the reserve, they have never visited a trapline, have never engaged in commercial fishing. With a Grade 12 education, a lucky few find work on the reserve, but there is little that the others can do except join "the $245 club" – the amount single people receive in monthly welfare cheques. Gordon Peter shakes his head when he thinks of the army of young people wandering around the reserve like wan ghosts, looking for a place of their own. They're lucky to have access to education, yet, without their parents' help, many couldn't survive.

Gordon Peter left school after Grade 8. He had forgotten to take a can of snuff out of his pocket, and two lay teachers beat him up. That was enough for him. As well, he was getting terrible migraine headaches, and most importantly, there were just too many kids at home for his father to support. "He was having such a hard time, especially in the wintertime, just feeding them. I told my parents the summer I turned fourteen that I wanted to go alone. They agreed with me, so I moved to Jan Lake.

"I lied about my age, told them I was sixteen so I could get my guiding licence. . . . I knew where the fish were. I knew where the reefs were too. As far as I can remember I never hit a reef. The first time I went guiding, I fell asleep near Harper's Island, and ran into some weeds. The guys in the boat all laughed at me.

"I lived alone there for a couple of years. In the winter I'd go onto the trapline with my cousins and cut wood for my dad. He was selling wood." The day his older brother Oscar got married at St. Gertrude's Church, Gordon Peter ran into his Uncle Dave from Deschambault, who asked him to help out with his commercial fishing enterprise, and Gordon Peter agreed. He was responsible for ten nets. "I had to get up pretty early in the mornings to check the nets. Any fish, I'd haul them in. We'd check them again in the evening. There was northern pike, whitefish, and plenty of pickerel in those days. My uncle used to pay me two hundred dollars a week. That was pretty good pay. I didn't have to buy groceries, he gave me a tent, everything I needed."

It was at Deschambault Lake that Gordon Peter first met Susan. She was thirteen years old and he wasn't the least interested in her. "I went out with her sister for about three years. We used to take a walk around town, and Susan would follow us and we'd yell at her to go home and not bother us." Neither sister had much education. Their parents went trapping every winter around Jan Lake – they had a log cabin there – and the nine children had been obliged to go with them.

One summer Gordon Peter was asked by some relatives to come along on a trip to Stanley Mission. When they got there, the older men disappeared and Gordon Peter wandered around, taking on odd jobs, until they showed up a couple of weeks later to fetch him home. Meanwhile his girlfriend set off for Grandmother's Bay. When she returned she told him that she had met her true love and would soon marry. "I was heartbroken," laments Gordon Peter.

The next time he met Susan was at a New Year's Eve party at his father's place in Pelican Narrows. By now she was sixteen and very pretty, and he, a hip twenty-year-old with some cash in his pocket. "How come you're not telling me to buzz off," Susan said. Gordon Peter just smiled. Midnight rang in. Everybody began shaking hands and hugging and kissing. Susan and Gordon Peter were suddenly in each other's arms. "From that time, we went out with each other. Ten months later we got married," says Gordon Peter.

For a couple of summers, Gordon Peter had helped his father build cabins at Amisk Lake, so he had some experience in construction. When a call came for workers for the federal-government-inspired housing project at Deschambault, Gordon Peter got a job as a labourer. When that work dried up, he and Susan moved to Pelican Narrows. There he began his twenty-two-year career working for the Peter Ballantyne Band, which is responsible for constructing houses on the reserve. But this work is on a contract basis only. If, for example, the supplier in Prince Albert doesn't send the lumber in time, Gordon Peter and his co-workers are sent home, and his paycheque is smaller than he anticipated.

Gordon Peter became highly skilled at construction but he had never taken formal training in carpentry. In 1991, he was funded to take a four-week upgrading course in Creighton, Saskatchewan, about 100 kilometres from Pelican Narrows. This was fine, because he could return home to his family every weekend. His big chance came two years later when he was selected to train as a journeyman carpenter in Saskatoon. It was not what he had hoped. He hated the city and missed his family; he was so lonely, he began suffering from excruciating migraines. As well, he was living on the federal government's unemployment insurance. After sending money home to care for his family, he was left with two hundred dollars to cover all his living expenses for a two-week period. It was all too much. After a month he returned to Pelican Narrows.

Eventually Gordon Peter was promoted to foreman of a six-man construction crew, building houses for the band, but his lack of formal education always rankled him. Leaving school so young, he was barely literate. And his salary was a sore point; he is still paid only fourteen dollars an hour. In 2002 he registered at the Saskatchewan Institute of Applied Science and Technology, Woodland Campus – courses were given in Pelican Narrows – and spent a year studying for his Grade 12 equivalent. He proudly shows off his marks: 88 in social studies, 86 in science, 84 in math, 77 in communications. "Peter is really smart," says Susan. "Not a slow learner like me." He's now on a waiting list for housing in Creighton, where he and his family hope to live while he completes his Grade 12. He'd like to study computers, and then who knows what the future will bring.

Since the beginning of the twentieth century, education has been regarded as the tool that would transport First Nations people into the Euro-Canadian world. If only it had been used gently and intelligently, underpinned by the philosophy that native culture was as successful in its environment as the white society was in its, the great tragedy might have been avoided. Instead, the classroom was used to force assimilation, and, in the process, became a dismal prison.

Before they became ensnarled in the white man's routine, Cree children were in school all the time, and every adult was their teacher. Two or three families often lived together in one wigwam during the hunting and trapping months so that a whole plethora of parents, grandmothers, grandfathers, aunts, uncles, and cousins were on hand to keep an eye on the kids and tell them what to do. Infants were swaddled tight and placed on *tīhkinākan*, brightly coloured cradleboards. With their arms and feet held down, about the only thing they could do was observe the world. Indeed, the essence of the Cree education system was that children were not so much taught but learned by observing what was going on around them.

Toddlers were breast-fed at least until the age of one and sometimes until three years. Childish shenanigans were a source of delight for the parents, not a cause for reprimand. Indeed, the carrot was always used, never the stick. Corporal punishment – slapping, punching, lickings with belts and other objects – was practically unheard of; only people gone crazy indulged in such things.

Philip Ratt sits in his little house, looking adoringly at his great-grandson, a well-dressed, healthy six-year-old whom he and Suzette are looking after while his mother is away taking a course. What disturbs Philip the most about modern-day life on the reserve is the neglect and abuse of children. "It's against everything the Cree tradition stood for," he says. Squads of social workers have been organized by the band, and these intervene when there is trouble. The kids sometimes are placed in foste
reserve or in Sandy Bay for a month, six months, o
ing on how much time it takes the parents to strai
out. Often it involves the parents spending time i

It all has to do with alcohol, the illness that is so hard to cure. It remains a disgraceful, collective shame.

In the old days, adults taught by persuasion, by cajoling, praising, distracting, and, in more serious cases, by embarrassing the youngster, by making fun of his or her behaviour. In a 1970 interview, John Dorion put it succinctly, "They listened to what the parents said to them, so that's why they never got spanked." For one thing, the children knew their very survival in the erratic boreal forest depended on the lessons they learned from the adults.

The workload was sharply delineated by gender (although no realm of labour was considered inferior to another). Boys were taught by the men of the extended family all the intricacies of hunting, fishing, trapping, making and repairing equipment, and canoeing. The camp was the women's domain, and daughters quickly became an integral part of daily life. They learned to pitch the tent, cut firewood, dress game, prepare hides and pelts, snare rabbits, fish, sew clothing, cook, and care for the younger children – the last task being the most important.

Every achievement was celebrated. The little girl who collected her first basket of berries by herself and the little boy who snared his first squirrel were treated as royalty of the moment. And, amazingly, the male sex was not favoured. A girl was considered a blessing, because, not only would she help in the hard work of the camp but, when she married, she and her husband would live with her parents, at least for a while. (Eventually he would want to trap and hunt with his brothers and father and the families would follow, but often this grouping also included the father-in-law and the wife's brothers.)

The functional aspects of life were taught in the camp or on the hunt, but the more ephemeral part of the culture – traditions, the spiritual, the arrangement of the cosmos, the ethical map – were conveyed through oral literature. As the scholar George Hamell writes, "Myths are seen as fundamental, narrative expresns of cultural truth. . . . Myths are not just charters of and for behaviour, but of and for ideal or normative behaviour in general. Myths are rational or sense-making systems."[1] Rock Cree chronicles were not of the Sleeping Beauty type, but more like a Brothers Grimm fairy tale. The message many relay is that the world is a dangerous place, full of wickedness, that sometimes is, and sometimes isn't, overcome. Marie Merasty, a member of the Peter Ballantyne Band who lived in Prince Albert and died in 1983, was a storyteller of the first order. Here is her "A Race for Life."

One time, after the ice had cleared enough to allow canoe travel, a man called Wetsoonesew went to visit a nearby camp. "I'll be back shortly," he told his wife. "I'm going to check on that camp. There were several people living there."

He arrived at the site to find the tipis in disorder. "I saw the bones scattered in a display of white," he related later. "I spied a small tipi with smoke rising from it, so I looked in. A human foot was being boiled!" He had the feeling that someone was heading for him, so he ran back to where his wife was. He knew what it meant and he ran swiftly.

His wife greeted him with, "The dog is lying in the sun in the brush."

"Quickly then!" he urged her. "Throw him into the canoe and get in yourself. I am going to make a fire and then jump into the canoe last. A Wetiko [*witigo*] is nearby."

The woman put the little dog in the canoe, got in herself and began edging along the shore. As soon as the man had made a fire, he jumped into the canoe too and started off across the lake. Just then a Wetiko charged into view! It managed to scratch the canoe, but failed to catch a proper hold of its bow. The couple were on a lake and, thus, in a position to leave the Wetiko stranded on shore. "Go and eat the foot you had boiling," the man taunted. "Don't bother us."

The Wetiko watched them leave and, since it was daylight, he could see them heading far out into the lake.

There, on an island, the man built a huge bonfire. He knew that a long portage and a winding creek were the last barriers between them and a major lake. That the Wetiko might catch them in the creek was the man's main concern. So he built the bonfire in the hope of fooling the Wetiko into thinking they were camping out on the lake.

Now they ran over the portage, the woman helping to carry their belongings. Now they wound their way through the creek, paddling furiously. They had almost reached the mouth of the creek.

"Oh no, here he is!" the man shouted.

It was as if the things along the path of the Wetiko were being tossed, it was rushing so fast. The couple were just gliding onto the lake, the canoe swaying with the effort, when the Wetiko launched itself at the canoe and into the water. But it was unable to grab ahold of the canoe.

"Go on, go on," the man taunted. "Go and eat that foot you had boiling." Once on the big lake they had no trouble escaping, because the Wetiko had no canoe in which to chase them.[2]

For anyone living in the northern forest, the setting of this drama would be vivid and real. And it would be gratifying. The *witigo* is as terrifying as he should be – killing people, eating them, and then boiling their feet – but the humans not only outwit him but taunt him. It's a horror story with a happy ending, the kind the Cree like best.

For the Woodland Cree, adolescence was not so much a time of rebellion as it was of challenge. Rites of passage were momentous learning experiences. The vision quest, three to four days without food or water in the wilderness, was physically dangerous, and emotionally unsettling. So was the desire, sometimes so passionate that it was hazardous, to prove oneself a good hunter. Once the son brought down the first moose or bagged a good number of geese, the parents threw a feast, featuring the protégé's contribution and other special foods, and welcomed the entire camp to applaud him.

Girls participated in vision quests as well, but so many perished during the ritual that parents were apt to discourage them. They had their own initiation into adulthood. On reaching menarche, girls were sequestered in a small hut set up near the parents' home. Every day an elder, usually an aunt or grandmother, would lecture the girl on the facts of life. One can imagine what tricks were discussed: how to make your husband happy, how to get the most for yourself out of the sexual experience, how to use birth control, how to abort an unwanted pregnancy. Afterwards the girl returned to her parents' wigwam, but for a month or so she was required to wear her hair dishevelled and a special hood with a fringe to cover her face. And she was made to drink only from a special water container.* The educational aspect of this ritual was important because in a short time she would be married.

Parental authority reached far into the lives of their sons or daughters. Marriages were most often arranged by parents, although if either of the young people hated the choice they were not forced into the match. So that kinship ties could be strengthened, cross-cousin unions were encouraged. A son could marry the daughter of his uncle on his mother's side, or the daughter of his aunt on his father's side. Likewise a daughter could marry the son of her mother's brother or the son of her father's sister. Roderick Ballantyne's two sisters, Rosie and Sophie, married the Goulet brothers, and this was considered the best pact of all. The reason for this complicated arrangement was that parallel cousins – the son or daughter of a mother's sister, the son or daughter of a father's brother – were considered siblings. Marriage between them was regarded as incest, and therefore prohibited. It was a

---

* As in so many cultures, the Cree had an abhorrence of menstruation. Whether they knew it was a function of child bearing is not known. At any rate, this repugnance is not one of the more appealing aspects of their traditions.

system that seemed to work. As the fur trader Harold Kemp observed, "The odd feature is that most of these marriages not only turn out satisfactorily, but they produce genuine affection on both sides. One seldom hears of an Indian couple separating."[3] Perhaps because bride and groom were usually so young, parents treated them like birds just flown from the nest. Morris Bear of Sandy Bay remembers how his father-in-law helped out when he was first married. "This old fellow showed us how to make the house, how to nail the house, and use other tools. That house, it's still standing there today."

Kemp also relates an incident that illustrates how much influence a Cree parent had over his grown offspring, and how much these children respected their elders. "I once offered a man a winter's job, one with Revillons. His father, however, was a staunch supporter of the Hudson's Bay Company; so, before he accepted the job, the man told me he would have to consult his father. When I inquired what his father had to do with it, he admitted, 'Nothing directly. But I never like to displease the old man.' When the old man gave an emphatic 'No!' I was the one displeased."[4]

The effort by white society to provide formal education to the First Nations people began in 1635 in New France with the assembling of Indian children into residential schools. The Jesuits taught the boys, the Ursuline Sisters, the girls. Both were considered dismal failures and abandoned. Two centuries later, day schools were opened in Upper Canada settlements where the Indians had asked for them or were willing to accept them. The government felt such training would speed along the incorporation of natives into white society, which was official policy at the time. The churches also liked the idea of assimilation, insisting that, only by learning to read and write English, could the Indian become a true Christian. And the natives could see that education was a necessity in a white-dominated world. In 1833 Chief Shawahnahness of St. Clair River in Upper Canada commented, "We agree to send our children to school that they may learn to read, put words on the page, and count, so that the white traders may not cheat them."[5]

What people like Shawahnahness didn't want was their children transformed into little Anglicans or Catholics, "brown on the outside and white on the inside," but that was precisely the choice that was presented to them.

By the 1880s, industrial schools, which provided training in reading and writing as well as in trades and agriculture were established along with boarding schools, which were usually set up on reserves to teach basic living skills and some academic subjects. (After 1923, both became known as residential schools.) Dr. Andrew B. Baird, general supervisor of the Presbyterian Church's work among the Indians, explained in 1889 why these were an improvement over day schools. "In the industrial school the children are withdrawn for long periods – and the longer the better – from the degrading surroundings of their pagan homes, and placed under the influence of all that is noblest and best in our Christian civilization."[6]

The government, of course, was very much in favour of religious organizations supervising the education of Indian children, for it was amazingly cheap. The 1902 annual government grant was between $50 and $100 a child per year, not nearly enough for the missionaries to hire adequate teachers or provide the students with decent accommodation, good nutritious food, or any kind of medical care. The main concern of most principals was how to save money; one minister came up with a scheme to spend only four cents a day on food for each child.

In many of the treaties signed in the 1870s in Canada's West, Indians were promised reserve day schools. Treaty Six, to which the Peter Ballantyne Band eventually adhered, was explicit: a schoolhouse would be built "whenever the Indians of the reserve shall desire it."

This was one of the first promises to be broken. In 1879 the publisher of the *Regina Leader*, Nicholas Flood Davin, was sent to the United States to study the "aggressive civilization" policy that had been implemented there. While Davin recommended that more money be allotted for Indian students, that proper teachers be hired, and that rewards be given to students and parents for attendance, he also insisted that separation of the child from his family was essential.

> Little can be done with [the adult Indian]. He can be taught to do a little at farming and at stock-raising and to dress in a more civilized manner, but that is all. The child, again, who goes to a day school learns little, and what little he learns is soon forgotten, while his tastes are fashioned at home, and his inherited aversion to toil is in no way combated.[7]

The Americans had convinced him "the chief thing to attend to in dealing with the less civilized or wholly barbarous tribes was to separate the children from the parents."

The Department of Indian Affairs seized on Davin's report. Bureaucrats were convinced that Indians in Canada's West were less advanced than those in the east – their traditions were seen as not only inferior, but evil – and a "harder civilizing" was needed. And if the church missions volunteered to administer residential schools in the West, well, again the financial benefits were so enticing. Congregating children all at one place to be taught by nonpaid or poorly paid missionaries – members of the "Standing Army of our Dominion" – cost a lot less than building large numbers of day schools and teacher's residences and employing people who might demand a decent salary. Industrial and boarding schools, it was decided, were a far better idea than day schools.

It wasn't as though some people weren't advocating a more humane and sensible policy towards Indian education. Dr. Peter Bryce, the federal official in charge of Indian health, recommended in 1907 that boarding schools with farms should be attached to the reserve; since only 30 per cent of the natives received any education, more schools should be built; and that the government should take them over and spend the required money to make them decent.[8] Even no less a worthy than Frank Oliver, minister of the interior and superintendent of Indian reserves from 1905 to 1911, wrote in 1908,

> My belief is that the attempt to elevate the Indian by sepa-
> rating the child from his parents and educating him as a
> white has turned out to be a deplorable failure. . . . The
> mutual love between parent and child is the strongest
> influence for betterment in the world and when that
> influence is absolutely cut apart . . . as in the education of
> Indian children in the industrial schools, the means taken
> defeats itself. Children must love and therefore respect their
> parents or they cannot and will not respect themselves. To
> teach an Indian child that his parents are degraded beyond
> measure and that whatever they thought was wrong could
> only result in the child becoming, as the ex-pupils of the
> industrial schools have become, admittedly and unques-
> tionably very much less desirable elements of society than
> their parents who never saw the schools.[9]

Oliver went on to describe his plan for Indian education: improved day schools on the reserve, manned by qualified married teachers, a good nutritious lunch served at noon, and, in the more popu-lated places, a nurse.[10] It would be another fifty years before his plan was realized.

By 1907, seventy-five Indian industrial and boarding schools, as well as about two hundred day schools on reserves were operat-ing in Canada, and nobody was satisfied with them. The day schools were particularly bad: the salary was so meagre and living conditions so bad, that teacher turnover was rapid, and what teaching there was was poor – in some instances the children did nothing but sing hymns all day.

The value of Indian education wasn't debated much at Pelican Narrows. There was no education. For the first twenty-five years after the Rock Cree signed on to Treaty Six, nobody thought it pos-sible to teach these "wandering gypsies." The closest institution was an Anglican boarding school established in 1906 at La Ronge, 150 kilometres from Pelican Narrows. Archdeacon John Mackay built a sawmill there to produce the necessary lumber and then constructed the schoolhouse with his own hands. But the only Pelican Narrows children who were accepted there were orphans. Thomas Ballantyne, whose mother died when he was a toddler, lived at the institution until he was eighteen years old. The standard age for leaving residential school at the time was sixteen, but, he says, "nobody knew when I was born." There's a picture of him at the school on his living-room wall. His hair is slicked back, his tweedy suit looks very British, and he's wearing a tie. What was unusual at the Lac La Ronge school was that children were allowed to speak Cree and there was little corporal punishment. "They were kind," remembers Thomas Ballantyne, "the only bad thing was the food. We had watery fish twice a day, with a slice of bread."

In the early 1920s, the Anglicans began clamouring for a day school at Pelican Narrows and the church and government authorities were considering the idea until the Catholic bishop Ovide Charlebois put the kibosh on it. He "is opposed to this proposal on two grounds," wrote the Indian agent in 1922. "First, the day school would not be successful here because of the nomadic habits of the Indians; second, the Indian population is largely Roman Catholic."[11] Indian Commissioner W.M. Graham certainly became convinced. "My advice to the department," he wrote, "is to discourage the day school as much as possible in these northern regions as it will not pay."[12]

The Anglicans kept campaigning, though, and finally in 1925 the first day school opened in Pelican Narrows. It was a modest, penny-pinching affair, operating only in the summer months, Monday to Saturday, from June to August, on the theory that this was the only time the children would not be on the trapline. No proper schoolhouse was ever built. Classes were held in St. Bartholomew's Anglican Church, and it must have been uncomfortable because there was no furniture or supplies. Three years after it opened, the Indian agent, the man responsible for dishing out treaty money, J.W. Waddy wrote, "No seats have been provided for the pupils and if the school is to be continued 24 single desks should be sent to Pelican Narrows via Ross Navigation Co., The Pas, Man."[13] The teacher was expected to live in a tent.

Nevertheless, the school was a big success, at least that first term. The teacher hired was Frank Dey, who held a First Class teaching certificate and was "single and of good spirit and presence." Class enrolment jumped from twenty-three to forty-one. So popular was Dey that in September, after the school closed, George Custer, a councillor on the Peter Ballantyne Band, wrote: "We the Indians of Pelican Narrows wish to recommend Mr. Dey . . . as being exceptionally capable in handling and teaching our children, none of whom ever attended school before. . . . If possible that Mr. Dey may return here we will be only too willing to build at our own expense a schoolhouse."[14] The interesting thing about the letter was that it was not only in Mr. Dey's voice, it was also in his handwriting. Obviously he was dedicated to the children and eager to return, but, by the following spring, he had disappeared from Department of Indian Affairs correspondence.

The school was never as good as it was that first year. For one thing there was no long-term financing from the government; whether the school would open at all was debated each spring. And it was always a scramble to find teachers. In 1926 the Bishop of the Diocese of Saskatchewan nominated Isaiah Badger: "Of course he is Indian, but at the same time a thoroughly good man."[15] Mr. Dey got a salary of five dollars a day, Mr. Badger four dollars.

It wasn't long before the Anglicans of Pelican Narrows realized that their children were not progressing at the summer school. The government was parsimonious beyond reason: the only thing it would pay for was the teacher's salary and forty dollars' worth of biscuits. Certainly no capital funds would be allocated, so a makeshift cabin was built by the parents. It was even hotter in there than the church had been. The pupils were forced to sit all day staring out the window at the Catholic kids swimming and playing.

It took each new teacher one of the three months the school was in operation just to determine the level of each student. And, over the long sojourn on the trapline, many of them forgot their three Rs entirely. At the end of the 1929 session, Indian agent Waddy wrote, "This is another miserable attempt at education. The pupils have no school at all here and sometimes the church is used for a schoolhouse, and at other times a shack is used. These unequipped summer day schools are useless."[16]

In 1929 the Anglican parents again pleaded for a full-time day school. Since the Anglicans and Catholics were then doing battle at Pelican Narrows, Sandy Narrows Reserve, about ten kilometres south, with its good fishing and many vegetable gardens, seemed the better location. The schoolhouse, they reckoned, might become the heart of a Protestant community. They wouldn't dare ask for an expensive, improved school, only a good-sized log building with a lean-to for the teacher. Finally the officials agreed: a schoolhouse would be built at Sandy Narrows and two teachers hired, but only if Parliament allocated the funds. The letter arrived from Ottawa in June of 1931: "As our appropriation for the current fiscal year was considerably reduced, the item to provide funds for a new building at this point was struck out." After that blow, parents and church officials lost heart, and the summer school closed. Fifty to a hundred children were left once again without any formal education at all. In May 1933, Indian agent John Weir received the following missive from the federal government: ". . . It is noted that you have supplied 600 lbs. of biscuits to the Pelican Narrows Day School. The Department has not provided any salary for a teacher at this school during the current fiscal year. Please advise to whom the biscuits were forwarded and why they were supplied."[17]

The Catholics, who represented two-thirds of the reserve's population, suffered an entirely different experience. If, after 1925, Pelican Narrows at times seemed a quiet, dispirited place, it was because most of the children had been sent away.

They'd leave every summer around the end of August, at first travelling by canoe and then, in later years, by plane. Their parents would gather on the shore of Macaroni Bay, hugging the boys and girls and then waving, waving goodbye, trying hard not to bawl or to shout out, "Come back!" Some of the kids, the little ones at least, would be crying, or having tantrums, but most simply looked dejected. Others ran away and had to be scooped up by the RCMP or someone else. "My cousin was swimming near Southend and this priest and the pilot came and got her," recalls J.B. Custer. "They tried to throw her into the airplane, but they dropped her between the plane and the dock. And this pilot grabbed her by the hair and just pulled her up and threw her in the airplane without letting her parents know. We were worth money. So much per kid." No one, except for the odd smart aleck making fun of the sorrow, was actually happy. No wonder. They would not see their parents again for another ten months.

The Guy Indian Residential School had been built in the 1920s at Sturgeon Landing, at the mouth of the Sturgeon River, supposedly because it was "central for the Indians whose children would live at the school." It was an odd rationale since the closest reserve it was supposed to service was 160 kilometres away. A report written by Father Laurent Poirier, the principal of the school, describes the journey inflicted twice a year on his students:

> From 100 to 400 miles one way, up and down rivers strewn with rapids over long, or steep, or swampy portages numbering as many as 40 on one trip, across lakes where wind and furious waves would hold them often for days on the shore, stormed by mosquitoes or drenched by heavy rains with only a light tent for protection, sweating by day and freezing by night.[18]

No wonder so many children arrived at the school exhausted and sick.

The school was a pet project of Bishop Charlebois's, but for years he had had little luck in convincing the federal government to build it. Finally, his former assistant, Father Joseph Guy, who was the Oblates' official representative in Ottawa, agreed to lobby the appropriate politicians and bureaucrats. He had a strong case. The government had passed the Student Attendance Act in 1920, making it compulsory for natives to attend school from ages seven to fifteen, but how were they to comply with the law if there were no schools to attend? Finally, in 1924, the project was given the go-ahead. Bishop Charlebois named it the Guy Indian Residential School, after Father Guy, the lobbyist, but hardly anybody called it that. It was known as Sturgeon Landing and later Guy Hill, although some people simply called it The Jail.

Because it was built in such a remote location, there was difficulty in shipping materials during construction, and workers were unreliable. As well, the inspector for Indian Affairs and the contractor's foreman were constantly battling each other. "This is partly due to the fact that the place is so isolated," wrote R.N. Wyatt, the contractor, "and weather conditions very bad (in fact, it rained nearly every night in July and quite a number of days) together with the mosquitoes, of which I believe they have never known them to be worse (in fact the Indians that we had engaged could scarcely stand them). Then the heat, and sand flies, we were all nearly bushed."[19] The wintertime was even worse, he noted. The north wind blasted down onto the isolated school. And there was no mail service for months on end. Wyatt wrote his wife, "How are the children supposed to take it?"

When the first batch of students, along with several Sisters of St. Joseph who were to work as matrons and teachers, arrived in September 1925, nothing was ready for them. They had to sleep on the floor, use an outdoor privy, make their coats do for blankets, and eat their dinner from pots, since no dishes were available. Immediately almost every student got sick, probably from culture shock more than anything else.

It's hard to imagine two environments more completely at odds than a cabin on the trapline and a school dormitory, than a relaxed home, where spankings were never given, voices seldom raised, and freedom taken for granted, and a military-style setting where rigid rules, corporal punishment, and humiliation were the order of the day.

J.B. Custer looks like the pirate Nick Adonidas, played so well by Bruno Gerussi in the television series *The Beachcombers*. He has been an angry man his entire life, and he blames it entirely on Guy Residential School. He and scores of other Peter Ballantyne Band members are currently suing the federal government and the Manitoba Oblates (now bankrupt) for the wounds inflicted on them from ages five to sixteen. They are convinced that the politicians and bureaucrats purposely set out to destroy their cultural identity by separating child and parents. Their years in residential school have clouded their adult lives. Suicides, drunkenness, depression, poverty, wife-beating, and the demolition of the Indian family is the mark of this "lost" generation. It is also casting a shadow over the next.

Horace Ratt is the fifth in a family of seven and, unlike his older brother Philip, he loathed residential school. He believes the experience not only wrecked his life but that of his children and grandchildren. "My father and I never bonded together. How could you bond with someone when you're away ten months of the year? My generation never had parents, so we never learned to parent." John Merasty adds, "The only thing that was missing at residential school was love. We had church, we had spiritual, but what good is spiritual if you don't have love. We grew up without being loved."

J.B. Custer was seven years old when he was first sent to Sturgeon Landing. "I was scared. I'd never seen people with black robes, especially the sisters. I thought they were floating around. I couldn't see their feet, these people in black. I'd never seen a big building like that before. Never seen white people before. I heard boys and girls cry day and night. Especially the smaller boys, five, six years old. It was like being in hell. Kids crying, fighting, screaming."

The school building, though, was an impressive structure, large enough to house 140 students, in the midst of rolling hills and with two vegetable gardens. By 1930 the staff included eleven sisters (several, however, were not qualified to teach, even though they did so), four brothers, one night man, one farmer, as well as the Reverend Principal and his assistant. Philip Morin, former chief of the Peter Ballantyne Band, remembers, "The church wanted us educated, but that was so they could teach you religion."

The day was divided into two: one part was devoted to academics, rudimentary reading, writing, arithmetic, and catechism, the only subject taught in Cree. The other half was designated for work, the girls in the kitchen, laundry, sewing room, the boys in the garden and on the small farm with cows and pigs that Bishop Charlebois had set up. They also hunted and fished to help feed the students and staff. With all that, the kids often went hungry. "We were always after something to eat, especially in the evening," recalls J.B. Custer. "We would go out and steal food in the night to feed other kids, 'cause they were always crying and hungry. Our diet wasn't very good. It was strictly macaroni soup, stuff like that, diluted milk. We had bologna once a month. That was like eating steak." Adds Roderick Thomas, who is a Peter Ballantyne Band member from Southend, "We were fed really poorly and dressed really poorly too." Guy Residential School operated from 1925 to 1978; some times were worse at the school than others, but many alumni are still haunted by nightmares.

"It was like an army. You used to line up to go to eat. You used to line up to go to classes. Line up to go to church. Line up to go to bed. Everything was discipline and very, very strict," recalls Roderick Thomas. And if the rules were broken, physical punishment was sure to follow. He recalls getting into a fight with a classmate while they were playing hockey. He was just coming into the school, when the principal caught up to him. "I was hit with his fists and he was kicking me at the same time. I couldn't run on the cement with my skates so I was kicked and kicked and hit. The next morning I had two black eyes, both eyes. That's the kind of discipline they gave." J.B. Custer adds, "Physical punishment was like a strap with little tacks in it. Steel rulers, fists, steel-toed boots

– the Brother had big boots – and hockey sticks. They used to hit us with hockey sticks real hard. The Brother used to stand in the door. He'd blow his whistle and start counting. There was a hundred kids out in the playground so anybody who was late got hit with a hockey stick real hard."

Oddly, the punishment for fighting was being made to fight. "When we were caught fighting, we had to stand right in the middle of the floor, there was about a hundred screaming guys around us, and we had to fist fight until one of us got knocked out. And the kids would be yelling, 'Kill him! Kill him!'"

"You couldn't even go one hundred yards away from the schoolyard or you'd be punished," recalls Gilbert Michel who attended Lebret Residential School, another Oblate institution. "The principal would make some little guy bow over and whip the little guy in front of the kids. It was awful. I got the strap a couple of times. Those priests! I hope they're burning in hell."

The girls at the school were not beaten as badly, but the nuns didn't hesitate to whack hands with a ruler. Everybody was subjected to this, but Suzette Ratt remembers one incident when the punishment almost resulted in death. Suzette was sitting with the other girls in the sewing room, darning and mending, when a Sister started screaming at one of the students. She was a big, heavy Cree girl, rather clumsy, from Pukatawagan, and many of the nuns didn't much like her. Suddenly the Sister grabbed the girl by the throat and pinned her to the wall until she began to make gurgling sounds. Suzette was ordered to fetch a cup of water; twice it was thrown in the girl's face but she remained unconscious. Finally someone slapped her face and she came to. "The next day that nun was gone," says Suzette.

It's to be expected that such sadistic physicality might turn sexual, and, of course, it did. "There was a lot of sexual abuse at Guy Hill," says J.B. Custer. "It was a sex-education school, I guess. There was a lot of dykes, a lot of homosexuals there – school teachers. I got sexually molested for about three years. This guy used to lure us with candies and little gifts. He treated us nice. He would con us, a little kid is vulnerable, and I hated that. He had mind control over us."

"Not everybody was abused," insists Susan Custer, "just the nice-looking kids. You know those beautiful girls you wanted to keep at home. You didn't want them to go there to be sexually abused, or molested, or whatever horrible thing you can think of."

Tomson Highway, renowned musician, playwright, and novelist, is a Rock Cree from Brochet, Manitoba. One of twelve in a fur-trapping family, he was sent to Sturgeon Landing when he was seven. He says that while he was sexually abused at Guy Residential School, his brother was tormented more often because he was such a beautiful boy. Much of Tomson Highway's novel *Kiss of the Fur Queen* takes place in a residential school. It's fiction of course, but smacks of reality.

When Gabriel opened his eyes, ever so slightly, the face of the principal loomed inches from his own. The man was wheezing, his breath emitting, at regular intervals, spouts of hot air that made Gabriel think of raw meat hung to age but forgotten. The priest's left arm held him gently by his right, his right arm buried under Gabriel's bedspread, under his blanket, under his sheet, under his pyjama bottoms. And the hand was jumping up, reaching for him, pulling him back down, jumping up, reaching for him, pulling him back down. He didn't dare open his eyes fully for fear the priest would get angry; he simply assumed, after a few seconds of confusion, that this was what happened at schools, merely another reason why he had been brought there, that this was the right of holy men.[20]

The March 1950 newsletter of the Oblate residential schools boasts about Sturgeon Landing's hockey team. They had played The Pas, Flin Flon, and Sandy Bay, and had whipped them all. "Father Girard's All Indian Team from Sturgeon Landing once again upheld the honor of the 'red-men' by defeating The Pas

Midgets, 6-4," reported the school's newspaper. "We had a good hockey team, that's for sure," says J.B. Custer. "For about five years I don't think we lost any games, especially against the white boys. We got after them because we came to hate white people with a passion because of the people teaching us. So we got back at them. A lot of ex-residential school students could have made it to the NHL, but no deal, no chance. Either they were drinking too much or they weren't recognized at that time. We weren't top priority like the white race."

Brother Nadeau was one of the hockey coaches at Guy and, according to many who played with him, he habitually sodomized them. In the 1960s he was hired as a coach at The Pas. The town honoured him by putting his photograph on display in the arena. J.B. Custer and other alumni were furious. "We told the big bosses at The Pas, 'Get that picture down or there's going to be media. It's a big reminder to us, him staying there.' They wouldn't budge until about two or three years later. Then one day it was gone."

It was not, of course, just young boys who were sexually abused – girls were even greater targets. When Elvena Pearson's mother and father separated, she was sent to St. Patrick's Orphanage in Prince Albert. She was still there in 1962 when she was sixteen years old. "On Saturday afternoon we'd do the chores, clean up, vacuum, polish the floors. When a different priest was there, we were allowed to wear jeans to do the chores during the day. But afterwards, when we were done, when Father La Bonte came, we had to change back into our skirts. So anyhow, I was changed and my name came over the speaker, he wanted to see me in his office.

"I knocked on his door and he said, Come on in. He was sitting in a corner. He wheeled his chair over, and there was a couch right by the door, so I sat there. He puts his legs on the outside of mine, like clamps on my thighs. And I was shocked. I think he was mad because my dad was behind two months with room and board. He starts yakking away. And I'm just looking at him and his hands started coming up my legs, feeling my knees under my skirt. He gave me the creeps and I just reacted. My right leg came up and I pushed his chair as hard as I could. As I was going out, I looked back and there he was sprawled, not on the floor, on the desk, that's how hard I pushed him. Because the back of the chair hit the desk hard and he flew right off. He was a pervert. In those days I didn't know what that meant. I just thought he was a dirty old man." Elvena was never reprimanded for the incident because, she feels, "the priest was embarrassed."

Many ex-residential-school students felt that, while the physical abuse was terrible, the denigration of their background and culture was even worse. Remembers Celena Bone: "In August, when you first came back from the summer holidays, what they used to do is delouse the kids. They put coal oil on the hair, and took a fine tooth comb and then twisted it." The students' clothes were stripped off and burned, they were scrubbed with a huge brush. Now you are clean, the nuns seemed to say, before you were dirty. Gordon Peter's mother, Sarah Ballantyne, arrived at the school with glossy black hair down her back. The first thing the nuns did was chop it short. "Everybody got the same kind of haircut, no matter what age" says Celena Bone. "Right across the forehead and down to the ears." When Sarah Ballantyne's parents saw her the following summer, they were horrified, and refused to send her back again.

The Cree parents were labelled backward and stupid, and, while most of the students at Guy had already been converted to Christianity, anything Indian was forbidden, including the Cree language, although at times it was more tolerated than others. Says Elvena Pearson, "I remember that one nun saying to me: 'I don't want you speaking that devil tongue.' Which is the Cree language. That's what she said to me. But I didn't listen to her. None of us did. Whenever we were alone, we would speak Cree amongst ourselves. Soon as we saw the nuns, we would switch and speak English."

"They used to call us savages. 'We have to educate you savages,' they used to say. That's why they didn't want us to speak our language," says Roderick Thomas. J.B. Custer remembers a scheme that backfired on the teachers. Each student was given thirty tokens for the month. If a child was caught speaking Cree, he had to give one to the kid who caught him. At the end of the month, whoever had the most tokens got a prize. "Well, we ended up ratting on each other and we decided we didn't want to do that. So we used the tokens for currency. If I want a cigarette butt from you, I give you two tokens. Or we'd gamble with them. We formed little gangs; we had bodyguards. They succeeded in a way. We didn't learn one damn thing about our culture."

There was no recourse at residential schools like Guy. There was no elder to confide in and seek advice from; mail was always censored; parents seldom visited, because the school was so isolated. About the only thing a child could do in protest was to run away, but the school was so far from their homes, or, for that matter, from any place, only a few attempted it.

On May 18, 1944, three students, Joseph Colomb, sixteen, Jeremie Colomb, fifteen, both from Pukatawagan, and Frank Morin, fifteen, from Pelican Narrows, were told that they would be the only students at Guy Residential School not to receive one of the rewards being given out that afternoon. "Bad behaviour" was the reason given, but, for the life of him, Jeremie couldn't figure out what he had done. He and the two others were angry at their exclusion and, at about four-thirty in the afternoon, they fled. The Royal Canadian Mounted Police were called. A constable and the principal, Father Poirier, searched Goose Lake to Rat Creek by boat, but saw no sign of the boys. Then, on May 20, the three showed up at the school. They had "borrowed" Father Poirier's canoe and had camped on an island in the middle of Goose Lake. They had run out of food, they were cold, and they were frightened by the wolves that were "thick in that area." They returned the canoe to the exact spot from which they had taken it, and had written a note: "We are going back home. We are sorry for what we have done." They then walked to the school. The principal decided to make an example of the three and expelled them all.

"This school is so far from all communications and from Indian reserves that it is fairly impossible for a child to run away with any chance of making it home. . . . And the failure of these boys to make it is likely to discourage any other attempt for a long time."[21] No attempt was made to investigate why they had fled in the first place. Indeed, not much effort was expended by any authority to ensure the children were being treated well. Government inspections were superficial to say the least.

In July 1929 the Indian Commissioner, W.M. Graham, wrote his boss in Ottawa, that visiting Guy Residential School would "entail a large travelling expenditure. I think an inspection of this school could be postponed until it is more accessible either by road or rail."[22] Never mind that this might take years. When the Indian agent did investigate the school, his report was always full of praise. Everything from the efficiency of the staff to the care of the sick was either "Good," "Very Good," or "Excellent." Obviously he made no effort to talk to the students. Only once did a small hint appear that perhaps not everything was perfect. In February 1937 A.G. Hamilton, the inspector of Indian agencies, reported, "The pupils read fairly well, but lack expression. These pupils appear more nervous than those in the junior grades and made more mistakes in spelling and arithmetic."[23] The remainder of the report deals only with the furnace.

It may be just as well the Indian Affairs bureaucrats didn't interfere too much as their ideas were often more racist than were those of the religious. In 1915, writing about Lac La Ronge Indian School, Paying Officer H. McKay had this advice: "There is one thing that strikes me as too bad, and that is, after these girls graduate or become sixteen or seventeen years of age, they get married and go back to the old life, viz the teepee and living on what their husband hunts. It seems to me it would be a very good thing if . . . these girls would be placed in some positions, such as washers or domestics with a good Canadian family."[24]

The former Guy Residential School students who are suing the government are mostly doing so for the physical assaults and sexual abuse they suffered. Roderick Thomas has a different complaint. He claims that the priests deliberately curtailed his education and thereby destroyed his future, and for the most trivial reason.

The Sisters of St. Joseph and the Oblate brothers were terrified that one of their wards might become pregnant: special deadbolt locks were placed on the doors separating the girls' and the boys' quarters and word was spread that sex before marriage was beyond the pale, a mortal sin. It was the main reason that all students were discharged from the school when they reached age fourteen, at about Grade 8 (age sixteen later on). A few academically minded pupils were chosen by the Indian agent and principal to continue to high school, at government expense, in Lebret, The Pas, or Prince Albert. Roderick was such a good pupil that he was told he'd be funded for further studies. He began dreaming of getting his pilot's licence.

The summer after he left Guy, he waited and waited for the news: where would they send him to high school? When September came without even a letter arriving, Roderick confronted his local priest, who found out what had happened. The previous semester he and some friends had been fooling around and decided they'd make a racket outside the girls' dormitory door. "All we did was look at them and smile, but that was a sin. Sex was dirty, that's what they taught us." The principal found out about their antics and a black mark was placed against Roderick's name. When the time came to select the students for high school, he was not even considered.

Guy was not the only residential school to which Pelican Narrows children were sent. In 1970, when Armand Ballantyne's mother died of cancer, he was devastated. "Even now it's really hard to talk about Mom. I really loved her. I was a momma's boy." He and his sister were sent to the Catholic residential school at Duck Lake. "I hardly saw my sister, my only sister. They wouldn't let me see her. They separated us. And that year everybody in the school went home for Christmas except the kids from Pelican Narrows and Sandy Bay. [It was considered too expensive.] We were treated really bad. I'm glad that place burned down."

Of course, not everything about the school was detrimental. "There were a few teachers who were very nice, very affectionate," remembers J.B. Custer. "They knew what was going on, but they couldn't go to the authorities, because it was a government-funded school." For Napoleon Michel, residential school was a godsend. His mother died when he was three, and his father was ill with tuberculosis, so he was sent to Guy. The nuns took care of him in their residence. A doctor's report prepared in February 1937 states, "The child has impetigo contracted from father's neglect to keep him clean; under the care of the nursing sister, the disease has almost completely disappeared." When he was old enough, Napoleon joined the school. He feels he got a good education; he's proud that he still knows some French. "When I went I had nothing to complain about," he says. "Quite a few people who went there, they know how to go about themselves in white society." He feels the people who are suing the government over their experiences at residential schools are doing so just for financial gain. "Personally I don't want to go against my church just for money."

Despite the horrors of being sent away, the Catholic kids did learn to read and write English, as well as some basic mathematics and a little science. The Anglican Indians of Pelican Narrows were entirely forgotten in the government's grand scheme of assimilation through education. After the summer school closed for lack of funds in 1930, the Anglican parents kept pleading with the government to establish a year-round school. In 1938, after the children had been without any education for eight years, the parents volunteered to loan two houses to accommodate the students, the fathers would provide meat and fish, and put up wood for the school, two of the mothers would keep house. The Anglican Church thought this was a sound idea, but the Indian agent responded in his usual racist manner: "The Indians no doubt promised to supply fish, meat, and wood, but getting them to keep their promise would indeed be a difficult matter. It would ultimately mean that the Department [of Indian Affairs] would have to provide for the entire upkeep of the children. Then again I would not think it would be wise to leave school children in charge of Indian women who were not their parents."²⁵ The request for a year-round day school was turned down at that time, but the appeal must have hit home somewhere, for the next June the summer school reopened, again under the auspices of the Anglicans. This time it would continue for thirteen years.

It was another feeble attempt at education. With holidays – Dominion Day, three or four days around Treaty time, Labour Day – and the weekends, there were only twenty-two days of classes. Most of the kids didn't know English, and it was nearly impossible to teach them in such a short time. Attendance was sporadic; many of the parents got jobs at the Rocky Falls dam and temporarily moved their families there. Many of the children remained illiterate. John Merasty believes this lack of schooling has resulted in another divide in the community: the haves and have-nots. "Economically, when you have education, you are able to get ahead further. So, it really creates a split when one side is getting more."

Finally, in 1948, the Department of Indian Affairs took over the summer program and, two years later, opened a year-round non-denominational public school in makeshift quarters. That first term there were ten students, mostly white and Métis children living in the settlement. The next year the governments of Saskatchewan and Ottawa jointly put up the money for a two-room schoolhouse built on land owned by the Catholic Church. When the doors opened in September 1953, twenty-two Métis and whites and thirty-six Treaty Indian children rushed in. Fifty-three years after signing a treaty that promised them a schoolhouse on the reserve, the Rock Cree of Pelican Narrows finally got one.

But Chitek Lake School, as it was called, was plagued with problems from the beginning. The preaching of the clergy had so turned the two denominations against each other, there was constant fighting between Catholic and Anglican children. "The teachers could hardly control it," remembers one former student. "It was just vicious. At every opportunity one kid would punch another, or throw something." Also, the priest did not approve of lay teachers or the fact that the children were receiving a secular education. And, from day one, the place was terribly overcrowded. A new school was built in 1957, a large, boxy affair, and the children moved in.

Behind the scenes, the Catholic establishment campaigned to have the new building deemed a religious school. The Bishop approached the Indian Affairs branch in Prince Albert, and, when he was turned down there, he flew to Ottawa and twisted the arms of politicians and bureaucrats until they finally said yes. In 1959 the Anglican children were marched back to the old school; the Catholics remained in the new one which was called Chacakoo Roman Catholic Day School. Close to St. Gertrude's Church, a two-storey convent was constructed for the teacher-nuns.

Ray Highway, currently the principal of Wapanacak, the elementary school in Pelican Narrows, attended the secular school for the first grades. "I can remember this very vividly, because it's still stuck in my head. I dropped a crayon and I asked a friend, in Cree, because I didn't know English, 'Can you pass that here?' The teacher came up and slapped me on the back of my head, and I kind of giggled, I thought it was for fun. And then I dropped it again 'cause I was so excited, right? Colouring this stuff and all. I said the same thing to my friend in Cree, and got hit again. It really hurt. I thought, why is this person doing this? Is this what school's gonna be like until I'm done?" "There was one teacher, she didn't like anyone to speak Cree," adds Isaac Custer, "even while she was talking to you, if you accidentally spoke the native language, she'd slap you on the head."

Ray Highway was pleased when the nuns arrived: "I thought it was cool watching these ladies in long black veils, these children of God. I thought, well this is going to change things, but it only got worse – beatings with knuckles or the ruler, or with a strap and they'd make you do unnatural things. I'm sure God didn't tell these people, this is what the Bible says and this is what you gotta do to these kids." "They used to twist our ears if we made them mad," remembers Cindy Ballantyne, "until sometimes they bled."

Gordon Peter's brother Oscar recalls, "We usually got a strap the minutes we were late. Fifteen minutes late, fifteen straps on the hand." "I remember one day," says Susan Custer, "the nun asked us what we had for lunch. The kids were saying macaroni and hamburger soup, some were saying egg-salad sandwiches and vegetable soup. The nun was surprised, you could see it in the expression on her face, like 'Oh my goodness, you Indians eat all those things? I thought it was only fish and moose meat.'"

Both schools held classes only to Grade 7, so, for the remainder of their education, Pelican Narrows students were sent off to residential school. Usually the Anglicans went to All-Saints in Prince Albert and the Catholics to Guy or Prince Albert Residential School, later Prince Albert Indian Students' Residence.

On September 4, 1953, Celena Bone was in the sewing room at Guy Industrial School, busy with her home-economics assignment. "We smelled smoke and somebody came by and said not to panic and not to run, try to be calm. We had stairs going outside that we had to use 'cause it was so smoky in the building." The children walked out in orderly fashion, carrying whatever they could, and, from the lawn, watched as the hay, the cattle shed, the barn, and the school building went up in flames. There was a heavy wind, so the blaze doggedly spread, but the bedding, clothing, personal belongings of the staff, the school records, twelve sewing machines, office furnishings, school desks, a piano, a kitchen mixer, and many books were saved, all carried out by the students. This was not the first fire in a residential school in Keewatin diocese; indeed, there seemed to be an epidemic. January 1920, the Lac La Ronge Anglican boarding school burns to the ground; February 1920, Île-à-la-Crosse Catholic boarding school burns down, one child dies; February 1926, Île-à-la-Crosse boarding school is gutted for the second time; February 1926, the Beauval Catholic convent and school is destroyed by fire, one sister and nineteen little boys perish; February 25, 1930, Cross Lake Catholic Indian School burns down; December 1943, the Onion Lake Anglican Residential School is destroyed by fire; February 1947,

Lac La Ronge is levelled by fire for the second time. While the fire at Guy Residential School was an accident, started by the sparks of a welding torch, many others were the work of arsonists, some of them students. It was one way of showing how they felt about their destructive education.

Guy School relocated to The Pas, the children at first being housed in a warehouse, and then in temporary accommodation built by the government. Finally it was decided that a permanent institution would be built at Clearwater Lake, about twenty kilometres south of The Pas. The site was chosen for two reasons: it was practically inaccessible – as the principal, A. Girard, wrote: "There is nothing like a school isolated from any Reserve, and the Fathers in charge of residential schools agree to this saying" – and a sanatorium was located not too far away. This was an advantage, since so many children were coming down with tuberculosis at Guy School.

The new school was opened to great fanfare in 1958. While the staff now included a few lay people who were better qualified, it was not a happier place than the old school had been. There was still the emphasis on vocational training, with the children doing most of the janitorial work, still the large dormitories, still the severe separation of the sexes, still the strictness. J.B. Custer describes it thus: "It was a big structure, made out of brick. It looked identical to a penitentiary in Prince Albert. On one side were girls, one side were boys. It was four stories high and it was out in the bush. We were imprisoned there ten months of the year." Horace Ratt remembers: "It was real bad. You lived inside a fence. There was a fence around the place. And you got up at six-thirty to go to church, at ten o'clock you went to mass, you went to benediction in the afternoon, and you went to church again in the evening. I developed calluses on my knees.

"The curriculum was outdated. They taught you how to read and write, but they never taught us anything about chemistry, biology, their math was old-fashioned. They didn't really push you to accomplish a lot – they only wanted you to attempt a certain level." Everyone in Pelican Narrows breathed a sigh of relief when, in 1974, a secular high school finally opened in the community. It had been a struggle.

Philip Ratt had always thought that the two-prong denominational education system was ridiculous for a community the size of Pelican Narrows. It was inefficient, with two administrations, and more important it had only intensified the conflict in the community. A new Anglican school had been built twenty-five feet from the Catholic, so the war had moved from the classroom to the outside. Instead of spitballs, stones were thrown. When Philip was elected to the band council in 1969, he was determined to force the issue, even though the Catholic Church was very much against the merger. "The priest preached all kinds of negative things to the people, but I think it was a ploy to keep the nuns and the convent in operation. Also the control of the Church would have been diminished." The consolidation went ahead anyway, in 1974, because the Department of Indian Affairs wanted it to.

The high school was overcrowded the moment it opened its doors, so that many young people were still being sent to Prince Albert, where they lived in residence. Even into the 1970s and '80s, it was the same old story.

Darren Highway's mother died at a young age. She had been raped by a white man in Flin Flon when she was only sixteen and gave birth to Darren, her only child, in 1967. She died young and, since Darren's grandparents were already looking after seventeen children, he was sent to Prince Albert Indian Students' Residence when he was only six years old. He remained there until 1981. He admits his experience at the place had left him an angry, at times violent, young man. In this instance it was the adult dorm-keepers, those hired specifically to supervise the children when they were not in the classroom, who inflicted the damage. Their favourite pastime was promoting hatred between the Cree kids and the Dene, and every Friday night they organized brutal fights between the two. "If you were in your room, they would call you by name into the living room and, if you didn't go, they would tell the person you were supposed to fight to go in there and beat the crap out of you. You had to scratch, bite, kick, punch, whatever . . . Everybody I was with in that dorm, everybody has turned to alcohol or drugs, has gone to jail, or committed suicide." What bothers Darren the most is that the students had no recourse. "Every time we told the people who kept sending us there about all the things these dorm-keepers were doing, they said, 'Oh, you're just exaggerating. You just don't want to go.' Well, fucking right I didn't want to go, I keep telling you what I'm going through. My granny asked me once, 'Why are you so angry?' and I told her about the dorm-keepers and she said, 'One day, it doesn't matter if it's today, tomorrow, next month, or next year, you will get even with those people who did you such wrong.' And every day when I get up, I say, I'm going to get even with everybody that has hurt me or my family. I don't care if it takes thirty years."

Education in Pelican Narrows finally moved into the modern age when the band council took over the programming in the late 1970s, including administrating the funds given for education by the federal government. Today, there are two schools with over 1,000 students, Opawikoscikan, Grades 4 to 12, built in 1990 for $11.3 million, and Wapanacak, nursery to Grade 3, which opened in September 2001. Although already overcrowded, both are beautifully kept and nicely decorated; at the junior school images from Cree rock paintings line the walls of the atrium. There is no corporal punishment. There is special education for everything from behavioural problems to speech difficulties. Ninety-five per cent of the teachers are aboriginal, classes in the Cree language are given – there is some talk of an immersion program – and native studies is an important part of the curriculum. Elders teach the children about the old, good way of life – the generosity that was once so prevalent in the society. There's a computer in every classroom, a lab with twenty to twenty-four computers, and more in the library, almost all of which are linked to the Web. Yet for all these material improvements, a heavy malaise hangs over the community.

Vandalism – especially popular are breaking windows and scribbling obscene graffiti everywhere – breaking and entering, alcoholism, drug use, gangs, and street fighting have become serious problems. The windows in the office of Hank Ballantyne, the principal of Opawikoscikan School, are cracked; kids threw rocks. "The respect is gone," he says. "It's a ripple effect. The ones that went to residential school passed it [lack of respect] on to their kids, and now they're passing it on again. It's a chain reaction from one generation to another."

But there's another deeper, more sordid reason for the ugly violence on the reserve: incest and sexual abuse. Celena Bone, a Cree and a nurse for forty years before she retired, says it is hushed up all the time but, "I think that's the major cause of violence. These kids don't want to bring it out, they're scared to bring it out. They keep it inside and they can't express it. They have so much hatred for the people that did that to them. They don't want to identify the person for fear of what would happen." How much of this goes on at Pelican Narrows remains a dark secret, but it's an indication of how far some Cree people have strayed from the principles of their forefathers.

The kids with the red bandanas worn like Arab sheiks are thumbing their nose at authority, though how serious this rebellion is on Pelican Narrows Reserve is hard to say. They are members, or more likely wannabe members, of the Indian Posse. This is a street gang prominent in such prairie cities as Regina, Edmonton, Saskatoon, and Winnipeg. Prostitution, break-and-enters, robberies, car thefts, tobacco fraud, assaults, weapons offences – IP is into it all. Members act as enforcers – trench troops – for organized crime groups such as the Hells Angels, and it's through this connection that they carry out their main money-making activity – trafficking in drugs (marijuana, cocaine, crack, and crystal meth). Writes journalist Sheila Steele, "The Indian Posse have emerged as a force in Saskatchewan lock-ups, jails, and prisons because a huge proportion of the people we lock up in Saskatchewan are natives."

One fact tells it all: of the 3,000 young people caught in the criminal justice system on any given day, about 1,800 are aboriginals, yet they make up only 12 per cent of the youth population.

Councillor Tom Sewap says some Pelican Narrows kids are identifying with the gangs. In the community, there's been a rise in break-and-enters, pawning stolen goods, selling drugs – and violence. "If you are one person, and you happen to be there to tell them not to do something, are they going to listen to you? There's going to be six or seven guys holding hockey sticks. It's like one against a hockey team. Sometimes it's golf clubs. And I'm pretty certain some are carrying concealed weapons." It's a phenomenon that is scaring the elders of Pelican Narrows. "They're starting to have little gangs. This is so bad," says Napoleon Michel. "There's quite a bit of drugs coming in. And fighting."

One afternoon in the fall of 2003, a free-for-all erupted near the two schools. More and more kids jumped in, and the situation quickly deteriorated into real violence. The brawl came near to being a full-fledged riot before the police were finally able to put a stop to it. An emergency meeting of the reserve's parents was called soon after, and ideas such as curfews and bush camps were discussed. The parents are worried, but nobody seems to know what to do about the spiral into anarchy.

Lisa Buettner's parents owned Danny's Store in Jan Lake, so she spent from June to September there every year, playing with the children of the Cree guides. Gordon Peter was one of her buddies. When she graduated from university with a degree in education, she thought it only natural to take a job in Pelican Narrows. She liked the children a lot and understood the cultural differences. "Your first reaction as a teacher when you've got a problem child is to say, 'You look at me.' Well, for a Cree child, looking at you is a sign of disrespect right off the bat. They do not look an elder in the eye, ever. It's something a teacher might not know, and it's very simple." Lisa loved the kids and her work, but around 1996 she and her husband, Kevin, who was posted there as a conservation officer, noticed that drug use, fighting, and drinking were on the upswing. In December, a Grade 12 student died from alcohol poisoning, a Grade 10 student froze to death in the school-yard after a school social – the kindergarten kids found his body the next day – and a kindergarten child was killed by a drunk driver. "That was at Christmas," says Lisa, "and then that spring I had a Grade 5 student who died from sniffing something, and that fazed me. I remember going to the funeral – it was held in the Anglican church, open casket and all that – and I was so angry, so furious, watching all these people wail and cry and scream, think-ing, 'This is your fault! This really is your fault! You are not there when these kids need you.'" Lisa quit her job the next June.

Of course, not every young person brought up on the reserve is so confused and angry. The school graduates about twenty-five to thirty students from Grade 12 each year. A few go on to univer-sity or college, but many do not. They live on the reserve, holding low-paying jobs or not working at all. "Out of the community there's so much stigma [attached to being a native]," says Lisa Buettner, "and so much fear that people are going to look down on them, and in a lot of cases they are looked down on, that they're not willing to take chances."

Timidity is not the only reason the Grade 12 graduates don't leave the reserve. The federal government does not consider post-secondary education a treaty right, and therefore, tightly controls spending. Says Judge Gerry Morin, "It's a misnomer to believe that we get free education. It's amazing as to how that myth got there. I get upset about it 'cause it is a damn myth. The money is just not there."

In 2001 sixty-one Peter Ballantyne students who qualified could not get funding to go to college or university. Since their families usually have many children and little money, and without collateral little access to bank loans, without government grants it's almost impossible for a nineteen or twenty-year-old to break away from the reserve. Where do you get the money for tuition and books? How do you find a place to live? In fact, how do you even buy a bus ticket?

Gordon Peter's eldest son, Peter Ballantyne Junior, is movie-star handsome, taller and more slender than his father, with a shock of black hair and a serious demeanour. He was a good student. "I got up myself, went to school myself, my parents didn't have to tell me." He particularly liked math, English, and physical education. Floor hockey, volleyball, basketball, lacrosse, soccer, he played them all. He graduated from Grade 12 two years ago. His father pushed him to become a provincial conservation officer, but the idea didn't appeal to him. "I have a lot of friends who hate the cops or anyone like them," he says. Eight years ago he received a guitar as a birthday present from his dad. He wasn't thrilled by it at the time, so a relative borrowed it for three years. "When I finally got it back, I started to play, and haven't stopped since." He was shown a few chords, and after that he taught himself. His tastes are fairly sophisticated: "I like the drums in rock and roll, the saxophone in jazz, the guitar in blues." He has no criticism of the reserve and insists that it isn't the violent place that people say it is. Still, he wants to leave. "I'd like to move out pretty soon. Getting pretty tired of this town." He's heard that the University of Alberta offers a good music program, especially for guitarists, and that appeals to him. The trouble is, he admits, he's a little lazy, a little apathetic. He has "an easy job" as a stock clerk at the Northern Store. He has money in his pocket, plenty of buddies, and a girlfriend. Whether he'll have the gumption to make a life for himself in the outside world remains to be seen. Many of Pelican Narrows's young people are balancing on the same tightrope. The reserve may be a turbulent place sometimes, but it is home and therefore fathomable; the city is so daunting and complex.

FALLEN ON HARD TIMES

It has been two years
since we last saw our one-time guide.
His face has aged ten years;
his paunch, grown vaster now
slumps over his jeans
as he limps past our doorway.
We invite him in for morning coffee.

He tells us how he broke
his ankle in three places last winter
falling down some steps. Barred
from the pub along with his son
they have both been relegated
to the filleting shed with the women.

But he voices no complaints,
harbours no grudges we can feel,
just bears this toll of shame
in silence, serves his time.

Glen Sorestad
Jan Lake Poems

5
niyānan

ONE INFECTS, THE OTHER IS INFECTED

PĪYAK ĀSOWIYĒW, KOTAK AKOSIW

New Year's Eve, 2002. It's minus 30° C in Pelican Narrows but that doesn't bother the party-goers who wander from house to house, some drinking heavily, others not at all. Laurie Ballantyne, Gordon Peter's sister, walks over to Crystal and J.J. Merasty's place at about 10 p.m., joining a group of young women crowded into one of the bedrooms, drinking Pilsner beer and Bacardi rum, laughing and talking. Among them is nineteen-year-old Joanna Linklater. Joanna has lived with J.J.'s brother, Jamie, for four years, and he is the father of her baby boy. At about 4 a.m., Jamie, who had been drinking heavily, and Joanna get into a loud argument. Not wanting his house wrecked, J.J. intervenes and the two brothers run outside, all the time punching at each other. Their father, John Merasty, who is also pretty drunk, gets involved. Then Jamie grabs a hockey stick and bangs on the window, demanding that Joanna come out. J.J. rushes inside, finds Joanna in the bathroom, and tells her to leave. "Fuck, Joanna, you always mean trouble. Get out of here," he screams, and bundles her out the door. Outside Jamie grabs the young woman and pushes her into the snow. At that point, Jamie's mother, Marlene Merasty, screams at her son not to hurt the girl. The last time the party-goers see Joanna that morning she is being pushed by Jamie towards their house.

7 a.m., January 1, 2003: the Pelican Narrows RCMP receive an emergency call – there has been a stabbing in the north-central part of the reserve. Two officers arrive at the house, which is in shambles. Furniture has been tipped over, broken beer bottles are strewn around. In the kitchen, Jamie Merasty is lying unconscious in a pool of blood. Joanna, also bleeding from an injury to her leg, is close to hysteria. "Oh God, how did this happen?" she keeps asking. She tells the police that she wasn't there, but she thinks Jamie might have been stabbed with a screwdriver. The ambulance carrying the paramedics arrives – there are few street names or numbers on display at the reserve so locating any particular house is not easy. They attend to Jamie. His shirt is torn and there is a shallow stab wound about five to eight centimetres long on the left-hand side of his chest, just above the nipple. He is gasping for breath. The two paramedics apply oxygen and hurry him onto a stretcher. Jamie regains consciousness in the ambulance, but suddenly a fountain of blood gushes from his chest.

7:26 a.m. at the health clinic: Jamie is hooked up to an intravenous, he has a weak heartbeat. Via the stethoscope, the nurses hear "muffled heart sounds." He is conscious, mumbling something, and breathing on his own. His blood pressure is low, but that would be expected after so much loss of blood. Joanna, who keeps moaning and hugging Jamie and getting in the way of the medical personnel, is told by one of the nurses that he is probably going to be all right. His heart seems not to be affected, the nurse says, but, because of the location of the wound, she thinks it best to send him to the hospital in Flin Flon. She calls the doctor there.

8:10 a.m.: Jamie is on his way to the hospital in an ambulance; Joanne is with him. He begins to scream and thrash about, trying to rip off the oxygen mask. The paramedics assume he is drunk. Suddenly the Code Blue alert is sounded. Jamie goes into cardiac arrest. CPR is applied, but it is too late. Jamie Merasty is only twenty-three years old when his life ends.

January 2, 2003: Joanna Linklater is charged with second-degree murder and released on five hundred dollars bail.[*]

There are many deplorable elements to this story. Pelican Narrows, with a population of about 2,800 people, has no doctor in residence. The health clinic is not equipped with X-ray or ultrasound equipment, so the seriousness of Jamie's injury could not be ascertained. A defibrillator is not available. The closest hospital is in Flin Flon, 120 kilometres away. There is no air service to Pelican Narrows in the winter, and, because the road is still gravel and so dangerous, ambulance drivers are not allowed to travel more than eighty kilometres an hour. Finally, because of the alcoholism on the reserve, all erratic behaviour is assumed to be caused by drunkenness.

If the Rock Cree's spirit and intellect have been assaulted by missionaries and teachers, their health, their physical well-being, has been assailed just as thoroughly. Since contact with the white man, there has been one devastating wave after another – epidemics, chronic diseases of all kinds, mental disorders, and, most serious, alcoholism. That there are any aboriginal people left in this country is something of a miracle.

The old trappers of Pelican Narrows like to brag about how healthy they were when they worked in the bush, how healthy the Indian was before the white man came on the scene. Philip Ratt explains, "There was very little illness among the Indian nations in those days because they were eating natural food. You didn't have the food that we eat today, the canned stuff and the frozen stuff. You don't know how many ingredients are mixed into the process. Here's why you have people like my father who is ninety-five years old. He didn't have the coffee and the Coffee-mate and the cookies in his day. The children were not even allowed to drink tea until they were a certain age." Their diet was pure protein, mostly meat and fish, and they drank clear, clean water, totally unpolluted and untreated. Everyone in the family was strong,

---

[*] At the time of writing, Joanna Linklater's case has still not come to trial.

even the children. Paddling canoes and lifting huge loads across portages, cutting firewood, hauling water, all the daily tasks, made for muscle-building.

Those fur traders who kept journals all agreed that the natives were fine physical specimens. Andrew Graham of the Hudson's Bay Company wrote in 1767, "The Indians in general exceed the middling stature of Europeans; are straight well-made people, large-boned, but not corpulent. Their constitution is strong and healthy; their disorders few, the chief of which are the flu, consumption, and pain in the breast caused by cold air being drawn in."[1] But, as the scholar T. Kue Young points out,

> the Indians did not live in a blissful world where diseases and suffering were unknown. The achievement of functional health in a population was not dependent on the total eradication of all diseases, disabilities, and discomfort, but rather on the maintenance of a "natural" equilibrium and the ability to cope with the challenges of the environment.[2]

The Rock Cree were perfectly attuned to the relationship between their environment and their physical self. The sweat lodge is a good example.

A chest cold was treated by sweating it out in a special conical wigwam. A fire was built and rocks thoroughly heated that were then placed in a central pit in the lodge in directions representing north, south, east, west. The door cover was then tightly secured. The elder who was leading the sweat-lodge ceremonies threw water on the rocks, others followed; the more elders in attendance, the hotter it got. Once you felt you could tolerate not one minute more, you dove into the nearest lake or rolled in a snowbank. It is not clear how much spiritual significance the sweat lodge had for the Rock. In most Indian societies there were pipe and other ceremonies, during which a kind of communal catharsis, group decision-making, and communication with the spirits went on. One's aches and pains not only disappeared, but one's greed and envy did too.

In Rock Cree country sweat lodges have enjoyed a comeback in recent years. "When I'm feeling down, I like to go to a sweat," says Elvena Pearson. "When I come out of there I feel rejuvenated, physically, emotionally, spiritually, everything. If something is bothering you, hurting you, you can talk about it and it stays there. I haven't been anywhere where somebody's pointing a finger and saying, 'Hey, remember what you said in the sweat lodge?' It's just not done. People respect each other, they do, we really respect each other. And we know that what I say here, stays here."

In 2003, Elvena underwent a profound experience at a sweat lodge in Thompson, Manitoba. "They had the sweat, and I felt good after coming out 'cause I prayed in there. I said, 'O Creator, give me a sign. I feel so unworthy, I'm not a good person,' or whatever. I was really down on myself. The next thing I know I could feel this gust of wind brushing my face, and I looked up to just above the medicine man, and I could see an eagle. He was flying around in the sweat lodge. So I said, 'Thank you, Creator. That's my sign.' I was happy again. When I went there, I felt black in my soul. When I came out I felt white."

There was a medicinal plant for almost everything, from irregular menstrual flows to back pain to earaches. Tinder fungus, cut into matchstick-shaped pieces, were placed on the skin and burned to relieve the suffering of arthritis; puffball spores were applied to the nose to stop nosebleed; reindeer moss was dried, and the resulting powder was mixed with water and taken to get rid of intestinal worms; water-dock was decocted and applied to aching joints; wintergreen was used to relieve chest pains caused by a heart condition; chewed dogwood stopped bleeding. Some plants cured so many ailments that they were considered magical. Yarrow, for example: the chewed root remedied toothaches, the crushed flower helped a headache, the flower itself eased the pain of burns. As well, it was used as a lure in traps.[3] Dried Rat root, *wikis*, was, and still is, a cure-all, the Aspirin of the Rock Cree.

Indian medicine was not a simple affair. One had to know, first of all, where to find a plant – not always an easy task for the rare medicinal variety – which part of it should be used, how it should be prepared, and how it would be administered. Medicine men and women were usually elders with a lifetime of experience curing people. Andy McKinley, a white trader interviewed in 1970, remembered watching a medicine man at work: "I walked into this old man's cabin. He had a bunch of these juniper twigs and he was carefully removing the outer bark, and then he scraped the inner bark and he brewed that in a copper kettle, just like tea, with boiling water. And this was the liquid he gave to people with gonorrhea. Apparently that cured it. And I've never seen any bad effects from that. He used to get guns and others things for doing jobs like that."[4]

Medicine men would perform amputations on frostbitten or injured limbs, bleed patients with leeches, and splint broken legs and arms. But since sickness was often attributed to someone intent on doing harm, medicine men also used their powers to cure illnesses caused by malignant forces. As well, these shaman could impose illness on people who were enemies for one reason or another.

Women were both medicine men and shaman. "Some of the women were more powerful than the men," said Angus Bear in a 1984 interview. "Some women were capable even of killing the *witigo*. They knew more because they could do more shamanism. Yes, the women were powerful. They were strong and that's the way it was."[5]

Part of a medicine man's method of treatment was to sing loudly in strange voices which sounded nothing like his own. Wrote Oblate missionary Father Marius Rossignol, "The medicine men had their own personal songs, but anyone could repeat them if his vocal organs were equal to the task. The sound of the medicine men's voices in their incantations seemed changed and no longer natural, and I am of the opinion that only ventriloquists made good medicine men."[6]

There have been many well-known medicine women/men/ shaman in Pelican Narrows country, including Adam Ballantyne, Jacob Ballantyne, Louisa Custer, and Wapaskokimaw (Joseph Bear). But it was Othapatchikew (John Alexander Custer) who was the most famous of them all. He remains a hero to many Rock Cree.

Othapatchikew was a half-breed with a Cree mother with whom he lived, and a white father, who deserted the family, and for that reason he was spurned by society. Othapatchikew and his mother often went without food. When he was a teenager and close to starving, he fell into a trance-like sleep. In a dream he was told that two arrows would be given to him, and with these he would become a great hunter. Sure enough, the first time he went hunting, he shot the two geese out of the air which everyone else had missed. After that, neither he nor his mother were snubbed again.

Othapatchikew became a great believer in vision quests. Solomon Custer remembered, "They built a big box out of a tree. They put Othapatchikew in there, right in the middle of the lake."[7] Bloodsuckers sealed the box to prevent it from leaking. A stick was poked through the ice and attached to a string in the box, which could be manipulated by the person inside. "That stick moves around in the water and the water doesn't freeze. As soon as something happens to him, if he's dead under there, the stick will stop moving and the hole will be frozen over." For Othapatchikew, the stick never stopped moving. "They put him in there right after freeze up and they took him out in spring." Amazingly, while he was an immensely strong man, he was tiny. John Dorion claimed he was only four feet tall. Yet he could take on any *witigo* and kill it.

Othapatchikew's favourite spot for collecting medicines was Big Rock Rapids, about fifty kilometres from Pelican Narrows. He'd travel there in a little boat which somehow became a magnet, drawn to specific rock formations. "Though the water was really fast going down," recalled John Dorion, "the boat just stayed there." For each trip, Othapatchikew made a medicine pouch from a new caribou hide as white as he could find. In this was placed something called *wagaman*, a rusty-red substance found on the rocks. When mixed with other materials, plants and animal parts, this was a cure-all with great healing powers.

There are many testaments given by whites to the skill of medicine men. On one occasion, the wife of A.A. McDonald, the HBC manager at Pelican Narrows in 1898, complained about tremendous pains in her legs. Medicine man Othapatchikew was called in and he found the proper herbs only two hundred yards from the post. It took a while for Mrs. McDonald's pains to lessen, but eventually she was cured. In many of the HBC post journals, the medicine man is referred to as doctor, which indicates the respect even whites held for him.

Gordon Peter's wife, Susan, is a Custer from Deschambault Lake, and Othapatchikew was her great-grandfather. "He never misused his powers," Gordon Peter writes. "They were used only for special purposes. When Christianity was introduced, he became very religious and through religion he lost his powers. It wasn't long after he lost his powers, that he passed away at a very old age." Soon the influence of every medicine man and woman would be challenged and then refuted.

In the afternoon of June 10, 1782, sixteen canoes loaded with furs arrived at York Factory. The news these Swampy Cree passed on to the HBC factor, Matthew Cocking, was alarming. "They inform me that a violent disorder has raged among their people which they described as a violent eruption on the skin," he wrote in the post journal.[8] All Cocking could do was hope that the stories were exaggerations. Then, thirteen days later, on a clear, blustery Sunday, another party of Cree arrived on foot, the wind forcing them to abandon their canoes some distance from the fort. They told Cocking "their Husbands & [children] died of a violent breaking out upon them all over their bodies and within the mouth and throat and which from their description must have been the smallpox."

Edward Umfreville, an HBC trader, documented the devastation.

That epidemical and raging disorder has spread an almost universal mortality throughout the country in the interior parts of Hudson Bay, extending its destructive effect through every tribe and nation, sparing neither age nor sex. . . . The distress of the Indians by this visitation has been truly deplorable. . . . As the smallpox has never before been among them . . . they at first imagined it to be no more than a simple breaking out on the skin which would disappear of itself. . . . Numbers began to die on every side; the infection spread rapidly; and hundreds lay expiring together without assistance.[9]

In the four decades after Christopher Columbus's arrival in 1492, massive epidemics killed millions of people in South and Central America. In the sixteenth century contagious diseases spread along the east coast of North America, and in the seventeenth century, Indians were killed off en masse. But it would not be until the late eighteenth century that the terrible *Variola* would reach the Woodland Cree in northern Canada.

In 1781 Sioux middlemen infected with the pox virus travelled along the upper Missouri River from one trading village to another. From these places the disease travelled in all directions, including northward to the Canadian prairies. By October it had spread to the South Saskatchewan River near the Red Deer River, by November it reached the junction of the North and South Saskatchewan rivers, by December it was at Cumberland House, and shortly afterwards it reached the heart of Rock Cree country. In February, Cumberland House traders reported what they had seen in the countryside. "They had found where four Indians had died, but nothing remain'd of three except the Hair of their Heads & a few scraps of their Coats, all of which had been eat up by the wild Annimals."[10] The Hudson's Bay Company men played a double-faced role during the smallpox epidemic. On the one hand they nursed as many afflicted Indians as they could, both at the post and in the bush. After all, they were customers; there'd be no business without them. William Tomison at Cumberland House reported that nine or ten sick Indians were on the premises, of which four were being nursed in the post house. They had, he wrote, "due attendance Night & Day."[11] On the other hand, it was not unusual to find the Bay men snatching a beaver robe right off a corpse to pay off the dead man's debts.

The death toll was devastating, because the Indians had no means of fighting the virus. One scholar believes it might have been the march through the Bering Strait from Russia to North America those thousands of years ago that resulted in the loss of immunity. The cold temperatures and low population densities would have killed off the pathogens of the old world, not just smallpox, but measles, influenza, whooping cough, and venereal disease, leaving the natives vulnerable.

After a two-week incubation the pox virus would bring on headaches, body aches, and drowsiness. This was followed by high fevers, causing delirium and sometimes blindness. Within two or three days what at first seemed to be pimples, then blisters, then pustules spread over the entire body. Finally, if the victim was still living, diarrhea hit. The Indians, William Tomison of Cumberland House reported, "chiefly Die within the third or fourth Night" of the disease.

Herbal remedies, medicine-man concoctions, did no good at all. And the sweat lodge, so long a panacea for all Indian ills, made matters worse, especially if the delirious sick person jumped into the freezing lake afterwards. Often he or she simply drowned. On top of that, as able-bodied men were felled, there was no one left to hunt or fish for food. Eventually, the Indians, frightened by the malignancy and the speed of the disease, gave up trying to care for the ill at all. "They think," reported Umfreville, "they need not look for any recovery. So when the person that's bad turns so feeble that he cannot walk, they leave him behind when they're pitching away and so the poor Soul perishes."[12] He estimated that about one in fifty survived the illness.

On his first visit to Regina, Gordon Peter was anxious to visit the Royal Saskatchewan Museum. I went with him. We spent hours studying the aboriginal people's exhibits, which nicely emphasize the successful side of Indian culture. Gordon Peter elaborated on many of the exhibits; a wooden slab with a movable metal arm on the bottom which the museum had simply labelled a "jigger" was used, explained Gordon Peter, to spread nets under the ice so that more fish could be caught. The beadwork on moccasins, belts, and cradleboards was stunning, and the displays accompanied by recorded stories lifelike and poignant. We were having a wonderful time until we spotted the display interpreting the changes in Indian society with the onslaught of white traders. The last sentence of the explanation read, "By 1800, at least one major smallpox epidemic had swept across western Canada, killing at least 90 per cent of the population between the Saskatchewan and Churchill rivers," the exact location of Pelican Narrows. Gordon Peter was reduced to painful silence and I felt much as I had when I visited the Auschwitz museum in Poland.

The suffering of Indian families was terrible. An historian put it this way, "This slaughter of the Indians by the smallpox was perhaps as shattering a disaster as any native race . . . has ever received from the white men; and it was all the more stunning because its destruction was compressed into a period of fifteen months or less."[13]

In 1838 smallpox returned again with a vengeance, but this time the white man performed some magic. The wizard was William Todd, chief HBC factor of the Swan River district, and a physician who had earned a good reputation among the various First Nations. It was Dr. Todd who persuaded the Indians to become inoculated. A vaccination for the disease had been developed in Europe in the late 1790s. Todd was able to get his hands on the serum, and inoculated as many natives as he and other post managers could. He also taught the Indians who came to his post to use the procedure on their extended families. He recorded, on December 8, 1837, that he had "fitted out the Indians and sent them off to the Strong Wood with particular instructions for them in case the reported Sickness should turn out to be the Smallpox. I likewise gave them a lassuch [lancet] and took great pains in instructing them how to use it in vaccinating others."[14] While it's not likely that many Rock Cree in the Pelican Narrows band were inoculated at the time, a buffer zone had been created by those who were. Almost all of the Woodland Cree of Saskatchewan and Manitoba survived.[15]

It was not only smallpox that proved such a deadly enemy. Measles, which usually was only an irritation when contracted by a European, killed a native person. In 1819 a dual epidemic of whooping cough and measles broke out on the western plains and woodlands. The HBC Edmonton district's journal reported, "This dreadful disease . . . as well as the whooping Cough prevailed during the greater part of the Winter among all the different tribes of Indians who trade with us at this District and proved equally fatal to all."[16] But it was the 1846 measles epidemic that transformed the Rock Cree in the Pelican Narrows and Lac La Ronge area – the proverbial straw that broke the camel's back. Belief in the medicine man, the power of the shaman, crumbled in the face of diseases that paid no attention to his herbal remedies or his occult knowledge. Many Rock Cree converted to Christianity during the late 1840s and early 1850s, hardly noticing that the epidemics continued anyway.

On August 19, 1907, the HBC manager reported that measles had become epidemic among the Indians in Pelican Narrows country. In the days that followed, his journal read like the script of the dead. "August 18: Eli Motto's little boy died this morning. August 25: John McCallum's young son died yesterday evening. August 28: Cornelius Bear's child died last night. August 30: Pas crew got back. Six of the men are very sick. September 9: R. Motto's little child died this morning. September 14: Tom's two daughters passed away last night. October 15: Noah Ballantyne brought in the body of Thomas Ballantyne [Chief Peter's brother], who has died of measles."

One fatal wave after another of devastating diseases pummelled the Rock Cree until they must have wondered how they had offended the gods, Christian or otherwise. In 1890 an epidemic of diphtheria broke out. Father Charlebois visited the sick near Cumberland House and wrote, "Nearly all the children are dead. The sight that meets my eyes when I visit the huts is most heartrending. I saw four, five, or six people lying upon the ground rolled up in miserable blankets, and so close to one another that I had to watch, so as not to tread upon anybody's arm or leg. I would often find a little corpse among the sick, and the poor mother exhausted by fatigue and broken by sorrow. Poor people!"[17]

By the turn of the century, the entire native population seemed to have been weakened. It was not just diseases; the lack of nutrition brought on by the shortage of game and fish made the people more susceptible. Sometimes even a mild flu bug, hardly more than a cold to a white person, quickly turned killer for the Indians. On February 19, 1900, the HBC post manager at Pelican Narrows noted that "Edward Sewap and George Custer brought in the body of old Benjamin. They are trading no furs as they are all starving, killing no fish." On March 29, 1900, the HBC journal reported: "Louis Morison's girl very sick. All the people are sick with 'La Grippe.' Those Indians that went to Prince Albert brought it back with them." April 3: "Indians all sick and starving, killing no fish." April 4: "L. Morison's girl died this morning." April 5: "Louis's girl buried today." April 7: "Indians are still sick. no fish killed today." April 18: "Indians are getting over their sickness. Only William Nateweyes' wife and John Rednose's wife are still very sick."

Sometimes a cloud of death seemed to be hovering permanently over Pelican Narrows, as bodies of children, grandmothers, uncles, cousins, who had died for one reason or another – accidents, sickness, old age – were brought in for a Christian burial. On September 18, 1902, the HBC manager waxed lyrically: "Mary Jane is dying." September 19: "Weep! Ye disconsolate, Mary Jane is dead. May she Requiescat in Pace. Such an angelic character was too good for this earth and she was called to share in the glories of the great Beyond." September 20: "Rain. Mary Jane was buried today. Nature in sympathy shed tears."[18] Who was Mary Jane? There's no clue to her identity, never a mention of her before or after in the journals, but whether she was human or, more likely, animal, her eulogy was in keeping with the mood of the times.

In 1904 in the Pelican Narrows neighbourhood scarlet fever killed one child, and made many sick. In 1910 five children died from whooping cough. Most shameful of all was the invasion of scurvy. It was the Indians who saved Jacques Cartier and his crew on their exploration to Canada in 1535 by providing the white explorers with spruce-needle tea, thus curing them of the dreaded disease. By 1920, the medicine man's remedy had been all but forgotten. As one doctor pointed out, "The church has relegated it to the realm of witchcraft, so that even such a simple thing as the brewing of spruce needles has disappeared. I saw an Indian child die of scurvy within 100 yards of a trading post, and yet not an orange or a tin of tomatoes could be bought there."[19]

Of course, it wasn't simply the white man's germs that were killing the Indians; the paraphernalia and psychosis of the industrial world was doing them in, as well. In 1913 the Royal North-West Mounted Police listed the nature of sudden deaths in "F" Division, which included most of northwestern Manitoba and northeastern Saskatchewan. There were eight deaths by suicide, seven by accidental poisoning (the report did not reveal whether these were homebrew or not), thirteen by drowning, eight by accidental shooting, three by falls, eight by injuries sustained in vehicle accidents, four by falling trees, four by mill accidents, four by freezing. Only ten people, 16 per cent, died from old age or natural causes such as heart attack.[20]

The pandemic that swept the world in 1918–19, and killed millions, was wrongly called the Spanish flu. It actually began in the south China province of Guangdong in February 1918, and travelled to France, perhaps carried by Chinese labourers. The infection invaded Canada via troop ships returning from the Great War in July 1918, but it was not until 1920 that it reached the north.

Millions of people died worldwide, an estimated fifty thousand in Canada, but native people were once again particularly susceptible. The Revillon trader Harold Kemp describes visiting an Indian camp on Montreal River south of La Ronge in March 1920:

> The woman lay on a bunk [in a log cabin]. A lone candle was burning. The woman was consumed with fever. It looked like pneumonia, but we could not be certain.
>
> "Should treat her for that," said Alex Ahenakew. "But what with?"
>
> Here was a settlement with a winter population of several scores of people entirely bereft of anything in the way of drugs . . . except those on sale at Alex's store – a few bottles of Painkiller, some liniment, and a few boxes of Little Liver Pills.
>
> "Could try the Painkiller," decided Alex. "I'll get some."

The woman died shortly after she took the pills.[21]

Kemp and the others realized the next day that it was not pneumonia that sickened her, but the deadly influenza. It swept through Rock Cree country like a firestorm. As Kemp reported:

> From outlying Indian settlements, from lone trapping camps, the people trickled in. Some brought their dead with them. Other dead they were forced to leave behind. Our attempts to help these people were given willingly enough, but they were pathetic in their ineffectiveness. We housed them, cooked for them, cut great stacks of firewood, and saw them die on our hands . . .
>
> We could not have dug graves had we desired. The ground was frozen feet deep. The hours spent burying the dead could be better spent caring for the living. Or for as long as they continued to live. We stored the bodies in the below-zero church. . . . At the end of three weeks things were beyond our control.[22]

Word came to the Revillon post that a family was in great distress on a nearby island. Kemp and two others went to the rescue.
What they saw was the stuff of nightmares.

One bunk held a dead woman. A dead man lay in his
blanket on the floor. Two more bunks held those that still
lived – a woman and a crying child in one of them, a man
of thirty, babbling insanely.

The man was a veritable skeleton, with fevered cheeks,
cracked lips, and stone-blank eyes. Now and again he
stopped his babbling long enough to stare across the room
where the dead woman lay, her eyes, wide-staring, fixed
ever upon her husband.[23]

At Pelican Narrows many people succumbed to the disease,
although the death rate was not as high as it might have been. The
old medicine people had come up with a cure. John Merasty was
told by his grandmother: "They killed a skunk, and they took a
cup of boiled water. They took a needle and you know where the
skunk smells really bad, that sack, they stuck the needle in there
and put it in the water. So they gave the sick person that drink,
with all the stinkiness. That's what killed the flu. Killed the virus.
And if you didn't drink it, you died. I know of cases where some
people didn't drink it and they died."

Underlying all the infections – scarlet fever, diphtheria,
chicken pox, whooping cough had been added to the list – was the
most insidious of all the diseases – influenza, highly contagious,
assaulting the most vulnerable, without cure.

Analysis of skeletal remains in Canada indicates that tuberculosis existed among some First Nations people before Europeans
arrived. At early contact, the disease was not uncommon; the
Jesuits found glandular tuberculosis among the Hurons as early as
1633. While Europeans did not introduce tuberculosis, they are
answerable for the appalling conditions created by the destruction
of the Indian society, which allowed it to flourish. By the twentieth

century, the tuberculosis death rate among natives of the western provinces was 10 to 20 per cent higher than among non-aboriginal people.[24] As one analysis put it, "the relocation of Aboriginal people to reserves with minimal resources, where people lived in crowded houses, and where children were concentrated in boarding schools, essentially guaranteed their complete and rapid tuberculinization."[25]

The situation was so severe that the Canadian government finally had to do something, and in 1904 the first medical official responsible for Indian health was appointed. Dr. Peter Bryce was a man who both cared about aboriginal people and was determined to do something about their poor health. He was particularly worried about the spiralling morbidity rate from tuberculosis, and said so in no uncertain terms. But he could not sway the niggardly government officials. His request for a special grant of twenty thousand dollars for preventive programs was rejected by Parliament in 1905. Two years later, he launched an investigation into the conditions at thirty-five industrial and boarding schools which he found to be rife with disease and lacking proper medical records and treatment. According to his statistics, in a survey over a fifteen-year period, from 25 to 35 per cent of all children who had been pupils at these institutions had died, most of them from tuberculosis. At some schools the figure was as high as 75 per cent. High-ranking government officials accused Bryce of exaggerating and, when he was passed over for a promotion, he quit. Fifteen years later he authored a pamphlet entitled "The Story of a National Crime: An Appeal for Justice to the Indians of Canada." "It is indeed pitiable that . . . this trail of disease and death has gone almost unchecked," he wrote, "by any serious efforts on the part of the Department of Indian Affairs."[26] Obviously, Indians dying of a disease continued to be a low priority. In 1940 Dr. P.E. Moore, acting superintendent of medical services, Indian Affairs Branch, wrote: "Prior to 1937, due to lack of funds Affairs Branch was able to accomplish very little in t concerted attack on the problem [of tuberculosis]." Dr certainly correct. In 1942 the death rate from tuberculosis among the Rock Cree of Saskatchewan and Manitoba was 1,400 per 100,000 people. The comparable figure for the white population was twenty-seven tuberculosis deaths per 100,000 people. As one doctor put it, "It was in the selfish interest of the white man, for his own protection, to take steps to control tuberculosis in the red man."[27] Gradually, sanatoriums, usually segregated, or beds in Indian hospitals were put in place for the native population.

Philip Ratt was ten when he was sent to Guy Residential School. Endowed with a lively curiosity, he was eager to get whatever education he could, but once the children discovered that he was an Anglican, not a Catholic, he was in for trouble. "I used to look forward to fights after class," he says. His schooling was so important to him, though, that he converted to Catholicism, "and after that everything was fine." He was there for just six months when he was diagnosed with tuberculosis and admitted to the sanatorium at Clearwater Lake in Manitoba. He would spend four years there, not once seeing his mother, although his father was able to visit a few times. Isolated and fairly well-fed, the children were kept busy knitting, looking at picture books, and, as a treat, listening to the radio. No academic subjects, such as reading and writing English, math, or employable skills were taught. When he was finally discharged at age fourteen almost fifteen, he was too old to return to residential school. Fortunately for Philip, he had the strength of will to educate himself. During the long winter evenings in his trapline cabin, and, in the summers, when he worked as a fire lookout, he painstakingly taught himself to speak, read, and write English, using a pocket dictionary that someone gave him and issues of the *Reader's Digest* as his textbooks. Today he is one of the most articulate people commenting on First Nation matters.

Philip Ratt was certainly not the only child to become ill as soon as he arrived at residential school. Sturgeon Landing's discharge records from 1937 to 1945 read like a health report from a prisoner-of-war camp. In any one year there were only 100 students in the entire school. "1937: Josiah Constant, 11, died at

The Anglican summer school at Pelican Narrows.

Log cabins replaced the wigwam once the Woodland Cree children were required to attend school. (Saskatchewan Archives Board, RB-5612-3)

A Woodland Cree wigwam greets visitors at the
Pelican Narrows reserve entrance. (Carmen Pauls
Orthner)

The sign indicates that Pelican Narrows is part of the Peter Ballantyne
Cree Nation. (Carmen Pauls Orthner)

A typical Pelican Narrows neighbourhood. (Carmen Pauls Orthner)

And a typical government-style house on the Peter Ballantyne Reserve.
(Carmen Pauls Orthner)

Gordon Peter with his father, Roderick Ballantyne, the long-time trapper. (Tina Pomeroy)

Philip and Suzette Ratt. (Gerald B. Sperling)

Susan Ballantyne with her daughters, Melissa and Vanessa. (Tina Pomeroy)

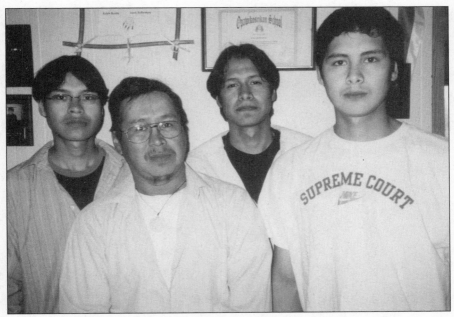

Gordon Peter Ballantyne with his three sons, left to right, Scott, Ronald, and Peter Jr. (Tina Pomeroy)

Fred Ballantyne, grandson of Peter, the band's first chief. (Gerald B. Sperling)

Chief Ron Michel.

The Pas hospital; Martial Castel, 15, sick at home, tuberculosis; Bibiane Bighetty, 10, died at school; Madelaine Head, 6, died at school; Arthur Ballantyne, 7, sick at home; Josephte Head, 10, died at Cumberland House; Domitilde Colomb, 11, sick at home; Marguerite Highway, 12, sick at home; Andre Castel, 10, sick at home; William Sauteux, 12, sick, cannot come back to school; Gabriel Colomb, 11, died at Pukatawagan; Gabriel Dumas, 13, sick at home, should be discharged. 1938 (incomplete records): Jordy Sywap, 15, not back to school for sickness; Cornelius Dorion, 9, sick at home. 1940 (incomplete records): Leon Merasty, 13, died at The Pas hospital; Baptiste Morin, 11, sick of tuberculosis. 1941 (incomplete records): Marguerite Linklater, 6, died at the hospital at The Pas; Jimmie Benaouni, 8, died at The Pas. 1942: Juliette Colomb, 12, sick at home; Madelaine Michel, 13, died at home; Wilbrod Dumas, 12, kept at home for weakness; Anthony Bighetty, 14, has been sick for two years. 1943: Joseph Michel, 7, died at sanatorium, Elie Caribou, 7, died at sanatorium; Elizabeth Linklater, 12, discharged [from school] on doctor's orders; Mabel Linklater, 7, discharged on doctor's orders; Emelie Michel, 11, died during holidays; J. Baptiste McCallum, 12, kept by parents, sick. 1944: Nelson Spence, 8, died at home; Ukald Nicolas, 11, died at home. 1945: Margaret Moose, 8, died at home; Emile Morin, 13, died during the holidays, drowned; Samuel Linklater, 20, poor health, going to day school at Nelson House; Flora Moose, 12, very poor health; Flora Cursiteur, 13, kept at home for her health; Helen Bear, 10, died at home; Madeleine Nicholas, 12, likely going to sanitarium."[28]

In his journal, that keen observer of the Rock Cree P.G. Downes, said of the desolation: "You see the romantic north no longer romantic; you see people working and starving for a precarious living, you see Indians losing everything hundreds of years have handed down to them – losing it through missionaries and other whites, so that they are but poor imitations of both whites and Indians. You see country burned, and game pushed out & trapped out. You see them dying of t.b. everywhere."[29]

The Chiefs who signed Treaty Six had suffered through the epidemics the non-aboriginals had brought, and had insisted, when negotiating the treaty, on being provided with non-aboriginal medicines to deal with them. This was the basis of the medicine-chest concept. Basically it was an undertaking by the Crown to make medicines available at the house of the Indian agent for the use and benefit of the natives. When the Peter Ballantyne Band signed on to Treaty Six, its members became entitled to pharmaceuticals. Since there was no Indian agent housed at Pelican Narrows, the job of storing, and then distributing, went first to the Hudson's Bay Company post manager, and then, in 1902, when it was discovered that Father Rossignol had two years of medical training, the task was given to him. It set a precedent; every priest after him was handed the same job. For dispensing the few drugs available, the priest was paid fifty dollars per year, twice the amount Peter Ballantyne received for being chief.

For the first half of the twentieth century about the only time an aboriginal person had contact with modern medical procedures was once a year on Treaty Day. While the Indian agent met with chief and council, the paying officer doled out the rations, and a Mountie meted out rough justice, a doctor would vaccinate against smallpox (beginning in 1902), and later, X-ray chests for tuberculosis, pull teeth, perform minor operations. In 1927 the RCMP commissioner for northern Saskatchewan wrote:

I would again emphasize the necessity of more medical men being stationed in the northern portions of Manitoba and Saskatchewan. From The Pas north to Port Nelson and Fort Churchill in Manitoba, and west to Isle à la Crosse in Saskatchewan, there is not one physician in that vast area. The Indians should be visited more often than once a year, and in cases of accident the medical officer should have every facility to travel quickly to where his services are required.[30]

But reports like these – and there were many similar documents – were ignored by government. Medical treatment for native people remained almost non-existent; until the 1950s visits to a doctor's office or a hospital were rare experiences indeed. Again it was the priest in the community who decided which ailment was serious enough for further treatment. "I know the priest tries to be fair," said James Ballantyne in a 1942 interview, "but if a Protestant and a Catholic are both sick, and there's one seat on the plane, you know who will get it."

By the 1930s, Pelican Narrows had grown in population, and there was a crying need for more medical service. Mrs. Lowrie, the wife of the HBC post's manager, became a substitute nurse. The post's journal of August 16, 1938, written by Mr. Lowrie, reports: "Old Noah Ballantyne chopped at a log this morning. The log moved and he just about took off his foot. Mrs. Lowrie sewed it up, and made a very nice job of it. Mrs. Lowrie is doing a great deal of unofficial nursing here, for which she receives nothing whatever, barring a very occasional word of thanks. There is supposed to be a doctor here once a month, and, as we have only seen him once since April, it would seem only fair to give Mrs. Lowrie an official position. At least it would save the Post the cost of the medicine." August 27: "There are one or two bad TB cases here, and once again it becomes apparent that a competent nurse should be in charge here, as these fellows get no medical attention at all." October 7: "Étienne Sinclair, who was referred to by the Priest last July as 'ready to die anyway, so why waste medicine?' walked down to the store on a crutch. He can, if he knows how, thank God and Mrs. Lowrie that he is alive now."[31] Nevertheless, it would take another fifteen years before a nursing station, with two beds and a poorly supplied pharmacy, was finally established at Pelican Narrows.

After the Second World War the Canadian government had a change of heart, and realized that if they weren't to receive a black eye in the world community, something had better be done about the deplorable condition of First Nations people. The budget for health services to aboriginals soared.

It made a huge difference. In the ten years between 1950 and 1960 the infant mortality rate among aboriginal people in Canada was cut by 50 per cent. Through inoculation, diseases such as smallpox, measles, and scarlet fever were all but eradicated. The tuberculosis mortality rate plummeted. The life-expectancy rate slowly crept up, yet by 1990 it was still only 63.8 years for native males compared to 73 years for white males, and 71 years for aboriginal females, compared to 79 years for women in the white population.[32] The reason can be found in one statistic: by the mid-1990s the leading cause of death, 30 per cent, was injury inflicted by violence – car accidents, shotgun wounds, drowning, fires, suicides. Underlying this tale of tragedy is the most devastating sickness of all – alcoholism. Says Ovide Highway, "We used to sit up with people who were sick until they got better. I was taught to respect the sick and the elders. Today we hardly see that because of alcohol." Almost every authority has linked illness, suicide, and alcoholism with joblessness and all that that entails – loss of self-esteem, boredom, confusion. First Nations people believe that this pathology, "this despair and depression of the human spirit," is the most devastating of all the diseases inflicted by the white man on the Indian. Pelican Narrows Indian Reserve is an unhappy example.

The health history of Gordon Peter Ballantyne's family is typical of others living on the reserve. His mother suffered a fatal heart attack at age fifty-four, brought on by diabetes, high blood pressure, and circulatory problems. His father was diagnosed with cancer, but was cured by a herbal remedy acquired from an Amisk Lake medicine man. As for his siblings, a sister died in infancy; brother Alfie Thomas died from a childhood illness; a sister, Jean Elizabeth, passed away at age twenty-four from a variety of illnesses; a brother, Melvin, died in a fire at age thirty-two. But what has played the most havoc with the lives of the Ballantynes, like all other families on the reserve, is alcohol.

In the early days of the fur trade, distilled liquor was the devil among the goods traded. The French used brandy liberally to get their hands on Indian furs; the British eventually did the same. Once the HBC and the North West Company began competing in the fur trade, "Fiery Double Distilled Rum" from the West Indies was dished out like water. In 1800 alone ten thousand gallons of the stuff were shipped to the interior of Canada; in 1803, as the competition became more fierce, twenty-one thousand gallons arrived. When the companies amalgamated in 1821, and George Simpson became the governor, he promised to get rid of the evil drink. He wrote to his superiors in London:

> we have taken steps as will tend to wean the Indians from their insatiable thirst for Spirituous Liquors by passing a res-olution that no more than half the quantity usually allowed be given as presents and that trade in Furs for that article (which was very limited) be altogether discontinued.[33]

Simpson's regime was so successful that, four years later, it was difficult to buy distilled liquor, even from a bootlegger. "The only time they had this liquor was before they went trapping," remembered Peter Linklater, in a 1970 interview.[34] "Sometimes the Bay and other traders would give the good trappers one or two gallons of rum. If you were a poor trapper, you drank water." The attempt at control went further; the Indian Act made it illegal for Indians to buy or use alcohol. How effective these laws were is open to question. "The traders' canoe brought whiskey and they are having a glorious drunk," reported the HBC journal, July 3, 1906.

The consumption of brandy and rum was not the only thing that had been copied from the Europeans; the natives also learned how to make homebrew. In 1970 Henry Dorion gave an inter-viewer his recipe: "In a two-gallon aluminum pail put three yeast cakes, two packages of raisins, each box four pounds, about a pound and a half of brown sugar. We'd set it for twenty-four hours and then we'd drink this stuff." "For sure, it tasted yeasty," says Napoleon Michel. He liked to add rice. "In the past," adds Ovide Highway, "the people only drank homebrew, no whiskey, wine, beer, or hair spray."

In lonely winter camps, or in settlements such as Pelican Narrows where entertainment was lacking to say the least, the brew party became immensely popular. As the anthropologist John J. Honigmann points out, for once, the stoic Indian could enjoy becoming "emotionally unrestrained." "They talked and joked, affirmed good fellowship, engaged in sexual badinage and overtures, and sometimes broke into quarrels and violence that a spouse or good friends sought to restrain lest serious injury ensue."[35] And this "having a good time" describes many a house party at Pelican Narrows to this day.

There are many people on the reserve who do not drink at all, and many who drink in moderation. Unfortunately, as the society has had to cope with the hierarchical white world, with the economics of cutthroat capitalism, which is so different from traditional Cree culture, the need for alcohol among many First Nations people has increased. The economically troubled times of the 1970s, the breakdown of traditional Indian spirituality and values, and the lack of viable employment all contributed to their travail. But it was the trauma of residential school that many believe did the most damage. Says J.B. Custer, "For twenty long years I was a real alcoholic, a drug addict. I was bootlegging, dealing drugs. I did a lot of fighting. The only time I ever talked was when I was drunk. I had no self-esteem and I hated white people with a passion, especially the cops and the priests. So all those years were wasted until, about fifteen years ago, I kind of made a comeback. We started this residential-school healing committee and that's when I understood the residential-school syndrome. And it helped. I stopped drinking, at least for a while."

Ron Michel, present chief of the Peter Ballantyne Cree Nation, says that the population of Pelican Narrows can be segmented as follows: 30 per cent are alcohol abusers, 50 per cent are social drinkers, and 20 per cent are abstainers. This echoes a report by the Federation of Saskatchewan Indian Nations, which demonstrated that between 35 and 40 per cent of adult Indians in Saskatchewan are problem drinkers and 20 to 25 per cent are drug-abusers. John J. Honigmann writes, "Heavy drinking became an occasion when people might release control, vent emotion freely and feel it intensely, and know that, within limits, drunkenness made such behaviour expectable and socially excusable."[36]

There is no indication that First Nations people are genetically less able to tolerate alcohol or become more readily addicted to it. Writes the anthropologist Hugh Brody, "I found no basis for the view that Indians [on Skid Row in Ottawa] have as a matter of chemistry constitutionally less resistance to alcohol. It may seem laborious to continue emphasizing this lack of evidence, but the insistence with which non-Indians hold the belief is disturbing since it provides . . . a rationale for discriminatory practices."[37] Gerry Morin, a Cree/Métis, and a Saskatchewan provincial court judge, has a simpler explanation. "How long have we been involved in majority society? Forty years. Forty years is a damn short period of time. How many has the white society had to deal with alcohol? A long, long time."

Everyone at Pelican Narrows agrees there's far too much booze and too many drugs. Everyone is touched by it. "Every day you see people drunk," says Charlie Sewap, "or getting beat up or medical emergencies. People despise each other because of alcohol." Isaac Custer, fifty-five: "Alcohol, that's my biggest problem. I've been wasting a lot of years drinking, broken dreams and sickness. As a result of alcohol, I've got a liver problem." Gary Thomas, thirty-five: "Alcohol was the worst thing in my life since childhood till today. It has gotten in the way of all my plans." Roderick Thomas, sixty-eight, of Southend: "It ruined my life 'cause I was so much in jail and breaking the law, in court. I was thrown in and out." Roderick finally stopped drinking after a month-long session at a rehab centre in Saskatoon, and got his life back together as best he could. His marriage, though, was destroyed.

Gordon Peter usually doesn't drink during the week, he never misses work because he is drunk, but on weekends, like many on the reserve, he sometimes parties. Drinking is his way of relaxing, of having fun. But on one occasion he was found guilty of drunk driving, lost his licence for two years, and had to pay an eight-hundred-dollar fine. The judge's lecture humiliated and frightened him so badly that he has not bothered to renew his driver's licence. At the moment he doesn't own a vehicle and he doesn't want one – not even a snowmobile. "I don't want to end up in jail," he says. His second oldest son, Ronald, spent a month in a Prince Albert rehabilitation centre in August 2003, and returned to school that September. But a month later he had dropped out and was drinking again. Gordon Peter's youngest child, Melissa, is a victim of fetal alcohol syndrome. "Susan didn't know she was pregnant until she was six months," he says. The family learned a lesson. On two occasions, when his daughter Vanessa announced she was to have a child, he made sure she neither smoke nor drank until the birth. But he admits his community is suffering badly. "And it will likely get worse before it gets better," he says.

One of Pelican Narrows's worst plagues is fetal alcohol syndrome (FAS). It's a condition caused entirely by a pregnant mother consuming alcohol. Children with FAS may have abnormal facial features, other physical disabilities, and trouble with learning, memory, attention span, problem-solving, as well as social/behavioural difficulties. Celena Bone, who was born in Pelican Narrows, had been a nurse in the north for forty years before she retired. She remembers one case of FAS that left her devastated. The child was born with a badly damaged heart and liver. He was sent to Saskatoon for heart surgery, but then was returned to Celena's maternity ward at Flin Flon's hospital. "We didn't want him to go to pediatrics because there were bugs down there. And you never know what he would pick up. We had him for six months and he died on our floor. He was so cute, and I thought, such an innocent little child, why would the mother do something like this just for her own satisfaction?

"Sometimes you can't detect it [FAS] right away. Your baby's born perfectly normal, the features are okay. But when they start growing up, they have behavioural problems, that kind of thing . . . a lot of them are not even diagnosed, probably because a lot of moms are in denial. Nobody likes to admit that they did this to their babies. It's putting a lot of stress on the teachers. Let's face it, those kids are hard to handle, and they don't readily listen to you. They just can't pay attention long enough for you to teach them anything. You have to be patient, you have to talk to them slowly, and be understanding. They need so much love."

Philip Ratt used to drink regularly until he saw what it was doing to him and his community. He laments, "I see my next-door neighbour, who is my daughter, and she has two boys who were both born with fetal alcohol syndrome. It's going from one generation to another." He sits at his kitchen table in his little house and draws a diagram which illustrates how alcohol abuse has afflicted his family. It's a triangular map of one small neighbourhood in Pelican Narrows. In the house in one corner, his grandson's wife committed suicide at age twenty-four while under the influence of alcohol. At the second corner is located the porch steps where another grandson, twelve years old, died from inhaling a noxious substance. At the third angle is located the home where a promising young man was stabbed to death on New Year's Day. Jamie Merasty was Philip Ratt's grandson.

Fred Ballantyne was a heavy drinker until he went to an Alcoholics Anonymous meeting in Flin Flon. "At that time I didn't know I was an alcoholic. I thought, 'I'm not an alcoholic. I know what to do. I eat, I never have welfare, I look after my children.' But I was mistaken. I was an alcoholic." Not only did he stop drinking, but he began counselling other abusers. "The people liked me so much, and I had to tell them, 'I'm not a saint, I'm just like you.'"

AA has been the saviour of many people on the reserve, and so have rehabilitation centres. Darlene McKay remembers the day in

1996 when she realized she needed help to stop drinking. "We were having a barbecue, and we had one of those baby monitors outside. We could hear my granddaughter stirring, so I said, 'I'll go and change her diapers.' I picked her up and hugged her and she pushed me away. An eight-month-old kid pushed me away! I said, 'What's the matter, baby?' She was looking at me so strange because I was half-cut and smelled of beer. That's when I said I would go to rehab and I stuck it out the full thirty days." Darlene still drinks the odd beer, but, she says, her heavy-drinking party days are gone.

On the Pelican Narrows Reserve there are those who are attempting to reinstate the ceremonies and philosophy of the old Cree religion as an antidote against drunkenness. Horace Ratt is one of this admittedly small group. "I wish people knew their native tradition, their native values, because there's no room for alcohol in native spirituality. If the people were taught about their identity, that would be a blessing. They wouldn't bother with drugs and alcohol. They would know their value system."

"Let's go back to our belief system," says the teacher Morris Bear. "Let's learn about the medicine wheel, let's learn about our justice system, let's learn about the power of the feather. We have to learn about diet. We have to get back to how healthy we used to be."

There has been one native tradition that has not entirely deserted the Rock Cree. The powers of the medicine men and their herbal medicines are still sought after, especially as a last resort. Deadly cancers, for example. Elvena Pearson relates the story of a Minnesota women, a non-native, who, along with her husband, came to see Raymond Ballantyne, a medicine man, living not far from Pelican Narrows. "Raymond told them they had to stay there for a week. They had to go to a sweat-lodge ceremony every day. He fed them; he looked after her. And he made her medicine and took in the sweats and doctored her in there. When she came up, she had six months to live and as far as I know that woman is still alive and that was four or five years ago." When Gordon Peter's father, Roderick Ballantyne, was diagnosed with cancer, he was one of those who sought the help of a medicine man, and was cured. Darlene McKay was another.

In September 1997, she felt a small lump near her nipple. A biopsy revealed that it was benign. But just after New Year's, Darlene discovered a bigger lump on the same breast. "I said, 'Holy, I'd better . . .' I had another biopsy and this time it was malignant." She underwent a radical mastectomy and then visited an oncologist. "I'm sitting in this little waiting room, and I'm thinking, whoop-de-doo, they took it and I'm going to be fine. The doctor opens this file and says, 'You've got really bad cancer. What you have is aggressive penetrating carcinoma.' Well, like what is that? Like, hello. And then I asked how bad was it. He said, 'In reality, you have six months to live.' I said, I guess my partying days are over."

Darlene did undergo chemotherapy and radiation, although the doctors more or less told her it was useless. She also went to see a medicine man. "He knew right away what was wrong with me. He said, 'Whoa, you're in pain on this side. Stand here.' He came out with a feather, waved it like this, and said, 'Your pain is gone.' I could hear this noise. I could feel this coming out of me. It was like a bloodsucker sucking on you. And then there was clipping noises. He told me it wouldn't hurt any more, and it didn't."

The medicine man put Darlene on a strict diet. "Quit eating beef, quit eating chicken, don't drink milk, don't use butter, no pork, no bacon, eat a lot of rice. I've eaten so much rice, I'm surprised I don't look like a Chinaman right now." He also gave her herbal medicine, assuring her it would kill the cancer "parasite." "He was just like Jesus. He took it right away."

Darlene returned to the oncologist. "He looks at me, then he looks at the chart, then he shakes his head and he reads my chart and he looks at me and he shakes his head. According to the white man I should be dead. But I'm not. Obviously God doesn't want me yet."

These days on the reserve, there's another epidemic that is plaguing the population: diabetes. There are now three times more

cases of the disease among natives than in the white population. It
has to do primarily with the change of diet; lard has replaced the
more nourishing natural fats for cooking and baking, which means
more fat in the body. But that's only the beginning: white bread,
potato chips, ice cream, soda pop, cookies, all the white "goodies,"
are damaging the health of the First Nations people. As soon as
Armand Ballantyne's father-in-law developed diabetes, he headed
for the bush. "For ten years he ate the right food, fish, game, anything from the wild. Now his health is just fine." "I went to a medicine man," says Napoleon Caribou. "He told me what foods to
eat: moose, pickerel, cranberries, bark soup, all the things I like
anyway. I don't bother with the diabetes any more."

In 2001 the Angelique Canada Health Centre opened in Pelican
Narrows. It's the largest of the Peter Ballantyne Cree Nation, which
spends some $5 million of government money on health services
each year. A handsomely designed building, with a teepee effect at
the entrance, it has become a community healing hub, where not
only medical services are provided – there are eight nurses on staff
– but also programs involving fetal alcohol syndrome, prenatal
nutrition, alcohol and drug prevention. It's the pride of the band
and, compared to the health care that existed in the past, it should
be. But there is still no hospital. There are still no resident doctors
– visiting physicians from Prince Albert or Flin Flon come during
the week, but are often late and are not available for emergencies
at night or on the weekend. Pregnant women must still travel 120
kilometres to the Flin Flon hospital to deliver of their babies.
(Gordon Peter's brother Oscar was born in an airplane on the way
to Flin Flon. He was named after the pilot. Elvena's sister was born
on a beach in Southend. Many babies caught their first glimpse of
the world inside a taxi.) While now there is a dental hygienist on
staff, who does everything from pulling teeth to inserting fillings,
there is no dentist in residence, never has been. The teeth, or rather
the lack of them, of Pelican Narrows people reflect this. There is

no nursing home for the elderly or severely ill. There's no labora-tory or X-ray services. There is a room set aside for dialysis, but no dialysis machine, which means that those with kidney disease, many of the elderly suffering from diabetes, must travel five hours back and forth to Saskatoon twice a week. Annie Custer, whose beautifully handcrafted birchbark baskets were symbols of the artistic spirit of the Rock Cree, is one of these perpetual trekkers. "I'm so tired from all the travel. The Chief and others ask me to make baskets for the band, but I tell them, I can't do it any more." Says Armand Ballantyne, "For years they've been trans-porting people back and forth. It costs a lot of money. Now if we had that machine it would make a lot of difference money-wise and people-wise."

Tisdale, Saskatchewan, is the closest non-aboriginal town to Pelican Narrows with a similar population. As of 2001 medical services there included a twenty-four-bed acute-care facility with twenty-four-hour emergency care, a laboratory and X-ray services, obstetrics, pediatrics, minor surgery, and pharmacy, five physi-cians, one dentist, one orthodontist, two chiropractors, two phys-iotherapists, two optometrists, four massage therapists.[*] Quite likely Jamie Merasty would still be alive if he had grown up in a prosperous farm town, rather than on a poor Indian reserve.

---

[*] The argument is made that the facilities are justified because the population in the hinterland is three times that of the town itself. However the same rationale can be applied to Pelican Narrows if the Peter Ballantyne reserves around Pelican Narrows – Deschambault Lake, Southend, Sandy Bay, Sturgeon Landing – are included.

FISH INSPECTORS

The walleye fishing has been spectacular
and we have limited out our three boats
in a matter of hours with eight fish apiece.
Arthur Custer has counted the fish like beads
and knows each boat has the number allowed:
nothing here will jeopardize his guiding licence.
He explains that the new game wardens
on Jan are real mean bastards.

On our way back to camp a boat hails us
and the two wardens pull us alongside for
        inspection.
They collect our licences, note details, then
count each boat's catch with the slow scrutiny
of electoral officers in a recount.

Custer sits impassive through his examination
until one officer turns to him and says,
"Pretty good fishing for so short a time.
Where'd you catch them all, Arthur?"

Arthur wears his disdain like mesh.
His face permits only a trace
of trickster impishness as he replies,
"On the lake."

Glen Sorestad
Jan Lake Poems

N   S

ọ   ﻟ

nikotwāsik
6

ONE RULES, THE OTHER RESISTS

PĪYAK WANASOWĒW, KOTAK NĪPUHISTAMASOW

Friedrich Engels once referred to the social organization of the Iroquois Confederacy as a form of "primitive communism." He was not being derogatory, not at all. In his sooty, cutthroat world of the Industrial Revolution, the social egalitarianism practised in the pristine New World forest was an ideal to aim for. On the Pelican Narrows Reserve there are still vestiges of communality. Houses and land are held in common by the band. Gordon Peter and Susan make no mortgage payments, pay no rent, nor any property taxes. Their drinking water, which is delivered, and their sewage, which is hauled away, are currently free services, although the band council has decided that next year, there will be a charge. Gordon Peter has electric heat in his house, but, like most people on the reserve, he finds his SaskPower bill too high, and, in the winter, relies on a big wood stove. If a rock is thrown through his window, the band will pay to have it repaired, although this can take months. On the other hand, the couple cannot use their house as collateral for a bank loan. Something like a snowmobile or a car must be bought with a large cash down-payment. If the family decides to leave the reserve to study or work, their house could be

from them in a relatively short time. Why then would
invest labour or savings in renovating or enlarging it? And
Gordon Peter and Susan must, like everyone on the reserve, live
with political decisions, big and small, that vitally affect every
aspect of their life.

Like a witches' brew, politics forever bubbles under the surface
at Pelican Narrows. One reason is that elections to the Peter
Ballantyne Cree Nation council, a powerful body consisting of one
chief and twelve councillors,* are held every two years, a remarkably short term given the complexity of band government. There's
hardly any time for a councillor to learn the system, or dig into
new business, before another election campaign is upon him. If
positions fall vacant, by-elections are held. And there's a whole
assortment of referenda and plebiscites being debated at any particular time.

The councillor's job is considered one of the best around.
The salary, paid by the band, ranges anywhere from $35,000 to
$80,000 depending on experience. There's plenty of travel and the
generous expense accounts that go along with it. But there are
drawbacks. Cynicism runs rampant among the Pelican Narrows
populace: anyone who is elected is considered to be in it only for
him or herself, no matter what he or she does. And yet it's obvious
that there are those who do care, those who are determined to
somehow make life better for their struggling, economically backward community.

Gordon Peter ran for council in the 2003 election. His plat-
form was a nostalgic ideal of a happier, healthier reserve. "I wanted
to go back to the old days. Everybody used to square dance, play
baseball and broomball, and go camping. There's been nothing
like that for years." He printed pamphlets and knocked on doors,

---

* All six reserves are represented; the number of councillors depends on the
population. Five councillors are from Pelican Narrows Reserve, two from
Deschambault, two from Southend, one from Amisk Lake, one from Sturgeon
Landing, and one from Prince Albert.

but he quickly discovered he didn't have what it took to get elected – money. Voters expected a cash handout, twenty dollars would do, or at least a couple of bottles of beer. "Have a cold one on me," is the standard opening line while campaigning. He lost, but he didn't do badly, placing seventh in a slate of twenty-four, the top four of which were chosen. He'll probably try again, but next time he'll concentrate on economic development and housing, the hottest political issues of the day.

Sunday, March 7, 2004: The last day of the Opawikoscikan Winter Festival. All week there's been Ski-Doo races, dog mushing, "the Moonie Memorial Dart Tournament" (in memory of Gordon Peter's brother), an arm-wrestling contest, a Come & Go bingo, a three-hour burbot fish derby, a square-dance competition, and, best of all, the King Trapper events – a competition in which heavy-set, determined men in plaid shirts build a fire and boil water for tea, make bannock, set traps, saw wood, bang nails, carry hundred-pound flour bags, dance a jig. Once the festival is over, the Miniquay Lodge quickly fills up. It's on the high end of the scale of northern bars, nicely panelled in wood, with a moose head on the wall, a pool table, VLTs, the Rez Brothers Band, and booze – Budweiser beer is by far the biggest seller. The Pelican Narrows party-goers must travel fifty kilometres to the bar in Jan Lake because their reserve is dry, a decision made by the community in a plebiscite ten years ago.

Wednesday, March 10: Quite a crowd has gathered in the gymnasium of the Wapanacak Elementary School; young, old, male, female, all are there. Seven of the twelve band councillors are present, as well as Chief Ron Michel. The issue they will debate tonight would not be so contentious in other communities – the construction of a fourteen-room hotel. But here it is a red flag. For the hotel to be economically viable, it must include a restaurant and a bar. Therefore, the dry by-law would have to be rescinded.

The chief, in his avuncular manner, lays out the reasons for the plan, but it is in reality the handiwork of Francis Highway, an energetic Pelican Narrows councillor, a neighbour of Gordon

Peter's. At the heart of the proposal is a question: why should all the funds generated by liquor consumption, about a million dollars a year, flow out of the reserve to the Miniquay Lodge Hotel in Jan Lake? If people are going to gamble, why not keep the slot-machine profits for the community? Why should the pawn shop at Jan Lake make all the money? Why not build a similar business on the reserve? There are other important considerations. Since the dry by-law went into effect the use of drugs has shot up, the by-law gives the RCMP far too much authority, and almost nobody has stopped drinking alcohol because of it.

Philip Ratt is the first up to comment. He is opposed to the idea, insisting that it would only increase the misery on the reserve. With a bar in their neighbourhood, the 50 per cent who are social drinkers might swell the ranks of the 35 per cent who abuse alcohol. The children would congregate outside the bar waiting for their parents. More access to alcohol would not deter drug consumption. He reads from his research: in one year the health clinic treated 150 patients who were victims of alcohol-induced violence, 650 who suffered from alcohol-related illnesses, and, saddest of all, thirty-five babies who were diagnosed with fetal alcohol syndrome.

All evening the debate goes back and forth. The group seems to be evenly split: the younger members tending to approve of the hotel, the older members standing against it. All the councillors are in favour of the plan. What bothers Tom Sewap the most about the dry by-law is the power it gives to the police. "We as native people have suffered so much indignity, and to be further humiliated by being stopped on our own reserve. . . . They confiscate [alcohol] and sometimes the police don't even have probable cause. This is an abuse of power."

"He's nuts," says Darlene McKay. "There'll be slot machines in the bar. Then everybody with a spare dollar is going to be throwing in that dollar, trying to make a thousand bucks. Please!" Dreams of riding his bicycle to a local pub dance in Gordon Peter's head, but he thinks of the children, and decides the bar/hotel will not be in the community's best interest. Maybe the band should buy the Miniquay Hotel, and ignore the consternation of the white cabin owners that would be sure to follow.

All during the long evening – the meeting was called for 6 p.m. and started after seven – the crowd sits quietly, listening intently to each speaker. Everyone is encouraged to speak their mind, there are no time limits placed on the long-winded, no one shouting she can't hear, no disparaging remarks about the opposite point of view. Respect and politeness reign.

Finally the meeting concludes with the reminder that a referendum will finally resolve the issue. Whatever the outcome, the people of Pelican Narrows will make the decision; it will not be imposed on them by an arbitrary, outside authority. If progress has been made among the First Nations, it is here. Aboriginal self-government is light-years away from the paternalistic, insulting, and nearly deadly rule by first the British and then the Canadian governments.

The political system of the Cree was as dissimilar to the European model as every other aspect of their society. Egalitarianism was the keynote that underscored the affairs in the Rock Cree camps. "The creation myth held that, from the *beginning*, all members of the tribe shared and participated *equally* in all privileges and responsibilities," write scholars Menno Boldt and J. Anthony Long.[1] Fellow citizens described their relationship with each other as "links in a chain," or "going down the road together." Their governing was informal, almost nonchalant, based on broad general rules that everyone knew, and an understanding that all voices must be listened to, including those of women. Because the Cree society was based not on the profit motive, but rather on collective responsibility, women's labour was essential for survival. As a result they were allowed a strong voice in all manner of decisions. The same holds true today in the governing of the Peter Ballantyne First Nation.

The hierarchical European system, in which power and authority was vested in a central source, a king, priest, or parliament, was offensive to the Cree. Their communities reached agreement through consensus, not by dictating and policing. This, however, left their leaders little more than lame ducks. The elders, for example, were revered, not because of their authority, but because of their knowledge, particularly of sacred tribal customs and traditions. They could hand out advice, but whether it was accepted or not was entirely up to the individual to whom it was given. Likewise, the chief or headman, called the *okimāw*, gained that position usually because he was the best hunter, the smartest, the most knowledgeable, the most generous, and sometimes the person with the strongest supernatural powers. And while his tent might be a little larger and his pantry full of gifts from his followers, he was still considered only one among many. As Boldt and Long write, "Self-direction (autonomy), an aristocratic prerogative in European society, was everyone's right."[2]

While sophisticated institutions and codes of laws did not exist, the Cree system of direct democracy – of community members meeting eyeball-to-eyeball – "performed all of the necessary political functions; it kept the peace, preserved individual life, and protected its members from injustice, abuse, and arbitrary actions by any of their number."[3]

The white traders and missionaries, however, could see nothing but anarchy in this political structure and set out to bring order out of the perceived chaos. The Hudson's Bay Company was keen on "good business practice," and insisted the native population conform to certain organizational behaviour, usually without much luck. In the methodical mind of the HBC servant, a "trading captain," a native who was articulate, knew the canoe routes, and had some understanding of the white man's ways would bring order to often unruly bargaining sessions. Special uniforms, flags, medals, and gifts were presented to the right man. Surely, in such an elevated position, he could persuade his comrades not only to return to the same post year after year, but also to spend more time trapping. The Indians paid little attention. They chose the person they believed could get the best deal for their furs; once the trading session was over, these leaders had no more influence than anyone else. As the Jesuit missionary Le Jeune wrote, Indians "have reproached me a hundred times because we fear our Captains [those in authority], while they laugh at and make sport of theirs. All the authority of their chief is in his tongue's end; for he is powerful insofar as he is eloquent and, even if he kills himself talking and haranguing, he will not be believed unless he pleases them."[4]

The Cree's political life was unique from another Euro-Canadian perspective; there was no sense of land ownership. "The territory belonged to the tribe in common," wrote the Oblate missionary Marius Rossignol. "It was the country of the Cree. There were no well-marked divisions of it. . . . Theoretically, anybody at all could wander around the country and shift from one end of it to another, just as he wished. But in practice such shifts were rather rare. Ordinarily a good hunter established himself near a lake or a river and was followed by his relatives who wished to live near him."

Indeed, the Indians laughed at the idea that man could possess the land, since it all belonged to the animals. When there was a moose shortage in their area, a hunting group had no qualms about moving into another band's territory. And the hosts were usually glad to see their guests. Food, and just about everything else, was shared, generosity a way of life. Father Marius Rossignol wrote the following in 1939, and much of what he observed still holds true today:

They [the Rock Cree] very rarely employ direct formulae: "Give me" smacks of discourtesy among them. Instead, they say, "Lend me this," or else, "I should like to borrow this from you." Another still more subtle method is to extol or praise the thing that one wishes [for]. Thus, you would never say to anyone: "You have a beautiful pipe" if you don't wish to possess it, for this would be the same as asking it of the owner . . .

I once had . . . a visit to a good old pagan woman. In the course of our chat together I saw coming towards me a small white dog who wanted to be petted. "You have a beautiful little dog, my grandmother," I said to her, thinking to please her. "Yes," she said to me, compressing her lips. "You speak Cree, it is true but I don't want to give him to you." I excused myself as best I could, telling her I did not have the intention of asking for the dog and that I would not be able to take him with me even if she gave him to me. But I had committed an indiscretion; by my imprudent remark made without reflection I had asked outright for the little dog as a present. This method of "asking without asking" is called "speaking Cree."

At the beginning of the nineteenth century, the federal government began to create distinct political units in Rock Cree country, primarily to keep track of those on the treaty list. The "trading-post band" was a painless way to organize. At Pelican Narrows, for example, this included everyone who did business with the Hudson's Bay Company. Thus came into existence the band named after its first chief, Peter Ballantyne. But neither the organization nor the chief had legal or political powers; the band administered no programs, spent no money. The chief and the headmen (councillors) met once a year when the treaty party arrived, but did little in the intervening months. Any but officially sanctioned meetings were discouraged by the government, and even during these sessions, the Indian agents were ordered to "take all possible steps to preserve order and decorum."

In his seventeen years in office, only one record exists of Chief Peter Ballantyne complaining to or even communicating with the Indian agent. It involved the flour given out as rations. "Nobody wants it, because it is not possible to cook with," Chief Ballantyne wrote to Indian agent William McKay, in 1915.[5] The flour had been double-sacked: the outside bag was stamped with the standard label of Indian Affairs, "Treaty Ten [*sic*], Peter Ballantyne Band," but the inside sack read "Hudson's Bay Company, Family Standard," a much inferior brand. "We want only to let Mr. Chisholm [in charge of buying supplies] know that the flour given to him is very poor, or if some fraud has been made, it could only be made at Cumberland House, where that flour laid at the Hudson [*sic*] Bay Company's Warehouse for a while."[6]

In signing the treaties, the chiefs believed that the Indian agent would not only be their liaison with the government, but also their advocate. They soon discovered what a misperception that was. These civil servants were given enormous powers: they were, for instance, investigator, prosecutor, and judge of whoever was thought to have committed a misdemeanour. Quickly they turned into tin-pot dictators. No less a light than the Anglican Bishop of Saskatchewan wrote that the Indians "are treated as irresponsible children . . . and they have no remedy or recourse against these officials." Well into the twentieth century, the Indian agent would dictate in what location a person could build his house on the reserve.

Sometimes the agents were simply mean-spirited. In November 1915 the inspector of Indian Agencies wrote a circular letter, pointing out that it was policy to pay an annuity to women who had married treaty Indians. The instruction was ignored. Five years later, in October 1920, the assistant deputy of Indian Affairs wrote that no payment had been made to half-breed women married to treaty Indians or their children, even though it was government policy to do so. "This is the third occasion upon which the matter has come to the attention of the Department. On the 17th December, 1917, and again on the 20th December, 1918, a letter in regard to this matter was sent. . . . It would seem that the instructions . . . have been disregarded." The Commissioner of Indian Affairs, Saskatchewan, then weighed in: "The wives of the Indians named have been deprived of their rightful share of annuity for some years, and I am surprised that the matter has not been corrected from Ottawa."[7] He might have added that it was the agent, William McKay, who had spitefully disobeyed orders for so long. Hopefully the women in question laughed a little when McKay was finally forced to hand over years' worth of outstanding annuities.

The Indian agent, the priest, and the Hudson's Bay post manager, the Unholy Trinity, constituted the power elite on reserves like Pelican Narrows. They were happy to do whatever the government asked to make sure "the Indian was taken out of the Indian." A long and sad history of legislation was there to back them up.

The Royal Proclamation of 1763, issued by the British government after the fall of Montreal, had been generous enough towards aboriginal people. Basically it was meant to protect reserves from land-hungry European immigrants: "no private person" was permitted "to make any purchase from the said Indians of any lands reserved to the said Indians." It was also intended to keep the warriors onside during the American Revolution and the wars following. After 1830, when the indigenous peoples were no longer useful as military allies, they became, in the eyes of the government, simple-minded wards in need of protection. The 1857 Act for the Gradual Civilization of the Indian Tribes was seen by bureaucrats as a gesture of goodwill towards the natives, but what it actually did was define an Indian as a "non-citizen." What was offered to the First Nations people was citizenship, never mind that they had been in the country centuries before any "Canadian" had arrived. All they had to do was be educated, debt-free, and of a good moral character, and they would be enfranchised and given two hectares out of reserve land. There was a catch of course – all treaty rights would be forsaken. The appeal of this "generous" offer is illustrated by one statistic: In twenty years only one individual, Elias Hill, applied for and received citizenship. He never got his land though. Six Nations Indians simply refused to allow the two hectares to be removed from reserve status.

In 1869 the new Dominion of Canada passed the Gradual Enfranchisement Act, which meddled even more in the Indian political process. Traditional leaders could be dismissed for dishonesty, intemperance, or immorality – determined, of course, by the Indian agent. Moreover, Indian women who married non-Indian men lost their status, as did their children. Men who married non-natives not only kept their rights, but their white wives became instant Indians. "This provision, like the whole of the statute, was a gross interference in Indians' management of their internal affairs," writes historian J.R. Miller. But that was only the beginning.

The 1876 Indian Act was the foundation for all of Canada's future legislation regarding the indigenous people. It has been declared "the most racist document ever produced by a western democracy" by native activists. Harold Cardinal, author and advocate, put it well: "Instead of implementing the treaties and offering much-needed protection to Indian rights, the Indian Act subjugated to colonial rule the very people whose rights it was supposed to protect." The act amalgamated previous paternalistic legislation, in the process regulating and controlling every aspect of Indian life. About the only concession to native sensitivities involved the elective system; it would be imposed only if the band wanted it. However, the number of councillors and chiefs for each band and who could vote in a band election was controlled by the act. In Clause 25, the government obtained guardianship over Indian lands with the purpose of surveying reserves into individual lots. The Indians were going to understand the European concept of private property whether they liked it or not. The Indian agent was given extraordinary administrative and discretionary powers. And the Act defined who was an Indian; basically anyone who happened to be present on the day when heads were counted. Finally it spelled out a means of obtaining Canadian citizenship, which once again meant giving up any right to land, and all other advantages – housing, tax benefits, identity – that came with status. With the passing of this act, "what becomes even clearer is the government's determination to make the Indians into imitation Europeans and to eradicate the old Indian values through education, religion, new economic and political systems, and a new concept of property," writes historian John Tobias.[8]

And that was not the end. Legislation to control First Nations peoples kept bouncing out of Parliament's doors. Indian Act amendments of 1880: it became possible for the Indian Affairs officials to impose an elected band council, whether Indians favoured the traditional choice by consensus or not. Indian Advancement Act 1884: those chiefs whom the Indian Affairs deemed unfit or unable to discharge their duties could be disposed. Indian Act amendments, 1894: Indian children were compelled to attend boarding and industrial schools. By prohibiting Indians from congregating on any reserve but their own, ceremonies such as the Sun Dance and Thirst Dance were essentially outlawed. Indian Act amendments, 1895: Parents of illegitimate children or neglectful parents were no longer eligible to receive government allowances, treaty payments, and rations for their children. Sir John A. Macdonald, Canada's prime minister, certainly understood what these laws were all about. The purpose of legislation, he wrote, was to "assimilate the Indian people in all respects with the inhabitants of the Dominion, as speedily as they are fit for the change."[9] Gradually, the Indians would gain the vote, own their land on the reserve (reserves would then disappear), and, in the process, happily give up their language, culture, and social and political identity.

There were Indians who agreed with what the government was planning for them, but not many. In all of Canada, between 1857 and 1920, only 250 individuals gave up their treaty rights in order to be enfranchised and obtain privately owned land. Among them was Cornelius Ballantyne, the son of Chief Peter Ballantyne and Gordon Peter's great-uncle.

Of all the Ballantynes in those early years, Cornelius, likely born in August 1885, was the one who opted for a different lifestyle. He worked for the Hudson's Bay Company as a tripper – he was always coming and going to The Pas, to the Churchill River, to Pukatawagan – and eventually ran a small post for the HBC on South Reindeer Lake. He was obviously responsible: any time a guide was needed for an expedition – surveyors, for example – he was the one chosen. For example, it was Cornelius who helped Tom Bear bring in the corpses of Tom's old father, Antoine, and Tom's little daughter for burial. He lived in a house in Pelican Narrows and was obviously considered part of the mostly white community. "Mrs. Cornelius Ballantyne increased the male population here by one this morning," reported the HBC journal on February 13, 1914. In 1915 he refused on principle to accept treaty payments while his father was still chief, an indication probably that he was moving away from a traditional Indian lifestyle. In 1919 he officially requested to be taken out of treaty. He must have been embarrassed when the Indian agent questioned his motives for doing so. "It was thought . . . that he wished to obtain liquor [illegal at the time] but this does not seem to be the case."[10] In 1924 he became enfranchised, perhaps the only Rock Cree to be able to vote for or against Arthur Meighen in the 1926 federal election.

In the 1920s it looked as though the government's policy of eliminating the Indian, not by force, but by assimilation, was working. With all that was stacked against them, poor health, inadequate schooling, encroachment on their way of making a living, the population began to dwindle. In reality, it was utter delusion that natives would conveniently fade away. In the 1930s their numbers rebounded, and their population has increased ever since. Today the First Nations have by far the highest birth rate in Canada. Nevertheless, it would be a never-ending struggle to gain control over their lives. The story of the successor to Chief Peter Ballantyne illustrates how often and how easily the wishes of the band members could be ignored or denied by government authority.

Chief Ballantyne died in December 1917, but he was not immediately replaced. There'd been so much conflict between the Catholics and the Anglicans in Pelican Narrows, that they hadn't been able to get together long enough to choose a leader. Finally, in August 1919, after Treaty Day, the man the Indian agent had singled out, Cornelius Whitebear, was elected chief. Born and brought up in Sandy Bay, he had married a Pelican Narrows woman, and settled in her community. A small man, he had a tubercular leg and walked with a severe limp. His father was Wapaskokimaw, the famous medicine man–shaman, and some people contended that Cornelius had inherited some of his powers. He certainly had a strong personality. "He was really straightforward in what he said," says Philip Ratt. "I guess he was also short-tempered." So short-tempered that he seems to have been universally disliked. A year after he was elected, there was so much friction in the community that there was talk of deposing all the headmen, including the chief. As well, the Protestant Indians were demanding that they be allowed to elect their own chief and councillors. Indian agent William McKay acquiesced. "As this is one of the largest Bands in the Agency, I would strongly recommend that it be broken in two and a Chief and two Councillors be appointed to represent the Protestants."[11] The request was promptly turned down by bureaucrats in Indian Affairs, despite the fact that the establishment of a separate Protestant band might have prevented years of turmoil.

By 1922 there was such a loathing of Chief Whitebear and a councillor, Angus Merasty, that a verbal petition to remove them from office was presented. After spending one day on the reserve, Indian agent W.R. Taylor reported:

It is my opinion that the chief is disliked because of his severity against evil. The younger men of the band are employed by the trading companies to freight supplies from Sturgeon Landing and I am told that they get hold of home brew, and have regular drunken sprees. It will also be noticed from the pay sheets, and the number of illegitimate children taken on this year, that immorality is rife among them.

This the chief is trying to fight, and he spares none of them. For this reason I feel certain he is disliked, and they would like to get rid of him, and elect another one who would wink at their evil ways. I would not suggest that the present chief be put out of office, but that he is confirmed therein.[12]

The man who gave Taylor this information was the Catholic priest; it's doubtful that he had much time to talk with anyone else. J.D. McLean, assistant deputy Indian Commissioner would write to his boss, W.M. Graham: "Mr. Agent Taylor scarcely allows sufficient time at each of the Reserves . . . to permit the Indians to discuss with him the various matters relating to their Bands, as he leaves very shortly after completion of the annuity payments."[13] Never mind, his word was law.

The following year, 1924, the settlement at Southend, some 280 kilometres north of Pelican Narrows, voted to secede from the Peter Ballantyne Band. They were so far away from Pelican Narrows that they were never visited by Chief Whitebear; none of their concerns were ever listened to by the band council. On their own initiative they had already elected their own chief, Peter Bird, and a councillor, Pierre Bird. Of them, Agent Taylor wrote, ". . . these people at South Reindeer Lake should be acknowledged as a separate band and allowed a Chief and councillor. Left alone they are constantly bickering and quarreling among themselves, whereas a Chief of the right sort among them is a great influence for good."[14] Once again the request was turned down by the Department of Indian Affairs, although Peter Bird was appointed a fourth councillor to the Peter Ballantyne Band.

Two years later, in 1926, the Indians of Pelican Narrows were again dissatisfied with their elected representatives, this time insisting that councillor Angus Merasty be forced out of office. Again it was up to the Indian agent to act as sole arbiter in the matter. Wrote Taylor, "I could not find anything against Merasty. No accusation was brought against him beyond the fact that he was lazy, and would not attend to his work."[15] Still, since the people were so adamant, Taylor allowed them to proceed with the election.

Forty-nine out of fifty-seven present cast their ballot for Joe Highway. However, as soon as Indian Affairs learned of these proceedings, the results were nullified. Under the Indian Act, a councillor could be removed from office only "on the ground of incompetency, intemperance, immorality, or dishonesty . . ." and, according to the Indian agent (not the people), "no charge of this nature was made against Merasty." Angus Merasty would serve on the band council until the 1940s.

Chief Whitebear was not involved in this latest dispute, because for eight months he had been bedridden with his tubercular knee. Whether he got medical help or not was entirely up to the Indian agent who in this case recommended Whitebear be sent to The Pas for treatment. There his leg was amputated above the knee. "He was furnished with a peg leg, but the thing does not fit him, consequently he cannot use it," wrote Taylor. "He asks if the Department would consider giving him an artificial limb. The old man is very proud, and I think feels the loss of his leg very much."[16] There's no record of whether Chief Whitebear got his leg, but, by the following year, he was dead. Fred Ballantyne says he fell asleep on his trapline and froze to death.

Naturally the Indian agent weighed in on who should replace Whitebear. "Personally, I think there is only one man who could intelligently fill the office. That is John Custer, who is now head councillor. The only thing that could defeat him on an election, is, he is a Protestant and the majority of these Indians are Roman Catholics." John Custer didn't even enter the race, so sure was he of defeat. Joe Highway beat his opponent Noah Ballantyne, Chief Peter's nephew, by three votes. Indian Affairs had the authority to cancel the election results, but the officials liked Highway – he "appears to be an outstanding man among them. He is 38 years of age, has a good house, which is kept in good order" – so he kept his job as chief. Highway was a strong family man, an ethical man, but he spent most of his time trying to make a living on the trapline. He was chief in name only, and then only on Treaty Day.

Band business fell into a state of lethargy. There were a couple of times, however, that that tranquility was shaken.

In 1929 Sedley Merasty was sworn in as band councillor, although he does not appear on the pay lists until 1934. The following year he was hunting in the bush when he spotted a towering figure charging towards him. He shot at it and ran, not stopping to investigate what it was that he had killed. In his tortured mind, he was sure it was a human although, in all likelihood, it was a bear. Two days later, he took an axe to his skull, badly injuring himself. A plane was arranged to transport him to the hospital in Flin Flon for treatment. It was a bumpy ride but, since the pilot's view was blocked by cargo, he couldn't check on his passenger. When the plane finally landed, no Sedley Merasty was found. He either jumped or fell out.

The second event that rocked the community would have profound consequences. It began with the arrival in 1934 of Shorty Russick. He was famous as a champion musher, having won the two-hundred-mile World Championship Dog Derby at The Pas in a record time of twenty-three hours and forty-two minutes. He had come first or second in so many sled-dog races that he had accumulated enough money through his winnings to start a business as an independent trader. Pelican Narrows looked like an ideal location at the time. Arthur Jan had left, the Revillon Frères store was about to go out of business, leaving only the Hudson's Bay Company post as competition. Shorty was not only short but "nervy as hell." The day after he arrived, October 21, 1934, he visited the people who would be his rivals, the Hudson's Bay Company staff, "requesting our assistance in finding a house to establish his business???? We had absolutely no suggestions to offer," the post journal recorded.[17] This marked the beginning of warfare between the two fur traders. Russick would do anything to win customers, from giving Indians a markdown of 20 per cent on goods on Treaty Day to ordering in the most gaudily patterned cloth which the native women loved. By September 1936, the HBC was complaining, "Russick, fur trader, stealing all our best customers, making heavy advances."

On November 19, 1936, Russick was returning home at night when his sled smashed through thin ice right at Opawikoscikan, Narrows of Dread. Shorty managed to struggle out of the water and crawl to shore on his hands and knees, but his valuable load of furs was lost, and most tragically, his precious dogs drowned. Russick cried for months after the accident, full-blown tears at which the stoic Rock Cree looked aghast. While he had no option but to continue in the fur business, he never did race again.

Most trappers liked Russick. He was polite to an Indian, and friendly, but it was a different story when it came to the people who worked for him. His brother Steve, who traded at south Reindeer Lake district, was in the habit of luring Indians away from the HBC by stocking liquor. As the post journal reported on August 13, 1938, "Steve Russick, trading for Shorty at Rocky Falls, was fined $200 for selling liquor (probably vodka) to the Indians." Steve Russick's shenanigans angered Chief Joe Highway and his councillors, who felt that the trader was taking advantage of his customers once he got them drunk. Then there was David Motherwell, who was Russick's clerk. He lasted only a short time at Pelican Narrows, but why Shorty hired him is a mystery. He was one of those white men – and they still exist today – who was so fundamentally bigoted towards aboriginal Canadians, he couldn't open his mouth without a flow of obscene, racist remarks spewing forth. "You red-skinned, stupid son-of-a-bitch" was the pejorative he used in place of a native person's name, including Chief Highway's. Pretty soon the entire community, including most of the whites, were up in arms. Coupled with the antics and insults of Shorty Russick's people, was the niggardliness of the Hudson's Bay Company. All of this provided fertile ground for Pelican Narrows's first dose of Indian activism.

On August 24, 1938, a cool, rainy day, the natives of Pelican Narrows gathered in a tent to hear Joe Nasipagō, a representative of the League of Indians of Western Canada, lecture on the

"Indians fighting for their rights." He spelled out how much money the Hudson's Bay Company made on a beaver pelt compared to what a trapper received. It's not recorded how the Rock Cree felt about the meeting, but certainly the priest and the HBC manager were outraged. The spokesman, claimed the post journal, "has nothing to do with the settlement at all, says his two bits' worth, and others whom we always thought were good men and true are proving themselves two-faced rascals." RCMP constable Wenzil threatened to throw Nasipagō out of town, but the organizer disappeared before he got the chance. A month later, the HBC manager was still harping on the incident. "The Indians are completely satisfied, or rather as much as they ever are, by the manner in which they are being handled at the moment. We are doing the best we can under the circumstances, and we have drilled that into their heads."[18]

In the eyes of the HBC the Indians might have seemed utterly content, but the dream of something better had taken hold. By 1940 band members wanted an activist chief and asked Joe Highway to step down. Says Philip Ratt, "He agreed. He said, 'Okay, I'm not here all the time. I'm not doing anything for the people. If you want to let me go, fine.' But nowadays, when the salary is sixty to seventy thousand dollars, it's pretty hard to get rid of them."

Solomon Merasty was elected in Highway's place. While Joe had been quiet, Solomon was one of the most gregarious Indians around. In 1936 he accompanied the writer P.G. Downes on his canoe trip from Pelican Narrows to Reindeer Lake and back. The two men quickly discovered they were kindred spirits; Downes called Merasty "an Indian with spectacles." "Solomon Merasty, my guide, is loquacious, speaks excellent English, & has some Scotch & English in his veins. . . . Very decent fellow & very curious about everything, particularly Chinamen, rocks, and where Cree come from. His favourite epithet is 'Holy Mackinaw.'"[19] Surprisingly, he didn't make the best chief. "Solomon Merasty was too much of a wanderer," says Philip Ratt. "He was a travelling person, curious about the world, and he would go anywhere there was a dollar to be made, so he was never in the community." It didn't much matter. Under the Indian Act, the band council could impose by-laws on minor police and public-health issues, but, before they became law, they had to be approved by the minister of Indian Affairs. This procedure took so long that, when the decision was finally made, the Indians had sometimes forgotten what the by-law was all about.

The most memorable event in Chief Merasty's tenure was his trip to Ottawa in 1944 as a delegate for the League of Indians of Western Canada, in the company of the famous activist John Tootoosis, a Plains Cree from Poundmaker Reserve. The main goal was to form a national organization from the various native groups that had evolved across the country, to be called the North American Indian Brotherhood. Once Ottawa got wind of the conference, everything was done to stop it. Indian agents were ordered to try and talk delegates out of attending, arguing that, since it was wartime, food and lodging would be in short supply. It was "their patriot duty" to stay at home and help with the war effort. The usual condescending, paternalistic missive was written:

> . . . the department is at all times willing to consider with care and sympathy any reasonable representations that the Indians may wish to make in the proper way which is through their Indian Agents, and also that where there are problems of special importance to be discussed, this Branch is prepared to receive small delegations of Indians who come with the approval of Indian Agents and duly established Councils for the Bands which they represent.

The delegates had requested that Henry Crerar, minister of Indian Affairs, attend one of the sessions. Crerar agreed, but only if John Sioui, secretary of the North American Indian Brotherhood, who was considered too much of a radical, was not in attendance. Sioui reluctantly excused himself and the meeting went ahead.

It must have made an impression on the politicians, because in 1946 a Special Joint Committee of the Senate and House of Commons was appointed "to examine and consider the Indian Act . . . and suggest such amendments as they may deem advisable." For two years the committee listened to Indian leaders outline their grievances – the interference by bureaucrats in their affairs, the problems with residential schools, lack of health care. The members of Parliament and the senators paid polite attention and then incorporated almost nothing of what they had heard in the new legislation. Indian Act 1951 was not much different in philosophy than Indian Act 1876. As the historian J.R. Miller put it, "The 1951 act assumed that the purpose of Indian policy was the end of Indians, as they became assimilated and chose to integrate themselves into the economic, political, and social life of Canada."[20] The Indians themselves had no remedy but to keep grumbling.

The Peter Ballantyne Cree Nation found itself behind the times. The old tradition of electing a chief, and then allowing him to remain in office until he either died or voluntarily stepped down, was backfiring. Simon Linklater was an example. He was elected chief in 1948 and there were several things going for him. He promised to spend time in the community, when he wasn't working his trapline, and he could speak some English, so he could talk directly to the politicians and bureaucrats at Indian Affairs. In 1954 he took a job as a caretaker in a newly built nurse's station at Pelican Narrows. When he was informed he probably had a conflict of interest, he resigned as chief. The problem was he told not a soul. "Nobody knew about it," says Philip Ratt. "It was only a couple of years ago that the community found out that we hadn't had a chief for two years." In 1956 Simon Linklater simply moved back into his job as chief as though nothing had happened. "He sort of stepped out, and then stepped back in without anyone knowing about it." He was one of those who put pressure on the federal government to dissolve the secular school and build a separate Catholic institution and a residence for the nuns in Pelican Narrows. In 1957 he finally stepped down only to be replaced by his older brother. Philip Ratt insists that Peter Linklater nominated himself. "He said, 'I've got experience on council, and I'm the only one in the community that's qualified to be chief. I'm going to run for that. I'm going to be chief.'" Peter's son Gilbert Linklater has a different version of the story. "Dad didn't want to run for chief. Then, while we were commercial fishing, a plane landed near our camp. They [Cree councillors] said to my dad, 'You were nominated to run for chief and you won the election. That's why we're here,' they said. So my dad became chief even though he didn't enter the race. But the people wanted him." Whatever the case, Peter Linklater served from 1958–69. "We had a lot of trouble with him," says Philip Ratt. "We kept asking for elections so that, well, they'd re-elect him if they liked him. But he wouldn't go for it. He said, 'Until I die or until I decide to quit, I'll be the chief.' He was more a dictator than anything else."

In 1967 both Philip Ratt and his father, Albert, were elected councillors. Both attended a banquet after the election. Remembers Philip, "Dad was the first to speak. He said, 'I would like to adopt the two-year term for the chief from the Indian Act and bring it into our band custom.'" It went into effect in 1969.

His four-year tenure as councillor was a liberating time for Philip Ratt. He was invited to visit the Gordon First Nation near Punnichy in southern Saskatchewan, to "look at how the other half of the Indian lived," meaning the Plains Cree. The first Indian administration office in the province had been set up on a Gordon reserve. They were much further ahead in taking control of their lives than the people of Pelican Narrows. "I learned they were looking after their own welfare, their housing, their children," says Philip. "I was just amazed." Even more astonishing was the attitude towards white authority. "We'd go to the Indian Affairs building, and the chief would sit in the superintendent's chair and put his feet up on the desk. I thought, God, this is out of the world, this behaviour. Where is the superiority of Indian Affairs? It shocked me. That's when I learned to be open-minded and outspoken."

The message he delivered to Peter Ballantyne Band members was that the government was not god. "I used to tell Indian Affairs, 'We're not working for you any more, you're working for us. We're doing the dictating and you're listening.'"

Probably because the reserve was so remote, it had not been caught up in that first wave of First Nations activism. There was not even a physical seat from which to carry out Peter Ballantyne business until Albert Ratt became chief in 1973. He had a band office built, just a small house, but a place from which to manage programs. It was the beginning of self-government for the Peter Ballantyne Cree Nation. In a few years it was administering an annual budget of $40 million and overseeing almost everything to do with the band members' lives – housing, family and child services, recreation, education, post-secondary funding, and the biggest expense of all – welfare. Previously, social assistance at Pelican Narrows had been administered by an Indian Affairs agent who gave out purchase orders at the local stores. In 1973 the first welfare cheque was issued from the new band headquarters. Says Horace Ratt, "What my dad wanted was for those people who were disadvantaged to have food in their stomachs. But the system went haywire."

For the first forty-five years of the twentieth century, Canada's indigenous people were almost entirely self-supporting. Only in times of real distress would they seek government aid, although they had a legal right to do so. Treaty Six had entitled the Cree to "relief in times of destitution." The Hudson's Bay Company took over the job of handing out rations "to starving Indians," with the understanding that repayment would come from the government. Basic foods and a minimal amount of clothing is what the bureaucrats considered as appropriate rations; post managers thought differently. They handed out to "widows, orphans, and sick old men" "combs, glove needles, kettles, swans-down cotton, parchments, seal mitts, wax vestas, painkiller, lavender, vials of saccharine, essence of coffee, Neave's baby food, baby-feeding bottles, putty, prunes, pins, handkerchiefs, printed moleskin, soda biscuits, sugar, tea, wavies, geese, rabbits, fish, partridges, nails, screws, brandy, portwine, and sherry." It was a scheme, of course, used to lure trappers away from rival traders without impinging on the company's coffers. Wrote an Indian Affairs bureaucrat in 1910, ". . . in every locality where there are rival traders to the Hudson's Bay Company, occupying and disputing the field, that Company is given an unfair advantage by the arrangement with this Department."[21] Indian Affairs sometimes simply refused to pay the ration bills presented by the HBC. In 1905, for example, relief payments in all of Northern Saskatchewan amounted to a grand total of $281.79. By 1915 the government had taken over the administration of public assistance, but the native people hardly noticed the difference. Rations came in the form of chits to be made good at HBC stores, at handsome profits to the company, of course. It was not until April 1959 that Indian Affairs issued cash or cheques to natives qualifying for relief. Today in the lineup for the checkout at the gloomy, expensive Northern Store, most people are still obliged to use chits as part of their welfare payments. It's not humiliating because they are now considered "treaty rations."

During the Dirty Thirties, many kinds of relief programs were created for the unemployed, but almost none of them penetrated into the North. After the Indian agent visited Pelican Narrows in 1936, he recommended that "no relief be given to Indians unless they agree to pay for same in whole or in part. If this stand is not taken it will develop into a racket as is going on in the white settlements on relief questions."[22] How, in this near-cashless society, people were supposed to repay their social assistance was not discussed.

The winter of 1939 was a terrible time at Pelican Narrows. The weather was frigid and the war news frightening. Shorty Russick ran a commercial fishing operation, and had left no fish for the Pelican Narrows population. The price of furs dropped, and fur-bearing animals, long over-trapped by whites and natives, became exceedingly scarce. That didn't prevent the HBC post manager from writing on January 30, 1939: "The Pelican Narrows Indians, having been pampered by an over-indulgent Indian Agent and other men who don't know the natives, are all set to live on easy street and they don't care who knows it." A short time later, the following journal entries were made by the same manager: February 9: "Few people here – mainly sick, destitute, and hypochondriacs." "Everyone is hunting and fishing to keep alive. Fishing is very poor, and it is too cold to allow any but poor hunts." February 14: "Put a net in close to Narrows in the hope that we can get something. Two dogs died last night – frozen to death, as we have had no feed, and oats and cornmeal not satisfactory." February 15: "Albert Ratt brought in a miserable unstretched red fox. Says natives are taking up traps and snares, as they see no use in leaving them down. Priest has given out practically whole of the rations already." February 18: "Indians sick at Manawan. Also, and we quite believe this story, starving." February 27: "Note in the mail from our local member of Saskatchewan House assures us that everything that is possible is being done." What was being done was nothing.

The trauma of the Second World War supposedly transformed Canadians into kinder, gentler people who had come to the realization that being poor or sickly was not entirely the fault of the individual. Legislation was passed to reflect this new altruism. In 1944 Children's Allowance (five dollars per child per month) was issued to all Canadian families, First Nations people included. "It helped a great deal," remembers Philip Ratt, "we looked forward to the family-allowance cheques. My mother would go to the store and buy as much as possible with what little meek allowance she was getting." Eventually it turned into a form of blackmail perpetuated by the government. If you didn't send your offspring to residential school, no Children's Allowance. "There's very few parents who would have voluntarily sent their kids to those dreadful schools if that threat hadn't been hanging over their head. They had to think how everyone in the family was going to eat," says Susan Beatty, who was born on Deschambault Reserve.

In 1947 Old Age Security became a reality for all of Canada's elderly people in need – except natives. They had to wait five more years before their elders received this little bit from the public purse. After that government largesse came to a standstill. By 1956–57, the entire welfare bill (not including Old Age Security or Children's Allowance) for the whole of Carlton Agency, which included Peter Ballantyne and many other First Nations, was six hundred dollars.

Fred Ballantyne remembers a particularly hard winter at Pelican Narrows during this period. Commercial fishing had gone poorly, and the Fisheries Co-op did not send the usual payment. "We had nothing, no money, no bonus, no food," says Fred Ballantyne. The provincial Department of Northern Affairs was situated in a small building on the reserve. Chief Peter Linklater asked Fred to talk to the agent there. "I said, 'You have to give us something to eat from the store, all the people. You have to give rations.' 'Oh no, no, no,' he said. 'I'll be fired if I do that. You people can live on bannock and water.'" Fred persevered, in his quiet but determined manner, and the agent agreed to think it over. The next day everybody, including the chief, was presented with chits for the HBC post. "They gave me fifteen dollars, five dollars a kid, and my wife and me nothing."

By the 1950s and 1960s, the children of Chief Peter Ballantyne and his siblings were dying out. Their estates reveal that theirs had not been a world of capital accumulation. John Ballantyne died June 25, 1950, at Deschambault Lake. After a lifetime of hard work, his total assets consisted of a cheque from the Saskatchewan Fur Marketing Service for $162.75, of which each of his four sons and his one daughter received $27.02. Seven grandchildren received $3.86 each.[23] Robert Ballantyne died on November 18, 1956. His estate included one log cabin, twelve by fourteen feet, valued at fifty dollars, personal effects, stove, blankets, dishes worth ten dollars, and an Agency Trust account of $132.11. Of that he owed $19.15 for funeral expenses, forty dollars to Saskatchewan Government Trading, and $7.50 to the town of Flin Flon. This last turned out to be the debt of another Robert Ballantyne, a mistake which became something of an imbroglio for the government department administering the estate. Finally in April of 1957, Robert's widow, Annie, received her legacy – a cheque for $72.96.[24] Thomas Ballantyne died on June 4, 1961, at age sixty-two at Clearwater Lake Sanatorium. He had a log house fourteen by sixteen feet, household effects valued at three hundred dollars, and a savings account of $88.50. The expenses at the Hayes Funeral Home were $165. An official at the Indian Affairs branch informed Thomas's widow, Eliza, that she would not have to sell her home or her blankets, her teapot or stove to make up the balance of $79.50 owing on the funeral. "The widow should be told that she has clear title to the log house and effects," magnanimously wrote the Administrator of Estates.[25]

In the 1960s the population on Indian reserves, including Pelican Narrows, was growing rapidly, but little had been done to provide these people with a way to make a living. "It's easier simply to hand out welfare cheques than to spend money on infrastructure – roads, hydro, airstrips – to create a northern economy. Of course, no bureaucrat ever thinks about what dependence does to a people," wrote Garth Smith, an economic-development consultant. The idea of social assistance as a substitute for not developing the north's economy remains a modus operandi to this day. Eventually almost all of the transfer payments available to the general populace were attainable by native peoples. The numbers on social assistance rapidly grew. If these payments were larger than what a fisherman or trapper earned – two hundred to three hundred dollars for a winter's catch in 1962 – why would anybody work? "For a long time," says Philip Ratt, "we didn't want to accept welfare because, as we said, it didn't make men out of men. But the trapping was active then and everybody was employable. After the road came in [1968] there was less anᵈ ˡ being done. Men began working outside t families had to be fed while they were away short periods of time, but gradually it was u people just don't want to work." Says C "The government gives us money [welfare], or the liquor outlet, only to bring it back to the reserve, only to have it confiscated by the police. So I look at it as one big cycle. Money in, money out."

Today over 60 per cent – three thousand members – of the Peter Ballantyne First Nation receive social assistance. The cost is $11 million a year. There is a lamenting chorus sung by natives and whites alike every time this figure is mentioned: If only that money had been put into developing the economy of the north, Canada's first people would not be suffering so.

Horace Ratt, like many other indigenous people, believe that social assistance is a conspiracy on the part of the government to finally get rid of the Indian: "In the long run the dependency took hold. That's probably how Indian Affairs analyzed things. They figured that's a way of destroying the social structures of the Cree. And it's been really successful too." "There's a story that I'll always remember that my mom told me," relates Susan Custer. "One day my dad said, 'Welfare is going to be introduced into the community and it won't be any good for the people.' Then he was sad. He cried, literally cried, saying, 'That'll be another form of destruction.' "

In 1985 a thirty-four-year-old education administrator, Ron Michel, a big, burly man, was elected chief of the Peter Ballantyne First Nation; nineteen years later he still holds the position. He is typical of his generation of native leaders.

His family, his parents, and his nine siblings were among the poorest in Pelican Narrows. His father, Solomon Michel, had contracted tuberculosis and spent four years in the sanatorium. He returned to trapping and fishing, but one day, while chopping wood, he suffered one of those fluke accidents, so common in Rock Cree country. The log he was sawing somehow kicked back. It hit in the chest, and his body was thrown twenty feet. Solomon lived, but he was physically handicapped, he went blind, hereafter unable to work. Ron's mother, Louisa, helped in any way she could, cooking and cleaning cabins each summer at Jan Lake, but basically the family of twelve existed on the meagre relief payments that the Indian agent handed out.

All of Ron's nine brothers and sisters were sent to residential school. He was kept at home to help his parents. "I always joke," says Chief Michel, "that I was the all-round maintenance man, the water and sewer man, sawing wood and hauling water." He completed his elementary grades at the newly built Roman Catholic school in Pelican Narrows. "When I finished Grade 8 on the reserve, it was a big deal. Eight of us were shipped out to Prince Albert. Dad was proud – someone who was going to high school and all that."

Ron Michel's experience was different than his siblings' and illustrates the kind of painless way education could have been provided for aboriginal children until schools were built on the reserves. He boarded in non-native households and attended the local public high school in Prince Albert. "We went into a school that had 1,500 to 2,000 students, then there was us – ten First Nations kids. There were fights here and there, and some name-calling – Red Indians and all that – but then quite a few of us got into sports and eventually we were accepted as part of the student body." There were several Pelican Narrows kids attending the Catholic Prince Albert's Indian Residential School "We couldn't even come up and visit them. They didn't allow us in. We were considered a bad influence." Ron Michel was one of the founders of the First Nations Youth of Prince Albert, and served for three years as vice-president, the first inkling of his talent for politics.

Michel's high-school career came to an end after Grade 11. "In the 1960s that was a major education for anybody," he says. An older brother got him a job cutting line and surveying for a subsidiary of Hudson Bay Mining and Smelting Company. In the fall, they'd go into the bush, return for a few days at Christmas, and then disappear again until the spring, when the work would come to an end until the next season. Even in the coldest part of winter, they lived out of canvas tents.

When Ron Michel married in 1972, his sojourns in the bush came to an end. He began working for the Peter Ballantyne Band "with housing and garbage disposal and things like that." In 1976 both he and his wife, Gloria, decided to go back to school. A pilot project had been established; teacher's training would be offered right on the reserve. And both took university courses during the summer. Eventually she became a teacher and he got a job with the Peter Ballantyne Band as education coordinator, overseeing the transition from federal-run to band-run schools. He was also a good hockey and baseball player, competing in all the communities. "So I got fairly well known."

In 1979 Alphonse Dorion, an uncle of Ron Michel's, decided to step down after a quarter of a century on council. "He asked me if I would run as councillor. I was twenty-seven years old. I said, 'Yeah, I'll give it a shot.'" Ron Michel won the next two elections, the third term he was defeated, and two years later he was nominated to run as chief of Peter Ballantyne Cree Nation. There was only one problem: the incumbent chief, Joe Custer. "He was under the influence of the older chiefs," says Philip Ratt. "The elders told him, 'You're elected chief. Don't listen to what others say. Do what you want.' Consultation was still fairly new and those in power didn't really understand it." Joe Custer decided he wanted to extend his two-year term to three, which would have enabled him to keep his job without running for the office. The election went ahead anyway, and Ron won. "I had a little trouble with Joe for awhile but then when we got the Minister's [of Indian Affairs] letter, that Chief Ron Michel and the councillors were accepted, that's when we started working."

Once in office, what Chief Michel had to deal with was not poverty and despair but a huge bonanza of cash and land, handed over by governments as Treaty Land Entitlement (TLE). Many of the First Nations in Saskatchewan had not received anywhere near the acreage they were entitled to under the treaty agreements. The Peter Ballantyne Band, for example, had been surveyed in 1919, and assigned 22,466 acres. Under Treaty Six, the land allotted was 128 acres per person. Since the population of the band at the time was calculated at 416 (it was probably a lot more), it should have received 55,424 acres. There was therefore a shortfall of 32,958 acres.

The federal government had already acknowledged this deficiency, if not to a specific First Nation, then generally. When, over the opposition of all Indian bands, in 1930 it had transferred all Crown land, minerals, and other natural resources to the province, certain conditions had been laid down, including that Saskatchewan would provide enough unoccupied Crown land to enable Canada to fulfill its land obligations under the treaties. Yet for years nothing was done. Finally, in 1976, the provincial and federal governments signed what was called the Saskatchewan Formula, in which Crown lands were to be used to fulfill the treaty obligations. That year, Peter Ballantyne was acknowledged as one of the First Nations that had a significant shortfall. Before the formula could be implemented, though, the socialist New Democratic Party in Saskatchewan and the federal Liberals were both defeated by right-wing, fiscally conservative governments. The Saskatchewan Formula had gone nowhere, but in 1987 negotiations began again.

Because there was not enough unoccupied Crown land to satisfy the various claims, another approach had to be worked out which included a cash payment. It wasn't easy to convince the governments involved. Protestors set up roadblocks at Pelican Narrows and elsewhere to emphasize the Indian point of view.

Ron Michel was one of the four Saskatchewan chiefs who sat at the table with the federal and provincial governments. "On the Indian side, our technical people sat behind us, while we chiefs did the negotiating. We didn't want any bureaucratic systems blocking the way." Eventually a complicated formula was devised which took into account the band's population in both 1919 and 1991, the amount of acreage shortfall, and the current average price of farmland, $248.85 an acre. In the end the Peter Ballantyne Band was awarded a shortfall of 22,466 acres and $62.4 million in cash.

Of the twenty-seven First Nations who were involved, only three held referendums on the TLE's initial Framework Agreement: Onion Lake and Poundmaker band members approved it; the Peter Ballantyne people, voting in November 1992, did not. They were quickly made aware that Chief Michel was not pleased. "I get very serious and I get very vocal when people don't understand. There is fear all the time [of governments], and I recognize that, but we have to move on. A lot of times, when I get vocal, people see me as mad, but deep down I'm not that kind of person." Says Philip Ratt, "The problem with Ronnie Michel is that he's very passionate, too passionate at times. And too generous at times."

The opposition to the Treaty Land Entitlement agreement harkened back to the Island Falls dam project of the 1930s. The Cree living in the area remembered how badly the government and the Hudson Bay Mining and Smelting subsidary had treated them, what a disaster it had been for their trapping and fishing, how they received no compensation. They wanted control over the two major rivers, the Churchill and the Reindeer, flowing through the Peter Ballantyne area. Since these waterways were not entirely contained within the reserve, the federal and provincial government vetoed the idea. The dissidents were sure another hydroelectric dam would be built, which would flood their lands without a penny of compensation being offered. The chief promised the band would buy land in the Churchill and Reindeer district that would block any future dam construction. But the provincial government refused to sell the land, and that roused suspicion even more.

There were other reasons for resistance to what seemed like such a sweet deal. Critics insisted that, in signing the Treaty Land Entitlement (TLE) agreement, the band was finally accepting the 1930 arrangement, whereby the federal government handed over the natural resources to the province without any consultation with the indigenous people. Many Cree insist that in an unwritten but not unspoken part of Treaty Six, they gave up land, but only the top six inches of it. The minerals and oil underneath were theirs. TLE gave compensation for natural resources, which in effect extinguished the rights that the Cree had always claimed were their own. "The only reason why the natural resources agreement is included in the TLE framework agreement," says Graham Linklater, "is that they [the government] knew full well that they were liable. They put it in such a nice fashion that, when it comes time for ratification, it goes through. You're accepting what was done wrong to you in 1930. And it is still not right." The intricacies of Graham Linklater's logic were understood by many of Pelican Narrows's elders, and they supported him.

There was also concern that the $62.4 million was to be handed out to the band over a relatively short time, twelve years. If it wasn't handled very carefully, there would be nothing left for future generations. "I think, in fifty years," says Fred Ballantyne, who was one of the leaders of the resistance, "our children will be angry at us for giving away so much."

After the referendum, which went against the deal, Chief Michel began travelling the land, explaining the complicated arrangements to the band members. Then he threatened to sign the Framework Agreement whether the community approved it or not. He told band members, "I didn't have to have that first vote. As a chief with direction from the council I could have signed the agreement, but I came to you guys first to see what were the fears." Then council decided to hold a second referendum, and that incensed the opposition even more. For a whole week protestors, some with small children in tow, occupied the band office. "We locked ourselves in," says Eileen Linklater. "The RCMP showed us a document through the windows that we were supposed to be out of there. We said no, we weren't going to let them in, and they didn't bother us." The occupying force used the telephone freely (more than fifteen thousand dollars in long-distance calls were chalked up), and plastered the windows with paper slogans. Finally the power was cut off, Philip Ratt's idea, and the sit-in ended. "When the media arrived, we did interviews. 'We got what we wanted,' we told them. 'Community meetings regarding the TLE, more information, and that's when the Chief said he'd give us these things.'"

But the struggle continued. Three applications against the TLE agreement were made to the Federal Court of Canada – several elders put up their own money to hire a lawyer – none of which were successful. Says Philip Ratt: "Misinformation was really rampant. A lot of people were told, the Chief is a sell-out, you're going to lose your treaty rights, your land is being sold off – our waters, our lakes, our natural resources. What they didn't realize was that all that had already been determined by Treaty Six 120 years ago."

On November 8, 1993, the plebiscite on the Treaty Land Agreement specific to the Peter Ballantyne Band was held. The result: 1,385 in favour, 400 opposed. The opposition quieted down, but there remains great bitterness. Once again the community had been badly split, and over something that could have been so beneficial.

Under the TLE agreement, the band was required to use the 22,466 shortfall acres, plus the same amount of purchased land, to be set apart as reserve land. Several new reserves were established, including Opawikoscikan in Prince Albert, Wapaskokimaw (named after Chief Whitebear) in Sandy Bay, and Kimosom Pwatinahk at Deschambault Lake. An urban reserve was also created in Prince Albert, on which the Northern Lights Casino was built; the casino is owned by twelve First Nations, including the Peter Ballantyne Band, and it pays rent to Peter Ballantyne.

There were two reasons why the formation of these reserves was so important. In the mid-1980s the government had announced that no longer would Peter Ballantyne Band members living off reserves be funded. Ninety-five per cent of the population of the village at Deschambault Lake were Peter Ballantyne members. Without reserve status no Indian Affairs financing was possible. Secondly under Bill C31, an amendment to the Indian Act which was aimed at alleviating past discrimination, thousands of people regained their status as Treaty Indians. They were living in places such as Sandy Bay and, as the population swelled, people wanted their own administration, which reserve status would make possible. Along with the creation of new reserves, the three existing reserves, Pelican Narrows, Sturgeon Landing, and Southend, were expanded.

Many parcels of land were chosen as reserves where no population existed; these are to be used for economic development – forestry, tourism, and in one instance, graphite mining. In 2000 the band came close to going into partnership with Ainsworth Lumber Company of British Columbia and Alberta. On the drawing board was a huge sawmill, to be built between Deschambault and Pelican Narrows, which would have employed more than three hundred people. The deal between Ainsworth and Peter Ballantyne Cree Nation had pretty well been thrashed out, but millions of dollars were needed to build infrastructure, including electricity, roads, and sewage-disposal systems. The Saskatchewan government was asked to contribute but, as Chief Michel puts it, "They said, 'If we're going to put something into this project, we want to be part of it.' We said no. We knew how Saskatchewan utility companies worked, and we didn't want any part of them." By that time, the Canadian forestry industry was in trouble, and Ainsworth finally pulled out. Another lost chance for the unemployed of Pelican Narrows.

By March 25, 1999, Peter Ballantyne had acquired its shortfall of 22,466 acres, which meant that they had much more flexibility with the remainder of the $62.4 million of TLE money. Businesses were established in Prince Albert, Saskatoon, and Meadow Lake – everything from motels to sawmills. Once those things are generating a profit, dividends will flow back to the Peter Ballantyne communities. "One of these days," says Chief Michel, "the Department of Indian Affairs is going to slap on cutbacks and then we will have nothing if we don't have economic development."

From the mid-1980s onwards, the focus of the Peter Ballantyne Cree Nation began shifting from Pelican Narrows to Prince Albert, 350 kilometres to the west. This is a city of forty thousand, although at present only about five hundred Peter Ballantyne members live there. A band office was built, and the chief and councillors began spending more time in Prince Albert than they did at Pelican Narrows. The politicians claimed that a central location was needed to administer all eight communities making up the First Nation, and that Prince Albert was convenient, since most of the band business, especially in economic development, is carried out there. But it was deeply resented by Pelican Narrows residents. "They are more or less hiding from the membership, from the community, that's what I think," says Eileen Linklater. She and her husband, Dennis, who was a Peter Ballantyne council-lor for eight years, have long been critics of the political manage-ment of the band. "It started in the 1980s, having community meetings down there. . . . Whatever goes on, they do [their busi-ness] behind the members' backs unless somebody steps in to correct it. But it's hard for us to get to P.A., because a lot of us don't have the funding to go there and protest, voice our concerns. They're out there so they can hide away from the people, so people don't bug them about this and that – why is it that they don't hold more meetings, give us more information?" Adds Dennis: "They try and hide information away from their own people, hoping that members won't understand. Because when you don't understand, things won't bother you." The politicians counter that one of the reasons they want to build a hotel in Pelican Narrows is so they can hold meetings there, and stay over, avoiding the long drive to Prince Albert.

Pelican Narrows, because of its large population base, was to receive 35 per cent of the $62.4 million TLE money. Since early times, the community had been made up of two reserves and a village which included the large holdings of the Hudson's Bay Company and the Roman Catholic Church. It was this land that the band bought to expand the Pelican Narrows reserve. As well, some $6 million worth of housing was built. "There's a housing crisis in this community, no doubt about that," says Bertie Dorion, one of Pelican Narrows's activists. "There's homeless people, single mothers without homes. Fifteen people to a house. I've seen mouldy houses. Holes in the floor, foundations are cracked, windows and doors broken." Yet she worries that Treaty Land Entitlement money is being spent in this way. "That area-fund money was supposed to be used for economic development in the community and for future generations, and growth so the money would generate itself. But it never happened." To address that complaint, a convention centre, a restaurant, a motel for 150 to 200 people, and a nine-hole golf course was planned; the proposed site, located near Philip Ratt's house, was cleared of bush and trees. Then it came to an abrupt halt; the leadership discovered that the people of Pelican Narrows were utterly opposed to it. "I still don't know why," says Chief Michel. Gordon Peter Ballantyne has an answer: "It was crazy. Nobody on the reserve played golf except the chief and the councillors. Everybody felt we were building it just for them." Darlene McKay says that instead of a golf course, what is really needed is a home for battered women. "Why do the women have to rush off to La Ronge when they're leaving their husband? Or to Prince Albert or wherever? It should be here." "Why don't they build a strip mall?" asks Eileen Linklater. "A store to call our own, to be operated by the band. The revenue it would generate would stay in the community." "What about the quality of life here?" says a teacher. "Wouldn't it be nice to have a hairdresser, or ladies' dress shop, or a pinball arcade, or even a funeral home? And all those things would put more money in the economy so people could start having a life here."

Some TLE money built the Napoleon Merasty Hockey Arena, a fine, modern facility. There were good hockey players on the reserve, and there were dreams of having one or more make it to the NHL. But there's been not as much interest in minor hockey as organizers would have liked. Says Robin Merasty (son of Napoleon), who is the arena's recreation director, "I don't know where all the kids are. They haven't come out this year. There's maybe a handful of kids in each age group." There are two very active girls' teams, the school uses the facilities as part of physical education during the week, and adults play hockey for recreation in the evenings. The paradox is this: the band can no longer afford to run the huge facility on weekends or during the summer so, during these times, when kids are running around with nothing to do, the ice lies unused. "We've got such a nice facility," says Robin Merasty, "but it has only limited use by the public." There is also a fitness centre in the arena, over two hundred thousand dollars was spent on state-of-the-art equipment. The problem was most people on Pelican Narrows cannot afford the thirty-dollar-a-month fee. "Mostly it's the white guys, the ambulance drivers, the Natural Resources guys, that use it," says Gordon Peter. "And if I'm out working in construction all day, I'm too tired to use it."

By the late 1990s, many people began to wonder if the Treaty Land Entitlement money was going to be all used up without any real benefit to the community. Where, for instance, were the jobs?

October 16, 2000: About fifty people have gathered in two rooms at the Imperial 400 Motel in Prince Albert. Most are women busy stapling, drawing, printing. The artist of the group holds up her latest handiwork: it's a picture of a fat drunk, his beer belly hanging out, passed out in front of a VLT machine. "Obviously chief and council," yells Elvena Pearson. "Where else do you find them but in a casino?"

October 17, 2000: A lovely fall morning. The annual meeting of the Prince Albert Grand Chief Assembly, of which Peter Ballantyne Cree Nation is a member, is taking place in a school gymnasium. Outside are forty protestors marching back and forth with the placards they assembled the night before. "Stealing from the POOR to feed the RICH," reads one. Another shows a drawing of a group of women washing and dusting: "Time to Clean House," it says. "Out with Chief and Council." Elyse Morin, an elder in her eighties, speaks to the crowd. Elvena Pearson translates her Cree into English. "I'm sure my grandfather [Chief Peter Ballantyne] would not like the way the chief is treating us now. He's taking money from the people. My grandfather would not have done that, would not have even thought about it. It's not a good thing." As cars go by, the drivers honk their horns and give the thumbs-up sign.

Elvena Pearson has resigned her position as justice of the peace so she can act as the group's spokesperson without a conflict of interest. To the media, she announces the main reason for their protest: In 1999–2000, Chief Michel had received a salary of $119,635, honoraria of $31,694, and travel expenses of $172,318, for a total of $323,647.[26] And this at a time when 70 per cent of Pelican Narrows adults were unemployed and a single mother with one child received $3,720 in social assistance a year.

Graham Linklater was the one councillor who joined the protestors. Among other things, he had discovered that two elected council members, with large salaries and travelling expenses, were also receiving social assistance. "That's actual fraud," says Linklater. "I started to do something about it. I think it was only Mr. Fred Ballantyne who was helping me at the time. The chief didn't want to lay any criminal charges, so nothing was done. Then I found out that life insurance was being deducted from the band employees' paycheques but those payments were not being made to the company. No dollars to London Life." The company was owed $144,000, but, after lengthy negotiations with the band, accepted $70,000. "I believe that the federal government is not really trying to help the First Nations," says Graham Linklater. "They're letting them do as much damage to themselves as possible. So in the eyes of the Canadian citizen, everybody looks down on First Nations people because they can't manage their own affairs."

There were other reasons for the growing dissent: rumours were circulating that Peter Ballantyne Cree Nation was badly in debt. For one thing, the band's cheques, even social-assistance cheques, bounced. "It was really embarrassing," comments Elvena Pearson.

October 27, 2000: Ottawa's Department of Indian and Northern Affairs announces that it will take control of Peter Ballantyne Band finances, at least the part provided by the federal government, $58 million in 2000. What this means is that a third party will manage the band's affairs until the financial mess is straightened out. The band had acquired a long-term debt of $15,032,036 and an accumulated deficit at the end of the year of $11,362,987. "That's a lot of money," says Elvena Pearson. "Think of all the houses you could build, all the economic development. That's why this community has nothing. Because all they're doing is spending the money in casinos, going to Las Vegas, going to China, wherever."

The more the dissidents looked at the financial statement the angrier they got. The Monday after the demonstration, about thirty people settled themselves in the band office, chaining the door, boarding some windows. Their demand was simple: Chief Michel and other high-flyers must resign. On the eleventh day of the sit-in, a group of elders arrived, as mediators. They claimed they were frightened for the protestors' safety. Some people had not received their welfare cheques and blamed those holed up at the band office, where the cheques were issued. Finally, after a petition was signed demanding that the chief be fired, the rebels relented and the protest ended.

The audit revealed that Chief Michel was not the only one receiving a large salary: ten other people, politicians and staff, received wages in the six figures. Yet another puzzling number was the $734,815 in outstanding advances or loans racked up by council and employees. "They [the chief and council] were co-signing loans but the people never went and paid for their loans. So who is at fault? Who is liable? Who has to pay? The entire Peter Ballantyne Cree Nation, of course," says Graham Linklater.

The 2000 financial statement by PricewaterhouseCoopers concluded: "There is a degree of uncertainty as to whether the band can continue to operate and deliver its programs to the members."[27] Although eleven other First Nations were in the same boat, it was a humiliating predicament, especially since the band has had to pay a million dollars a year to have itself managed by the third party. There were other reasons, besides big salaries and oversized loans, for the financial mess. About half of the Peter Ballantyne Band members live off the reserve, but the council still felt it necessary to help them during difficult times, even though no government funding was provided. And the eight communities making up the Cree nation all wanted administration offices and health centres of their own, an expensive proposition. "When we made all these decisions," admits Chief Michel, "we didn't look at the financial situation we were getting into. We made good decisions, giving everybody their own thing. Then our debt started going up, going up, going up, and wasn't coming down. We ended up in third-party management."

In December 2000, Chief Michel was diagnosed with a non-malignant brain tumour and an operation became necessary. He would eventually recover, but he did not contest the election in 2001. He did run for the job of vice-chief of the Prince Albert Grand Council and he was outside campaigning when Elvena Pearson, who by then had been elected a band councillor from Pelican Narrows, spotted him. "We [Elvena and a friend] took off running towards the group. We pushed our way into the circle and I stood close to him. He was addressing a group of northern Dene delegates. I piped up, 'I can't believe you have the nerve to run for a position such as this after what you did to our band.' Then I walked away to my car. I was furious with Ron Michel for having the audacity to run for vice-chief when his mismanagement brought our band into such a deficit."

The chief elected in 2001 was a feisty schoolteacher, Susan Custer, the first female in the band's history. "We were in debt in the millions. We still are, but we were able to cut down a lot of programming and just make it by on what we had," she says. "Pay the bills, just enough so we could survive. I think I managed pretty good, cause I can do that here at home. I have those skills and so it was just a bigger amount of money, but it could be done." Chief Custer and her council, under third-party management, slashed the deficit by half, but programming suffered so much, many band members grew disgruntled.

In 2003 Ron Michel decided to run again. "I just wanted to come back," he says. "It was me who got us into this financial mess to some degree, and I wanted to be the guy to get us out of it." And, as Michel pointed out to the voters, since his illness, he had stopped drinking and gambling. It was an exciting race, with seven candidates for the top job, but in the end it was a battle between the two chiefs. Ron Michel beat Susan Custer by sixty votes. The majority of people in Pelican Narrows had voted for Custer but other reserves had gone Michel.

Chief Michel claims the debt is currently at about $2.6 million, and financial administration will return to the band once it's paid out. But the third-party manager has made it clear that this will not occur unless "accountability structures, financial reporting and disclosure is transparent for both INAC (Indian and Northern Affairs Canada) and non-INAC programs." In other words chief and council will be forced to inform the band members about what's going on in enough detail that they understand. And this will be a major step forward.

It's part of a political malaise that has infected the community: favouritism, cronyism, clan bias. Everyone talks about it; indeed it could be the chorus in a Greek tragedy. Oscar Ballantyne: "If you're not related to the councillors or the chief, you have a hard time to find a job. They're just looking after themselves. They're not looking after their people. Like the white man says, 'The rich get richer and the poor get poorer.' That's what it's like right now." J.B. Custer: "A lot of people here, they cover their past with religion or materialism or nepotism. That's why there's so much corruption, especially in our band here. A lot of them went to residential school, but they're still in denial." Eileen Linklater: "If the chief and councillors are not in favour of you, or don't like you as a band member, they shut the door on you. If you don't try and do something about it, they'll just step on you." Anson Ballantyne: "Their families get the jobs, no matter how qualified you are. They don't see you as someone who is important. Right now, because of the deficit, the overspending, there's nothing left for guys like me." Cindy Ballantyne: "Favouritism, there's lots of that." Charlie Sewap: "Too many times, when the government gets money for our use, a lot of times we don't even know where the money goes or how it is spent. Especially in housing. We lose part of that money to the deficit, and they put some for their own use. They buy cheap materials for the housing." Glen Ballantyne: "They're only there for themselves and their families. Like the council that just came to office, they all have new vehicles. In the meantime people need new houses or renovations. One of the councillors has bought everything, boat, Ski-Doo, and it wasn't very long ago that he got in." Mary Anne Ballantyne: "They'd rather pick someone that is closely related to them. Then the others get angry at the way things are run." Ida Swan: "Economically there's only a few people that work and most of the jobs are somehow connected to politics, so nobody's job is totally secure. Even me, I've been teaching for thirty years, and twice I've been fired for no reason. I always think it's for belonging to the wrong side of the tracks." Armand Ballantyne: "I would like to kick a few councillors out of there. They're just there for themselves and their relatives."

Because of her political involvement, Eileen Linklater lost her job as a community worker with the band council and was never rehired. She started a medical taxi service, transporting people back and forth to Prince Albert and Flin Flon for dialysis and other treatment. But now she finds herself being edged out – the band does the hiring and finances this transportation – and says she's on the point of bankruptcy. She feels that there is a conflict of interest: Councillor Alex Morin is one of those who is involved with the health portfolio. His brother Otto owns the other taxi business in town, and, according to Eileen, is getting the lucrative trips – $840 a return trip to Saskatoon, for example. "Don't you think that's a little bit of nepotism?" she asks. The band claims she was driving too slowly, she wasn't efficient enough.

Gordon Peter is deciding whether to run in the next election, but the prospect frightens him. He asks, "How can you handle such a big debt? How can you provide the housing that's so badly needed? Where would you get the money to build a community centre so the young people will have something to do and won't drink and take drugs? What if you disappoint the people?" The future of the Peter Ballantyne Cree First Nation depends on decent, caring, bright people such as Gordon Peter not losing hope. If they despair, the long struggle for self-government will have been for nothing.

ONE MAN

The easy laughter is gone now.
Face pinched, a darkness has settled
for John. Last year his son. Dead,
victim of another's jealousy, cut
down by a shotgun blast at a party.
A few days ago, his sister,
one who was closest, gone.
John wears his grief in his eyes
as long as he can. Then breaks
as we all must. As we must
wear his grief with us
this night, and tomorrow,
carry it away when we leave.
There is no other way.

Glen Sorestad
Hold the Rain in Your Hands:
Poems New and Selected

7

tēpakohp

ONE SINS, THE OTHER SUFFERS

PĪYAK WANĪTIW, KOTAK KIPAWĀW

Gordon Peter and Susan Ballantyne were sleeping late one frigid winter night when they heard a sharp rap on the door. Gordon Peter yelled, "Who's there? We're in bed already. Go away." The knocking continued. Gordon Peter, thinking it was a drunk, told the intruder to get lost. But the pleading didn't stop.

"Open the door, I'm cold."

"If you're so cold, go home," was Gordon Peter's response. "If you keep this up, I'm going to call the cops."

"Go ahead, call them, but please open the door."

Susan finally intervened: "There's something wrong. Open the damn door!" Gordon Peter obeyed.

The young guy standing there was covered in snow, he had no gloves, and his face was a mess of blood. Gordon Peter sat him down by the wood stove and asked him what had happened. "The last thing I remember, I was being beaten," he replied. "Then I woke up down by the lake on the ice."

As the nineteen-year-old bent towards the fire, blood began to drip from under his jacket. Gordon Peter called the police.

The RCMP depot is located only three minutes away. Since there was no ambulance service at the time in Pelican Narrows, and Gordon Peter did not have a vehicle, he expected them to come immediately. Instead the officer kept questioning him. "What's happened there?" he kept asking. Gordon Peter related what he knew of the assault, and told the officer that blood was dripping all over his kitchen floor. The cop would not promise to send a car, so Gordon Peter hung up on him. He knew the boy's parents were playing bridge at his brother's place, so he called there. The mother ran over, took her son's jacket off, and carefully lifted up his bloodied shirt. There were seven stab wounds on his back.

This time the mother called the RCMP. Again they kept stalling, kept asking her questions, even though she told them everything she knew. Finally Gordon Peter grabbed the phone and yelled, "If I was calling about an injured white person, you'd have no problem, you'd be here. If you don't get your butt over here, I'm going to call the chief." The police cruiser arrived ten minutes later and rushed the injured man to the hospital in Flin Flon – just in time.

Of all the occasions when indigenous people have bumped their heads against the white institutions that rule their lives, none has been as painful as dealing with the criminal justice system. And no place is this more obvious than at Pelican Narrows Indian Reserve. There are nine regular officers and two auxiliary police assigned to the Pelican Narrows RCMP detachment. None are native. With their shiny white vehicles, with their haircuts that would make a sergeant-major proud, their clean, sharply pressed uniforms, they are so out of place on the reserve they seem an occupying force, Pelican Narrows an armed camp. The law enforcers intrude in the daily lives of the people in astonishing ways, primarily because of the power derived from the dry by-law, which was passed by the band council itself. They arrest anyone walking down the street with a glass in their hand. They charge into people's houses without search warrants. They wait at the entrance to the reserve, at

Opawikoscikan, the Narrows of Dread, stop anyone they like – seldom is this a white person – search their car and confiscate whatever booze they find. Almost every wedding or graduation or anniversary, people end up spending the night in drunk cells, often with no charges laid against them. Gordon Peter's sister Laurie worked one summer as a cell guard. "One time there was some sort of graduation or wedding, and a lot of people were drinking. And they just kept throwing guy after guy after guy into the same cell. There were about ten people in that cell. I thought, 'You can't do that!' That was one of the things I saw that made me want to shoot them [the police]." If an officer feels someone may be suicidal, the prisoner, often a young boy or girl, is stripped of their clothes. "It's awful degrading," says Doug Pearson. "Some of them [the RCMP officers] are just here for two years, they come north, and they sure let the world know that they don't like it here. You get the feel of them right away. I've had many arguments with cops. I told several of them I'd be ashamed to pick up their paycheques for what they do and the way they act. It's the old story. An Indian kid has a brand-new bike. They stop him and say, 'Where did you get that?' It's all got to do with attitude."

Tom Sewap, who is thirty-five years old and a band councillor, explains how the power, derived from the dry bylaw, sets off a chain reaction that can escalate a small matter into a serious offence. "They [the police] pick somebody up who's been drinking. The guy would go willingly, but the cops bang him around. The guy sooner or later has to defend himself. Then they charge him with obstruction of justice or resisting arrest and he's in big trouble. . . . When white people come here, especially the police, they start dictating to us how we should live, how we should speak, how we should listen, and I get upset." He will never forget the police officer who told him, while looking him straight in the eye, that the only good Indian was a dead Indian.

In early Rock Cree society there were no laws, no policemen, no prisons. There was, of course, a moral standard, to which each person was required to conform, but this was a matter of the conscience, not imposed by some outside enforcer. The principles by which one lived were laid out in oral literature, which the Cree believed originated from the Creator, much as the Judeo-Christian tradition relies on the Bible. As Menno Boldt and J. Anthony Long point out, "Rule by custom, without a separate agency of enforcement was possible in traditional Indian society because a face-to-face society can maintain order with few but broad general rules known to everyone." Since the society was egalitarian rather than authoritarian, based on sharing, generosity, and hospitality, with little private property, there weren't many ways to commit crimes – not as we understand them anyway.

There were, of course, individuals who were selfish, wrong-headed, short-tempered, but the method of dealing with them was through persuasion, cajoling, and lecturing, usually by the elders. And there was always the shaman standing by. The threat of an evil spell, of being attacked by a beaver or an eagle or a *witigo*, or being sent an illness that could kill you, served to make you mind your ways. For those who refused to change their behaviour, banishment was imposed; the deviant man or woman was simply not allowed to follow the group when they moved to another camp. Oblate missionary Marius Rossignol, writing in 1939, had this observation about the way justice was meted out in Rock Cree society:

There was no tribunal of justice, but the chief or leader of the group with his principal associates would talk over and discuss the case and would express their views on the matter. This expression of view was equivalent to a verdict and had the force of law. The guilty one recognized this without hesitation. Ordinarily no hand was laid upon him to start with; he was boycotted in order to force him to betake himself away in case he did not do so at once and voluntarily. He was not given any further aid, he had no share in anyone's food, his traps were put out of commission, his tools were sabotaged, his implements of hunting were broken. Then, seeing himself up against it, he would depart and never come back.

Finally, in the case of truly serious offences, murder for example, the kinsfolk of the one transgressed against would take revenge on the family of the transgressor. These clashes often proved deadly for both sides, which is probably why they were very rare. As Joseph I. Dion put it, "In all the many established home sites, the Crees lived at peace with one another. No case of mass violence has ever been recorded in our oral history."

As the raid by the Sioux on Pelican Narrows in the eighteenth century illustrates, war was the most serious violence inflicted by one Nation on another. This usually took the form of raiding parties of young warriors on the margins of a territory. Father Rossignol:

> No doubt they [Rock Cree] often tried to increase their territory. It is related that they fought with the Chipewyan (Dene) at many points to which they had advanced, but that having suffered a defeat of the first order, they had to fall back in full retreat – to Reindeer Lake, Snake Lake, and Cree Lake, to mention only some of the more important points. Later on they succeeded in encroaching peacefully upon the territory of their neighbours whom sickness and other causes had weakened and who withdrew, incapable with their small number of hunters of further maintaining their ancient tribal territory.

Thus the Dene people to the north became the traditional enemies of the Rock Cree, although both tribes periodically raided Athapaskan neighbours to the north and west. It was an animosity that would last a long time.

When the fur traders arrived in Rupert's Land, they tried to put an end to extra-tribal fighting. How could someone trap beaver if they were off battling their enemies? As Paul Thistle writes,

"Europeans did not understand the role of warfare in Cree society and they attempted – again largely unsuccessfully – to divert them from this time-honoured pursuit to trapping." At a time when there was near-constant warfare in Europe, the white traders had the audacity to moralize to the Cree on the subject of peace. But by the time the fur trade was well-established, warfare was almost non-existent. Rock Cree country was remarkably peaceful, right up until the 1960s.

Once the indigenous people encountered white society, they had to deal with representatives of state authority. The North-West Mounted Police was formed in 1873 to bring Canadian law and order to the Dominion's vast western domain, and basically to protect the Indians from white abuse. But they had so much power, acting as investigator, judge, and jury, that natives were often terrified of them, as the case of Thomas Ballantyne reveals.

In the first band election that saw Peter Ballantyne become chief, his brother Thomas was chosen as headman. He was smart and energetic. The HBC journals are full of his success as a trapper. "Thomas Ballantyne in with a good collection of furs. Got about forty dollars." "Thomas arrived, he brought in 333 M.B. [Make Beaver]." "Thomas Ballantyne came in, brought a good lot of mink and other furs." A renowned hunter and trapper, Thomas was also a respected medicine man.

From late summer to fall of 1907, a measles epidemic had killed several adults and children in the Pelican Narrows district. It was no surprise, then, when Noah Ballantyne showed up with his brother's body. Thomas had died from measles on October 13, Noah said. Since there was no Anglican clergyman in the settlement, relatives buried the dead man in St. Bartholomew's Church cemetery themselves.

Three weeks later, the Mounties in Prince Albert received a dispatch from the manager at Revillon Frères trading post, claiming there were suspicious circumstances surrounding Thomas Ballantyne's death. Corporal W. Munday set out by canoe for the settlement, arriving there November 3. Later he wrote this account:

On the afternoon of the 4th Novr. in the presence of Mr. Simpson [the HBC post manager] and the priest I exhumed the body; it was recognizable as that of Thomas Ballantyne. The coffin had been made of ¾-inch rough lumber and was covered with a black shawl. The corpse was slightly decomposed and had evidently been laid out carefully; it was dressed in old but clean overalls, drawers over them and socks and a shroud of muslin. I examined the body thoroughly and found a small bullet wound 4 inches above the navel and a wound above the left hip, nearer the back than the side, where no doubt the bullet had escaped.

There was a piece of old shirt on the body which had evidently been worn by the deceased at the time of his death, it was saturated with blood and had two holes in it, pieces of leather were covering the wound and two handkerchiefs were bound around the body. There appeared to be some bark on the leather as though Indian medicine had been tried. There were no marks of violence on the body.[1]

Corporal Munday and some Indian guides set off by canoe for the Ballantynes' camp at Bear's Point but, when they arrived, they found it deserted. The group decided to camp there. During the night, a thin sheet of ice covered the lakes, and the next day it snowed, with strong winds blowing from the north. Travelling that day or the next was out of the question; it became obvious that the corporal would be unable to proceed to the Ballantyne camp. He made it back to Pelican Narrows by keeping to the larger bodies of water. By that time the true story of Thomas's death had surfaced anyway.

Thomas and his nephew Jacob had gone hunting together in the bush, but they soon separated, each going a different direction. Jacob circled around and there, standing on the riverbank, was a moose. He took aim, and shot it. Then came a sharp human-like yelp. He ran over and found his uncle on his knees, blood gushing from a wound in his stomach. Thomas has been standing under a willow tree and Jacob had thought the branches were antlers.

The Ballantyne family had been so frightened of white authority that they had made up the story about measles being the cause of death. "The case appears to me so far to be one of accidental shooting, and that is the general opinion, and the Ballantyne family are too afraid to say anything about it," wrote Munday.[2] Yet six years later, police investigators were still showing up, questioning various family members about the death. Jacob Ballantyne finally moved to Pukatawagan permanently.

This was not the first time the Mounties had made the long journey to Pelican Narrows. Four years before, Inspector W. Parker had travelled there to formally charge Mary Linklater with murder.

The complaints directed at the police usually originated with the trading-post managers, who often had an axe to grind. In the Thomas Ballantyne case, it was H. McLeod of the Revillon Frères post who had provided the information. He wrote "the Ballantynes are a very bad outfit," not mentioning that they dealt with the Hudson's Bay Company and refused to do business with him. In Mary Linklater's case, it was the HBC manager, Horace Belanger, who wrote the damning letter:

Owing to the bad treatment and bad usage, the son of Peter Linklater, aged about 11 or 12 years wandered away during his Fathers absence and was found four or five days later stiff and cold. This was the fourth time the poor lad had wandered off after getting a pounding, but in former times had been followed and saved. . . . Everybody looks upon it as if he had been murdered.

The woman is a notorious bad character. I think it would be right to make an example of her, or at least give her a good scare. She is a Catholic and of course the Clergy will not be in a hurry to report it and shove it through.[3]

The NWMP decided to send Inspector Parker to investigate, but it took weeks to arrange the trip. "Cannot find Pelican Narrows on any map. It must be somewhere the other side of Cumberland House," one official wrote. Fred White, the NWMP comptroller, reported: "I am unable to locate Pelican Narrows, but Pelican Bay and Pelican Lake are, I think, within the boundaries of Manitoba."[4]

Inspector Parker finally left Prince Albert on March 7, 1903, by canoe and arrived at Pelican Narrows two weeks later. He was told that the Linklaters' house was about sixty kilometres north of the Churchill River, and the family was trapping thirty kilometres north of that. He set off with three trains of dogs, his assistant, Constable Dunning, a Métis interpreter, and an Indian as guide and forerunner, breaking the way for the dogs. The group arrived at the Peter Linklater house on March 22 and found his brother Magloire and his family in residence. The Mountie thought the place too dirty, and he demanded that it be cleaned up. He then sent Constable Dunning off to the Linklater camp to arrest Mary Linklater.

The next morning Inspector Parker went fishing with Magloire, who netted a sturgeon seven feet long and over a hundred pounds. The policeman was thoroughly enjoying himself, but, when Dunning arrived with the prisoner, the trial began immediately. It lasted three and a half hours, during which time four witnesses were heard, including Mary's husband, Peter. He insisted that his wife never beat their son, ever. Since the accused was too frightened to give a statement, he related to the court what Mary had told him: "I took the boy in a canoe to go and set some snares, the dogs followed along the shore. I put the boy ashore, telling him to drive the dogs back to the house. I waited for him for a long time but he did not return. We searched for him for four days." One of the Linklaters' neighbours testified, "I helped to dress the body, there were no bruises on it, the swelling on the cheek was caused by lying on the ground. The face was marked as if picked by birds." Finally, Inspector Parker concluded that, while trying to find his uncle, the boy walked for about six days, until he perished from cold and hunger. "There was nothing in the evidence to warrant me in sending the prisoner up for trial, so I dismissed the case."[5]

Given the distance Inspector Parker had travelled and the expense incurred, it was perhaps fortunate that he had something else to investigate. "John Rednose is, at times, as crazy as he can be and wants to kill his children. Last summer he was in the act of hitting his boy with a big stick when the Mother got between, and at other times he is as sane as anybody. Nobody knows when he may do something serious," Horace Belanger of the HBC wrote.[6]

When Inspector Parker arrived at Pelican Narrows, he called on Fathers Charlebois and Rossignol to discuss Rednose's behaviour. Father Charlebois told the police officer that he had known John Rednose for a long time. He was a hard-working trapper, often trading his furs at the HBC post. As Parker reported, "Father Charlebois said he would not think of laying an information against him as a lunatic, that he was not bad enough for that, he being a good working man and supporting his family, always regular in paying his debts, but thought it would be a good thing if a Doctor could see him to try and cure him of his hallucination, principally the hearing of voices which he, Rednose, claimed interfered with his hunting. On the strength of their statements I decided not to proceed any further in the matter."[7]

It might have been a good idea if Inspector Parker had talked with Rednose's family, his wife, and Rednose himself. In a few months the Mounted Police depot in Prince Albert received the news that John Jones (he had changed his name) was growing more violent and threatening the lives of his wife and children frequently, so much so that they were all afraid to sleep at night. It was decided that Inspector J.H. Heffernan would make the long trip again. At least this time they knew where the place was.

The inspector reached Pelican Narrows on March 14, 1904. Three days later, with Rev. James Settee, an Anglican clergyman, as translator, he arrived at Amisk Lake, 130 kilometres southeast of Pelican Narrows, where John was camping. "Through Mr. Settee, I told John we had arrived to take him to see Prince

Albert," reported Inspector Heffernan. "He replied that he would not go etc. etc. After resting the dogs and boiling the kettle we coaxed John from the house. I immediately put a pair of shackles on him. With Constable Dunning we put him into a carriole, and without loss of time, departed."[8] According to Heffernan, the wife of John Rednose Jones thanked the police profusely for taking her husband away.

It was a terrible trip back, but not because of the "lunatic"; he gave the police no trouble at all. It was the weather. As the inspector reported, "Taken as a whole, the trip was the hardest I was ever on, having to sleep out on the snow with the thermometer away below zero [F.] was anything but nice, and I got a nasty attack of rheumatism in my groin, legs, and shoulders." There was something else that truly disturbed the inspector – the food. "Const. Dunning did his work well, but he is not the really first-class man I expected from reports made of him. He has no more idea of camp cooking, than I have of flying." The "lunatic John Rednose Jones" was handed over to authorities in Prince Albert and was never heard of around Pelican Narrows again.[9]

There was little or no real crime in Rock Cree country, and what misdemeanours there were, almost always involving home-made brew, were looked after by the priest in the community. The Indians were children, there was no doubt, in the mind of Oblate missionary Father Charlebois. He had devised a system to keep order among the "savages," which he imposed on Pelican Narrows when he arrived in 1900. He named three to six "police-men," from his congregation, who were to patrol the settlement. A strict curfew was laid down; everyone had to be in his or her own place at nine o'clock, except the policemen and the dogs. "No one had the right to roam about the camp and anyone found outside his own tent was reported to the priest who would reprimand him publicly on the following day," wrote Father J.M. Pénard, "or, on occasions when the case was serious, impose a heavier punishment." What that heavier penalty was was not described by Pénard, but he was sure the system worked at Pelican Narrows. "After the curfew, silence reigned in the camp, or perhaps one heard the singing of hymns, the recitation of the rosary, or a little pious reading from one of the tents."[10] In reality, the playing of poker and the making of homebrew went on as usual.

Over the next couple of decades, the Mounties patrolled Pelican Narrows, although seldom more than once a year. Usually only one kind of crime was committed – all alcohol was banned, particularly the homemade variety. In 1922 the Indian agent recommended that a RCMP officer should be stationed at Pelican Narrows for at least a year. "He should be a strict man, one who will not mix with them [the natives], and who will get right after them, in regard to this homebrew drinking and immorality."[11] His superiors paid no attention to his recommendation.

The priest and the manager of the HBC store told the Indian agent, on his arrival in 1924, that bootleggers had visited the hunting camps during the winter, and several Indians had been drunk. While no charges were laid, the Indian agent gave them a good lecture. "I took occasion to read to them the penalties they lay themselves open to by drinking, gambling."

The settlement's morals continued to be the major concern. In 1925 the Indian agent reported, "When landing at this place [Pelican Narrows] I found Const. Peacock of the RCMP had passed through on his way to Du Brochet. He had gathered the Indians together and had given them quite a talking-to. This meeting with the police created quite a change among these people. They needed an awakening and Const. Peacock is just the man to wake them up."[12]

Another towering figure of authority, much resented by the natives, was the justice of the peace appointed to act as a judge and overseer of the laws of the land. In 1924 Arthur Jan took on this job as a sideline to his trading business. Only months later, allegations were made against him by Father Nicholas Guilloux, who insisted that Jan intimidated and threatened the Indians and treated them harshly, using his power as justice of the peace. Emile

McCallum claimed that Jan had gone right into his house, taken his stove, and put it in his warehouse as payment for a debt that McCallum insisted he didn't owe. The agent who was ordered to investigate the case talked to not one native person, only the priest and the trader. Not surprisingly, he reported, "I am quite satisfied from what I could learn that there is nothing in the charges."[13]

On January 13, 1926, Corporal J.J. Molloy left The Pas by dogsled and arrived at Pelican Narrows five days later. He was there to set up the reserve's first RCMP detachment, a room in the Hudson's Bay Company house, which served both as Corp. Molloy's bedroom and police headquarters. The following year, six acres were leased in the southeast corner of the HBC's fifty-acre lot. There, a log building, twenty-four by twenty-eight feet, which would serve as the detachment and residence, was built, as well as a storage shed with a jail cell at one end, and a small storehouse for oil and gas.

From Pelican Narrows, Corp. Molloy and Special Constable Jewel went on extensive patrols, by dogsled and motorboat, to places like Reindeer Lake, Pukatawagan, and Stanley Mission. Their most time-consuming tasks were enrolling people on the census list, handing out beaver-trapping permits, and lecturing the Indians. "Corporal J.J. Molloy . . . has made a number of long patrols," the RCMP commissioner wrote in 1926. "During January he made one to the Upper Churchill River, in the course of which a drop in the temperature to fifty degrees below zero was welcome, as it froze the slush which had hindered travel. This patrol was marked by much good advice to Indians."[14] But arrests were few and far between. In 1927 only one person was taken into custody. She was a young girl under sixteen years of age who had done away with the dead body of her baby. She was escorted to Dauphin, Manitoba, made to stand trial, given a two-year suspended sentence, and sent home again.

In 1931 Inspector G.G.P. Montizambert arrived to inspect the Pelican Narrows depot. The HBC post journal sardonically reported his findings – "No Crime! (To be found.)" The following year, the detachment was closed down because, "there was very little work of a police nature in Pelican Narrows." Business would be much better in La Ronge, the RCMP decided.

Pelican Narrows was thereafter served from the La Ronge detachment, 150 kilometres away. Police officers often arrived by air to patrol the reserve, but there was so little crime that one sergeant suggested that even that service be suspended. On February 9 Albert Ballantyne was arrested for trapping a lynx before the season opened and was fined $5 and $3.75 in costs, and that was the major crime of the year. Perhaps the Mounties were keen to justify their existence, because they were always looking to uncover the makers of homebrew, the one crime that never went away. On July 21, 1938, the HBC journal reported, "Const. Wenzil is trying to get on the tail of some of the homebrew with which this settlement is apparently well-supplied."[15] On July 23 the Treaty Party arrived, and, after rations and money were dished out, "a good time was had by all." Except by Abraham Ballantyne and Zaccens Ballantyne. They were arrested for making and distributing homebrew. On July 25 court was held with Const. Wenzil as investigator, prosecutor, and judge. Not unexpectedly, both were convicted and sentenced to jail terms. The next day they were flown by plane to Prince Albert. The HBC post manager was indignant about the proceedings:

> The "mock" trial, for that is all it could be called, convicted two men who were undoubtedly mixed up with the brewing that went on last winter, but they were certainly not the principals. The small fry, as usual, got the sentence, while two if not more, who are still carrying on their winter "business" are not even found out. Disclosure of certain caches could scarcely have been avoided if the constable concerned had gone about it in a more reasonable manner. We are handicapped in that they are all fairly good customers of ours.[16]

When Abraham Ballantyne was released from jail a month later, he had no transportation to get back to his home at Deschambault Lake, so he decided to walk the two hundred kilometres. Fortunately, his family found out he was on his way and met him halfway with a canoe. They were surprised at how healthy he looked. "The food was great and you could eat as much as you wanted," he replied. When he next met Const. Wenzil, he told him, "I had a real good time."[17]

Philip Ratt's father, Albert, was known as a smart, capable man about town. As the HBC post journal pointed out, "With men like William Merasty, Buster Flett, and Albert Ratt in town, the men are afraid to go out and leave their wives alone for even one day." Albert's poker playing was legendary. He was in partnership with the trader Shorty Russick. Philip remembers: "Shorty would use up all his cash to pay out the trappers and then Dad would get into a poker game and win most of the money and he would give it to Shorty and Shorty would make out a cheque for my dad. . . . Shorty said one time, 'I was sleeping and I got up at seven in the morning and there's no Albert. He's still in the poker game.'"

Albert Ratt was also a violent man. He had terrible temper, which he often took out on family members. On April 10, 1939, he was tried before Constable Bain, "for beating his wife continuously throughout the winter."[18] Several witnesses were called who testified to his cruel treatment of her. He was found guilty, but was given only a reprimand, a sentence which raised eyebrows in the settlement. Obviously, in the eyes of the police, flogging one's wife was not nearly as serious as making some homemade brew in your shed.

Over the years, the main policework in the north remained focused on Indians and booze. In his 1949 report the RCMP's commissioner was shocked: "There has been a large increase in the number of infractions of the Indian Act. This year the number is 355 as compared with 290 last year. All of the infractions were connected with intoxicating liquor." Hardly statistics of a frightening crime epidemic.

Over the next three decades the population of Pelican Narrows grew and, along with more people, came more crime. In 1968 the RCMP re-established their detachment there. At first, it consisted of two rooms in the recreation centre. Then, in 1972, a transportable office-cell complex was constructed on a lot owned by the Hudson's Bay Company. (In 1977 it burnt to the ground, and a more permanent structure was built.) This was at a time when the road had just reached Pelican Narrows, and the people were not as yet very worldly. A police officer could play God if he were so inclined.

Certainly they were wild girls. Because she kept running away from residential school in Prince Albert, Darlene McKay had been sent to Pelican Narrows to stay with her grandparents. She was sixteen, and immediately linked up with her cousin Marleen, fourteen, who had also been raised in the city. They considered themselves beyond sophisticated. "I came to Pelican Narrows in 1969, but it could have been 1920, the way they dressed," says Darlene. "They didn't wear regular clothes like us. They wore dresses, old-fashioned, with scarves tied around their necks. And we had miniskirts. We shocked the priest. Everybody said, 'Oh my God, they're showing their asses in church now.' But we were young and that was the style.

"There were girls who used to envy us. I heard that just last year from my friend. She said, 'Remember when you guys were young, coming out of the store, looking so cool. You had bell-bottoms on.' And we went swimming down at the dock. We just swam in our panties, you know, what the heck, we weren't evil. I was a virgin for the longest time, until I was over sixteen.

"Marleen was the oldest in her family, she had nine brothers and sisters. She more or less had to raise them, because her mother was drinking and her dad was driving a taxi. He'd just kind of look in on his kids and leave and come in a day later, check up, are they all there: one, two, three, four . . ."

It was another cousin, Joanne, who suggested that the three-some take off. "She said, 'Come on, let's go to Thompson.' 'Thompson? What's over there?' we asked. 'Guys!' So then off we went hitchhiking. We stayed in Flin Flon one night, two nights, partying and then we hitchhiked to Thompson." The girls remained in the Manitoba mining town for about two months, until Darlene heard that her grandfather had died. They hurried back to Pelican Narrows.

It was at that point that Darlene met the RCMP corporal who had arrived to take over the reserve depot. He had ordered a pair of mukluks and mitts from Darlene's mother, who did beautiful beadwork. "He would come and check every couple of days, see how it was going. I was kind of shy of him. I didn't know anything about him at the time. 'Here comes Jack!' somebody would say, and I'd go running into the bedroom."

One night, not long afterwards, Marleen came over to Darlene's. She was dishevelled and couldn't stop crying. "She said, 'Can you keep a secret?' We were closer than anybody else, the two of us, and so I said, 'Yes, of course.' Then she told me, 'That Mountie raped me.' "

When Jack Ramsay was growing up on a farm near Biggar, Saskatchewan, he had read everything he could get hold of about the Royal Canadian Mounted Police. "As soon as I'm old enough, I'm going to join," he told anybody who would listen. In 1957 at age twenty, he graduated from the RCMP academy in Regina. Over the next seven years he was posted to seven different detachments in Manitoba towns, and he spent four months in 1958 touring as a member of the RCMP's Musical Ride. Then it was back to duties in small towns, only this time in Saskatchewan. In 1969 he was promoted to corporal just before he was sent in May to Pelican Narrows as head of the two-man detachment.

Ted Merasty, a former councillor for the Peter Ballantyne Band, remembered Corporal Ramsay well: "He struck fear into the people who he was supposed to serve and protect. His type of justice was swift, painful, and not often recorded." Chief Ron

Michel was a teenager when Ramsay was around, and he too remembered him. "He arrested me a couple of times. He was really gung-ho. He wore black gloves and used to walk around the reserve at night looking for parties. He broke up a couple of mine. He was one of those guys, 'My way is the only way.' He was the law. Nobody could touch him." When years later Chief Michel heard that Ramsay had been charged with sexual assault, he wasn't surprised at all. "I said, 'Yeah, I'm sure it happened.'"

Doug Pearson was one of the few whites who lived on the reserve at the time. He too has vivid memories of Jack Ramsay. "In the springtime, he'd wear a red plaid jack shirt, blue jeans, and he'd wear his gun and holster Matt Dillon-style tied to his leg. If he wanted information, he'd get a person alone and take him down to the bridge and stand him on a rail and say, 'Now start talking or you'll go swimming.'" About the only people who liked him were the whites working in the community – the nurses, teachers, and shop manager. "He was the finest RCMP officer and the most decent man I ever met. I would trust him with my life," insisted Abigail Nedd-Isaacs, a former nurse at Pelican Narrows.

Marleen did not tell anybody about the assault at the time, and in a newspaper opinion piece, Ted Merasty explained why. "In 1969 our people were still looking at the RCMP as men with almost godlike powers. Here in the remote northern communities these were judge, jury, and punishers." Says Darlene McKay, "Nobody would have believed us if we told about it. Because he was a cop. He was a cop."

Many years later Darlene was confided in by another friend, Susan, who said she had come close to being sexually abused by Ramsay at about the same time Marleen was. "She was fifteen at the time. She said Jack Ramsay took her to the RCMP office in the old community hall. She had a dress on – all girls wore dresses then – and he asked her, 'How come you don't go to school?' She was young, and native girls are very shy, especially back then, and she didn't say anything. He told her, 'Take off your panties. If you try running away, I'm going to shoot you in the back.' Then somebody came in and that's what saved her." She also was too frightened to speak out against the policeman.

In 1970 Corporal Ramsay was transferred out of Pelican Narrows, and the following year he quit the RCMP. In July 1972 he became a celebrity. *Maclean's* magazine's cover story was entitled "Confessions of Corporal Jack Ramsay: Shattering a Great Canadian Legend." But this was not an admission that he had sexually molested young girls, far from it. It was an indignant outcry against the strict, sometimes ridiculous, rules by which the police force was run. "Inside the RCMP: The Conscience of a Good Cop" was the headline on writer Peter C. Newman's interpretation of Ramsay's exposé. The ex-corporal's picture was on the cover: a clean-cut young man with severely short hair, his ears sticking out, his smile revealing a gap in his front teeth. It could have been a Norman Rockwell portrait of American wholesomeness. But when Darlene McKay saw the photo, all she could think of was "ugly": "I will never forget that ugly face. Look at how ugly he is. Fucking sleazy eyes. That ugly smile."

In the years that followed, Jack Ramsay remained in the spotlight. He was hired by federal Indian Affairs as the department's Alberta Ombudsman. He then worked as a consultant and private investigator for several First Nations and individual native families. He played a key role in getting the conviction of Wilson Nepoose overturned. The Alberta Cree had spent four years in jail for a crime he didn't commit. Ramsay seemed dedicated to the welfare of indigenous people, but every time Darlene saw his face on television all she could think of again was "ugly."

Ramsay's primary interest in the 1980s and 1990s was politics. He created the separatist Western Canada concept, and served as its leader for four years. His main difficulty in launching this alienation party was that the idea of separating from Canada was absurd to most people. In 1988 Ramsay joined the right-wing Reform Party, and five years later he was elected as a member of Parliament in the Crowfoot, Alberta, constituency. For several years, he was his party's outspoken, hard-edged justice critic; in the words of one commentator, he was "a firebrand speaker who fought for tougher sentences for criminals, particularly sexual predators who assaulted or raped young women."

Meanwhile, the cousins were living more mundane lives. Darlene and Marleen both married in Pelican Narrows and eventually had children. But in 1974, at age seventeen, Marleen packed her bags and took off for Alberta, leaving her husband and two kids behind. Says Darlene, "I lost track of that woman for the next seventeen years. We were so close, and then all of a sudden she vanished. I never heard from her, she never wrote me a letter, she didn't phone me. And then when my husband died in March 1992, there was a knock on the door and there she was." Darlene discovered that Marleen had completed a carpentry apprenticeship and was working as a cabinet-maker in Alberta. Before that, though, she'd led a desperate life.

After leaving her husband and her relatives in Pelican Narrows, she had ended up in Vancouver an alcoholic, a drug addict, living on the streets, working at odd jobs and supplementing her income as an occasional hooker. Abusive men dominated her life. Marleen later told a reporter, that after her run-in with Ramsay, "I was depressed all the time, suicidal, had low self-esteem, and was always afraid of authority. I would do things to forget, like abuse alcohol and drugs. But the more I tried to forget, the more I thought about it. Not a day went by that it wasn't on my mind." Finally in 1979 she moved to Edmonton, joined Alcoholics Anonymous, and discovered her native spirituality, which became extremely important to her. Then she pulled herself together and became a carpenter and a maker of scaffolds. Says Darlene, "She's tough. She's got good jobs and makes money, and she goes on vacations to Mexico with her son."

Darlene had always been close to her Aunt Catherine, who was Marleen's mother. "My auntie drove up here one day in '96. I think that she knew maybe that she was going to die, but out of the blue she mentions friggin' Jack Ramsay. She said, 'You know what? He raped me too.'" Catherine died soon after of lung cancer. At her funeral in Prince Albert, Jack Ramsay, whom others had thought of as Catherine's friend, was listed in the program as an honorary pallbearer. "And there he was, big as life," says Darlene. (Jack Ramsay has always denied he was at the funeral.) That got the cousins thinking. They looked up their friend Susan, who had told Darlene that Ramsay had threatened to shoot her in the back if she attempted to run away from his sexual advances, and the three-some talked long into the night. Marleen decided to go to the RCMP.

As part of the investigation, the police asked her if she would meet with Jack Ramsay and surreptitiously tape his conversation. The spot chosen was a Tim Hortons near Ramsay's constituency office in Camrose, Alberta. Marleen was strapped into a body pack, and a tape recorder was hidden in her gym bag. But the recording was poor, with too much clanging of dishes and people talking. That same day Marleen phoned Ramsay, and this time the conversation was properly recorded. At the end, Marleen let out a shocked laugh. "Jesus!" she exclaimed. The three policemen who were with her were aghast at what they had heard.

If the phone call had caused such a reaction, the statement given by Ramsay a month later must have been greeted with sheer incredulity. RCMP sergeant Bob Laidlaw visited the politician in his Camrose constituency office on July 15, 1998. Journalist Christie Blatchford, in her usual inimitable manner, later described the meeting:

> Mr. Ramsay began to talk, and talk, and at some point Sgt. Laidlaw suggested he take a breather, and read to him then the standard police caution about having the right to silence. He also suggested Ramsay might like to have a lawyer present.
>
> Pshaw, said Mr. Ramsay in effect, and kept on truck-ing. Several more times, Sgt. Laidlaw said, he warned him he need not say anything and impressed upon him that he had a right to call a lawyer . . . but, by God, nothing would stop Mr. Ramsay.

On August 14, 1998, more than a year after the investigation had begun, Jack Ramsay was charged with sexual assault, attempted sexual assault, and confining a person without appropriate authority. Marleen was relieved. "I've had a lot of rough spots in my life," she told a reporter. "It's time for me to do some healing. It was time for me to open up."

Few people on the reserve believed that Ramsay would be convicted. Even if he was found guilty, he wouldn't go to jail, they were sure. He was a big shot, a powerful politician, a friend of the rich and influential. It was his word against that of a native woman with a tainted background. Said Ted Merasty, "I feel I speak for many people when I state the Reform Party member from Alberta will, in all likelihood, walk out of court a free man." In a way he would be proved correct; Ramsay would not spend a night in jail.

After the charges were laid, Ramsay had resigned from the Reform Party's shadow cabinet but he retained his seat as a member of Parliament. He felt good about the support he was getting. "What that woman said was a lot of garbage," a supporter told a television interviewer. "Why would someone like Jack Ramsay want to rape an Indian girl?" "If he's guilty, I'm crazy," said another fan. A Canada-wide fundraising campaign went well; his constituency association was particularly generous, as was the anti-gun-registration crowd. "It's vital that members of the firearms community support Jack. He has been a staunch supporter for our rights," said a gun lobbyist.

The preliminary hearing was held at Pelican Narrows on February 3, 1999. Darlene arrived at the court – a.k.a. the bingo hall – with a hood covering a completely bald head. A few months before she had been diagnosed with breast cancer, and was undergoing chemotherapy. That didn't prevent her from having her say. "I was the one making the most racket. I was yelling, 'Jack Ramsay, if it's not going to happen to you, sure as hell it will happen to one of your kids, or grandkids somewhere down the line.'"

As well as the accusations outlined by Marleen, the preliminary hearing heard the evidence regarding Darlene's friend, Susan.

She claimed that she was saved just in the nick of time by someone arriving at the detachment. In this instance Ramsay was charged with attempted sexual assault and confining a person without appropriate authority. The attempted sexual assault charge was dismissed, but the judge decided that there was enough evidence for the other two charges – one count of having sexual intercourse with a female person not his wife, without her consent, (the rape charge), involving Marleen, and one count of unlawful confinement involving Susan – to proceed to trial. Since the crimes were alleged to have been committed twenty-nine years before, the 1953–54 version of the Criminal Code was used. Two years later, Justice Gene A. Smith dismissed the charge of unlawful confinement, Susan's complaint against Ramsay, on grounds of reasonable doubt. Susan admitted she might have been a year or two out in recalling the date on which the alleged offence took place.

Almost ten months later, on November 25, 1999, in the elegant yellow-brick courthouse in the prosperous farm town of Melfort, Saskatchewan, member of Parliament Jack Ramsay stood trial on the charge of raping Marleen. There to give him support was his wife, Glenna, his four children, three of his brothers, and some constituents. The Pelican Narrows people who were in attendance, including Darlene, were frustrated by the manner in which witnesses were questioned. "The judge kept saying, 'Answer yes or no.' 'Can we try to explain ourselves?' we'd ask. 'There's more to the question than yes or no.' 'Well, then,' said the judge, 'did he have his penis out? Was he circumcised?' These are the questions the judge is asking Marleen, twenty-nine years later. Who the hell is going to stop and look at his dink while they're getting raped?"

Marleen, slender and petite, with her hair coloured dark blonde and wearing little glasses – journalist Christie Blatchford called her "a dead-ringer for tennis star Martina Navratilova" – was on the witness stand for three hours. At one point, prosecutor Robin Ritter asked her why she didn't fight or try to stop Ramsay. She replied, "Do you expect a fourteen-year-old-girl to start fighting a man? A policeman?" It was that kind of question that made Darlene McKay want to stand up in court and scream, "What kind of idiot court is this?"

An important part of the evidence was the telephone conversation between Ramsay and Marleen taped by the police in August 1998. It was clear that something had gone on, for Ramsay was heard saying: "It was all my fault, it was all my fault. And, ah, you know, I want you to be very, very clear on that." He admitted he'd caused her pain, but he does not say that sexual intercourse occurred. "Ah, well, you know, when I say sex never took place, I mean penetration never took place." Marleen replies: "Oh, it did take place, believe me, I remember. . . . It hurt." Ramsay: "Okay, okay, I, you see, I don't remember it that way, because I, I realized what was happening and I just felt so ashamed about it." Marleen: "I had to keep it a secret for a long time and I . . . couldn't turn to my mother, she's an alcoholic, couldn't turn to my dad, he's abusive, so I kept it, I kept it in me all these years, you know, but, it just got to the point where I had to phone you."

Even more lethal to the defence was Ramsay's statement to Sergeant Laidlaw. He remembered Marleen being in his office. Why she was there? He wasn't sure, but he might have been questioning her as part of his investigation into a series of sexual assaults against young girls that had occurred in the area. He was trying to find out if they knew what intercourse was. So perhaps that's why he asked Marleen if she had ever had sex with anyone. She said she had, but he thought perhaps she was trying to be worldly wise, so he challenged her. "I asked her whether she would like to have sex with me. . . . It was more of a joke than anything else," he could be heard saying on the tape. But then the gag got ugly. He told Marleen that he was going to leave the office for a minute. If she wanted to have sex with him, she should unzip her pants. Sure enough, when he returned, "her top button of her slacks was undone, her zipper was undone, and I could see her, ah, panties." He became sexually aroused, approached her, "and I believe I touched her waist. At that moment, the disgusting nature of what was happening caused me to turn away and I went back behind the desk." The fault was Marleen's, he suggested: "Had she not [undone] her zipper and undone her clothing as indicating consent to have sex, it would have never happened, and that's the only thing I can add."

Marleen's version was, of course, very different. In a soft, low voice she recalled that fateful day in 1969. "There was a knock on our door and Jack Ramsay was there. My mom said he wanted to see me. He told me to go with him to the community hall. That's where he had his office. He closed the door and asked me, 'Are you a virgin?'" She replied she wasn't, because a few years before she had been raped by a junior hockey player. Ramsay said that, if she agreed to have sex with him, he'd agree not to tell her mother that she was unchaste. Marleen said she was too frightened to do anything but acquiesce to his request. He unzipped his pants – she remembered the yellow stripe of his uniform – and told her to come over to him. Then he penetrated her, standing up, leaning against the front of his desk. It hurt, she said. "It was embarrassing. It was dirty. It was humiliating."

The jury of eight men and four women deliberated for over five hours, now and then asking questions of the court. Finally, the foreman announced that a verdict had been reached. The accused was found guilty of attempted rape. Jack Ramsay's family collapsed in tears, but Ramsay himself stiffened his upper lip, "It was an inappropriate situation . . . but I do not believe it was a criminal offence of any kind." This from a man who once argued in the House of Commons for zero tolerance for sex offenders.

The following May he was sentenced to nine months in jail. Justice Ted Noble thought he was imposing a harsh sentence by sending the former MP to prison. "Retribution is clearly called for, given the accused's moral blameworthiness. His actions were a serious assault on her privacy and an attempt to invade her body. They indicated a contemptuous disregard for her dignity and her feelings." But the Pelican Narrows community were stunned by what they considered an outrageously light punishment. "Is this how we are to be treated? Is this how we are going to be dealt with by the police?" Chief Ron Michel asked. Darlene, too, was shocked: "I thought to myself, 'Is that all? Is that mother-fucking all?' But then I thought, what goes around, comes around. Sure as hell, Jack Ramsay, before you go to your grave, you are going to pay for it!"

Ramsay would remain exactly six hours in custody. The verdict was appealed on the grounds that the judge had improperly instructed the jury on matters relating to reasonable doubt and presumption of innocence. On January 24, 2001, the Saskatchewan Court of Appeal ordered another trial. Ironically, it was a victory for the Crown. The mistake was so obvious that the prosecutors agreed with the defence that the initial verdict must be overturned. But Ramsay's lawyer had gone further and argued strongly that the charge be dropped altogether. This was denied by the Court of Appeal.

Marleen agreed to testify again, although she wasn't happy about it. "I don't regret having brought it up, but I thought it was over the first time. I thought it was all over, it was finished. Now they have to bring it up again." She was reluctant because the first trial had been such a gruelling experience. The defence lawyer had questioned her credibility, insisting that years of alcohol and drug abuse, including heroin, had fried her brain, destroyed her memory. How could she remember events that occurred so long ago? She knew she would be attacked again, but, as she told a friend, she didn't care. She wanted the second trial to go ahead. "Marleen is the strongest woman I've ever met," commented the prosecutor, Robin Ritter.

In May 2001, Ramsay's lawyer, Morris Bodnar, announced that Marleen's sister would provide evidence that would prove the attempted rape never took place. "She's dropped a real bombshell," exclaimed an excited Jack Ramsay. "Thank goodness the sister has come forward. At least now there's corroborating evidence of my story." Bodnar demanded that the case against his client be dropped immediately, and that police investigate the possibility of laying charges of perjury against Marleen. But Marleen claimed her sister was an unreliable and vindictive alcoholic who was also mentally ill. "We haven't been in contact for a long time. This is a woman who ran over my two-year-old with a Ski-Doo. I wouldn't pay too much attention to what she says, especially as she was only eight years old at the time I ran into Ramsay."

Ramsay's second trial on attempted sexual assault was scheduled to begin October 16, 2001. The Ramsay family, the friends and supporters of Marleen, and the media gathered once again in the Melfort courthouse. They were in for a surprise – a last-minute plea bargain had been struck. The prosecutor and defence lawyers jointly submitted a deal whereby Ramsay would plead guilty to the lesser charge of indecent assault. He would be given a one-year suspended sentence and perform 120 hours of community service in Camrose, where he lived. The maximum sentence for the offence under the 1969 Criminal Code (which applied in this case because it happened in that year) was five years in prison.

By that time everybody was pretty worn out by the whole affair. Marleen, particularly, seemed to have mellowed. "I don't know what jail does for a person," she said. "I'm hoping he'll get some help for himself. . . . I've done my part and the justice system had done their part. It's good enough." Even Darlene was somewhat philosophical. When asked if justice was done, she hesitated. "No! Like, I don't know. When a guy rapes a young girl, nothing is right, ever. You end up hating the rest of the cops because of one asshole."

It's hard to see how there can be a reconciliation between police enforcement and the people of Pelican Narrows; their philosophies are so far apart. The police seem unable to comprehend the traditions of the Woods Cree, unable to be in sympathy with their painful emergence into the white world. On the other hand, in the violence that erupts on the reserve, almost all because of drunkenness, the police do protect one citizen from another. "This place would be a zoo without them," says Gordon Peter. Maybe the answer is a Pelican Narrows police force with Indian officers. It's worked with educators and social workers on the reserve, almost all of whom are now native. This will require overcoming the aversion the aboriginal population has about meddling in another's business. And it isn't just the enforcement arm of the legal system about which the citizens of Pelican Narrows are leery. When the very person who is paid to protect their interests, who swears devotion to justice, can turn into a devilish tempter, who is there left to trust?

THE LEECHES

In the morning before the guides set out
with their paying parties to the fishing grounds
the parasites ready their own boats and depart,
but only to nearby bays and coves where they
will anchor, pretend to fish, and wait . . .
then they will weigh anchor and pursue,
strung out behind a guide's party of boats
and shameless as lampreys attach themselves
to the guides and the fish – free.

But some Crees are not without a love of sport
and when one sees the string behind him grow
a faint grin breaks like a wave on his face
and he initiates a series of maneuvers
through reefs and shallows, loops like a wolverine
and leaves behind an unreeling of curses,
damaged propellers and broken shafts.

. . . . .

Glen Sorestad
Jan Lake Poems

8

TRANSGRESSION

PĀSTĀHOWIN

Although Gordon Peter doesn't like to talk about it, one of his relatives had the dubious honour of being Michael Bomek's most beloved. The lawyer carried a photograph of Daniel[*] in his wallet and would show it to anybody who was interested. "Isn't he cute as a button?" Bomek would ask. "He looks like he's fifteen."

In fact Daniel was twenty-six years old and a father of six children, three of whom are looked after by his parents, and three by his common-law wife's mother and father. He is one of Pelican Narrows's lost generation, a school dropout, who drinks too much and smokes marijuana for "breakfast, lunch, and supper." But he has a sweet personality and he's good-looking, slender with thick black hair and refined features. "Fabulous eyelashes," as Bomek liked to say. "Daniel provided me with such absolute joy. We did so much together. We'd leave the car down a railway track on a mining road, walk, find a spot, park the blanket, have some lunch, lay on our backs, and watch the jet stream go by." What the young man saw in the fifty-something portly lawyer is hard to say.

---

[*] By court order correct names cannot be used.

Perhaps it was his lovely house right on Lake Athapapuskow, his supply of liquor, his home-entertainment centre. Probably it was more than that – the thrill of sleeping with a white guy who had so much power and money, a guy who was a somebody.

The downfall of this aggressive and effective lawyer who worked for ten years in the north serving the native population is important to Pelican Narrows's history if only because his tale can be seen as a microcosm, a case study of white-Cree relations over the years. Once again a white man in authority, who had something valuable to offer, has instead transgressed. Bomek must now join the long line of fur traders, missionaries, teachers, judges, social workers, police officers, bureaucrats, and politicians who imposed their will on the Rock Cree and did incalculable damage in the process. Yet, his is not a simple, black-and-white story.

James Michael David Bomek, the eldest son in an Orthodox Jewish family, was brought up in the prairie city of Brandon, Manitoba. His parents were hard-working immigrants from Russia. His almost-illiterate father was employed by the city as a labourer all his working life. He was a meticulous man in everything he did. "He taught me a lot," Bomek says. His mother was better educated; she had completed Grade 9 and could read and write. She remained at home looking after the three children.

Even as a kid, Michael loved being the centre of attention; he was loquacious and outgoing. Partly because of his quick mind, partly because of his ability to "work the system," he was very good at school and thought it lots of fun. But the family had little money, so, after he graduated from Grade 12, he got a job in the food industry.

By the time he was twenty-six he was the president and manager of two companies, Bomek Investments Ltd. and Dynamic Foods Limited, which ran Dauphin Pizzeria near Riding Mountain National Park in Manitoba. Something happened at this point, though, which illustrated, as a psychologist would later report, that he was the type of person who would violate positions of trust.

In 1977 he borrowed $395,000 from the Dauphin Plains Credit Union to cover an existing loan, as well as to finance the construction of a restaurant at Clear Lake, Manitoba, and to cover operating expenses. In just a few months he was forty thousand dollars overdrawn on his operating account, and the credit union demanded five thousand dollars a month in repayment, a sum he could hardly manage. At that point he asked his parents for a twenty-five thousand dollar loan. When they told him they didn't have that kind of money, he suggested that they mortgage their modest house in Brandon, the only asset Mr. and Mrs. Bomek possessed. He did not mention that he was in financial trouble, only that "he had a lot of money but couldn't put his hands on it." He promised that he'd make the mortgage payments each month. The Bomeks agreed to their son's request and signed the papers without reading them or seeking legal advice. "It was Jim we were signing for, and he was our son and we had no reason to discuss with him, so we just didn't bother." A year later both of Bomek's companies went bankrupt. He was able to make only two $250 mortgage payments, and his parents had to come up with $3,600 so as not to lose their home. In 1982 Mr. and Mrs. Bomek sued their son, and later the credit union, claiming they didn't realize what they were doing in signing the mortgage papers. Fortunately for the elder Bomeks, the Court of Queen's Bench and the Manitoba Court of Appeal agreed with them. The mortgage was set aside. Both Bomek and the credit union were ordered to pay Mr. and Mrs. Bomek's legal expenses.[1]

By then Michael must have realized that he didn't have the makings of a capitalist, for in 1978 he had returned to school. He was already thirty-two years old when he graduated with a Bachelor of Arts degree from the University of Manitoba in Winnipeg, and he was thirty-six when he was called to the Manitoba bar in June 1985. Two years later he moved to Flin Flon.

The mining town perched atop volcanic rock is a bustling place with a young, affluent population of 6,500. The city was named after Josiah Flintabbatey Flonatin, a character from a paperback novel *The Sunless City*, which prospector Tom Creighton and his companions had found on the trail while hunting for gold. Al Capp of "Lil Abner" fame dreamed up the visual image of the character. A huge statue of Flinty used to sit high on a cliff, dominating the city, but the citizens decided that this was a bit childish and moved him to a park. He's an appropriate mascot, a short, fat, balding white prospector wearing round glasses. For years the role of David Collins, the Cree trapper who actually found the copper-zinc ore body that became the city's *raison d'être*, was not acknowledged. Indeed, there is very little about this city that reflects the people who resided on the land thousands of years before Flinty showed up.

The Pelican Narrows population have never felt comfortable in Flin Flon. It's where many got their first taste of hard-core bigotry. "If you walked into a jewellery store, the owner looked at you as though you were going to rob the place," said Josephine Morin. "If you went into a restaurant, you could stand there for hours before you'd be seated. When you were going along the street, somebody would say Dirty Squaw, or something awful like that." But it was more than snubs that frightened the Indians. Philip Ratt, in a 1979 interview, explained: "There's a gang of six or seven of them. The native people call them the 'Channing Boys.' I think they live somewhere in Channing [adjacent to Flin Flon], and they have a knack for ganging up on Indian boys, particularly when they notice a boy is under the influence of alcohol. They gang up on him and beat him, the police force don't usually show up until after it's over, until the white boys make their getaway."

The Flin Flon police, in fact, added to the natives' fear of the place. Philip's brother Horace found out first-hand how violent they could be. One day in 1979, he and a friend, Rob Merasty, were approached by a couple of cops on the street. One of them punched Horace in the face, "for doing nothing." When he tried to defend himself by grabbing hold of the officer's shirt, they were both taken to the police station. There, Horace recalled, "They took all our clothes off. Then four of them grabbed me and the other one was pounding me." Finally, they handcuffed the two Indians and threw them in the cell for the night. No charges were ever laid. Horace thinks that someone saw what had taken place and volunteered to act as a witness.[2]

Michael Bomek, on the other hand, thrived in Flin Flon. He eventually opened his own law office, employing a half-dozen or so people, dealing with everything from family law to bankruptcies. What he enjoyed the most, though, were his criminal cases. He travelled all the time, to courts in Thompson, Lynn Lake, Lac Brochet, Cross Lake, and Norway House in Manitoba, and Pelican Narrows, Sandy Bay, and Southend in Saskatchewan.

He was prescient in setting up shop when he did. The crime business began to boom. More and more indigenous people were being charged and thrown in jail; by 1999 they made up 8 per cent of the Saskatchewan population yet comprised a huge 76 per cent of inmates in prisons. On top of that, justice-department funds were cut back, so that legal-aid lawyers found themselves with heavier and heavier client loads. "In Pelican Narrows, for example," says Bomek, "they had so many files that they couldn't possibly do justice to them." There was more and more pressure on the accused to plead guilty, saving the province time and money. "I found with my native clients that so often they would sit with the policeman, and the policeman would put the words in their mouth that he wanted on the statement. And native people are invariably shy, so they'd agree simply to get the matter over with." Bomek says that many of the legal-aid lawyers would not challenge these statements. "What you heard so often in court was, 'Oh, just enter a guilty plea. Nothing's going to happen to you today. You're not going to go to jail so get it over with.' But by the second or third offence, things started to get serious, because you would be sentenced to a prison term. Then you wanted a private lawyer who would give your case some attention. . . . I remember this police officer screaming at me, after court, 'How did you get that fucking cocksucker off? You know damn well he's guilty. You saw the pictures. How in good conscience . . . ? What kind of person are you, you goddamned Indian lover?' I'd reply, 'If this was St. Catharines, Ontario, would you be saying that to me? Everyone is entitled to a defence.' That'd make him even angrier. 'Oh, you're just an Indian-lover. You make so much money off these people. You don't care about them at all.'"

As private lawyers go, Bomek wasn't that expensive, but often it was hard for the accused to come up with even the minimum amount. "Everybody, all their friends and relatives, would dig deep into their pockets and suddenly there would be three hundred dollars," Bomek explained. He had one rule: if someone didn't pay him, he wouldn't represent them the next time they were in trouble.

By mid-1990s the realization that filling the jail with aboriginal people wasn't accomplishing much dawned on Canadians. Reforms were implemented, and one of these was to set up a Cree-language court at Pelican Narrows. It was headed by Judge Gerry Morin, a Cree Métis who had been brought up in Cumberland House and whose first language was Cree. He had left a thriving law practice in Prince Albert – he had been the Peter Ballantyne Band's solicitor during the Treaty Land Entitlement negotiations – because he thought a Cree court was such a good idea. "You've got to have a little more respect for the language than just pulling somebody off the street to be a translator. . . . Part of having a Cree court is being able to explain yourself in a way that is meaningful, that is understood. 'This is how I am. This is where I'm coming from. This is what I'm doing.'"

The prosecutor, former Mountie Don Bird, had been brought up on his grandfather's trapline near La Ronge, and he too is fluent in the language. The only one who couldn't speak Cree was arguably the most important person in court – defence counsel. Fran Atkinson occasionally acts as a defence lawyer in Pelican Narrows. She says, "We needed something, but I'm not sure the Cree court was it." Adds Bomek, "If I had a trial, I would have to use one of the court clerks, who would whisper in my ear what was being said. It made cross-examination very, very difficult and cumbersome." If someone is found guilty or pleads guilty, Judge Morin often gives that person a lecture in Cree. He says, "I explain a lot of things when I'm talking Cree to people, I'm always saying *kinistōtahin*, which means, 'Do you understand me?' I'm also talking to the rest of the people sitting behind [in the court room]." The problem is the defence counsel can't understand a word of it. Says Bomek, "What it ended up being was one man's ego blown out of proportion." Elvena Pearson, who worked as a court clerk and justice of the peace, says, "The answer is not more judges, lawyers, or JPs who are Cree-speaking, that's not the answer. I think they [the offenders] need treatment centres. Learn how to set snares, how to cook a rabbit, how to skin a moose, sweat lodges, all those traditional values that are missing. Would it work? I don't know but it's worth a try, but nobody wants to try it. . . . The police keep asking me to come back as JP. 'We need you,' they say. Well, I'm sorry, I don't want to be part of a system that is not working any more and myself, healing inside spiritually, I don't see it as part of the medicine wheel, slamming someone in jail."

August 15, 2002: It's a nice day, so people amble about outside, waiting for the judge to arrive. A big fellow wears a black shirt which taunts: "I DID *NOT* ESCAPE. THEY GAVE ME A DAY PASS." On one side of the building is located the community hall, which serves both as bingo parlour and courtroom – when a trial runs too long, the bingo players bang on the door to be let in – and on the other side is the village office. All the windows have bars or are covered with wire mesh, which is why it seems such a dismal place. The railing on the stairs has mostly fallen away, and the floor of the entranceway has a gaping hole in it. How someone hasn't broken their leg is a wonder. On the outside wall of the village office, in bright blue paint, is scribbled "FUCK" in huge letters; on the community-hall side, there's a smaller "Fuck" painted in the same painful blue. Piles of garbage and rubble are scattered around. Why the band doesn't cough up the money to clean the place remains a mystery.

The interior is not much better. The walls are streaked and need a paint job, the grey-white floor has tiles missing. An old, faded red Christmas decoration hangs from the Exit sign, which has not lit up in years. The smell of cigarettes, smoked during frantic rounds of bingo, hangs in the air. A steel door right near the judge's chair opens onto the "executive washroom," a small space with toilet, sink, and one chair. This is the defence lawyer's consultation room, where he or she discusses a client's case – often for the first time. The lawyer sits on the toilet, the client on the chair, or the other way around.

The first group of accused file in. Since they are being held in custody, all are handcuffed and shackled, looking haggard from lack of sleep. There's a boy who looks nine but is fourteen, so skinny the shackles clank and clang around his ankles. The captives sit in chairs directly behind the prosecutor, which, he admits, makes him very nervous. Quietly, a toddler escapes from his stroller and runs towards his father. Despite his fetters, the man lifts the child to his knee and kisses him. Another young prisoner, wearing a red Indian Posse bandana, sits and smooches with his girl, who is about seven months pregnant. She is oblivious to his chains. Another shackled captive explains that he is trying to get back into school: the judge listens as he munches on an apple. An attractive young woman is called to the witness stand, which consists of a rickety chair. She wobbles, obviously inexperienced at walking with her legs chained. The court is told that, under the influence of alcohol, she stabbed her husband twice. The wounds were not life-threatening. She has a history of depression – twice she has tried seriously to commit suicide – and no previous record. She is given a suspended sentence, and ordered to attend an alcohol treatment centre. The RCMP officer undoes her handcuffs and shackles and she joins the crowd in the back of the courtroom. It seems she was not Hannibal Lecter after all.

Elvena Pearson worked as a court clerk for fourteen years, involved in what she calls "the sausage factory." She despairs of the justice system ever improving for the native person. "When I worked for that judge, he was making $125,000 a year and I, as a clerk, was making $2,100 a month. That's a lot of money fifteen years ago. I can't imagine what they're making now. Pardon my English, but they don't give a shit if they fix the system because they're all getting wealthy on it. They don't care about the individual . . . Pelican Narrows is a big community but there's nothing here to help the people. Why?"

The day rolls along, as the sorrowful chorus moans on. Assault, assault causing bodily harm, sexual assault, sexual assault with a weapon, public mischief, break-and-enter. One man is charged with failing to check his gill nets once every forty-eight hours and he pleads not guilty. This is the only alleged crime that does not stem from drunkenness. Crown prosecutor Don Bird puts it bluntly, "If there was no alcohol problem at Pelican Narrows, we wouldn't have a job." Here, more than anywhere, it's obvious that alcoholism is a sickness that stems from a great bruising of the soul. Yet it's important to remember that only a minority of the Pelican Narrows population ever appears in court. As Judge Morin says, "If I say that there's 40 per cent that I'm seeing go around and around, that tells me that there's 60 per cent out there that I'll never see. If we're seeing 30 per cent of young offenders, that's 70 per cent that are doing great."

This was the environment in which Michael Bomek defended his clients, and most often he was successful. Not only was his law practice flourishing, but he was a popular man about town – it was not uncommon to read about his activities in Flin Flon's *The Reminder*. He was a member of just about everything: Lodge 153 of the Masons (where he served as Master), North of 60 Shrine Club (Circus Daddy Club), Flin Flon Chamber of Commerce, the Downtown Businessmen's Association, the Arts Council, and the crime-prevention committee. He served on the board of the Woman's Safe Haven Resource Centre and helped establish the

Northern Neighbours Foundation, a charity, of which he was chairperson. He took over command of the local army cadet corps which was on the verge of collapsing, and made it popular again. He donated land to the City of Flin Flon for a park on Main Street. He gave free workshops on wills and estates, buying and selling your home, and divorce and property law at the local library. He played Santa at the food bank's annual Christmas dinner. And he was the popular and funny emcee at the annual Mother's Day brunch at the Miniquay Hotel in Jan Lake. Wrote Arni Goodman, a lawyer working in his office, "If someone was down and out, Michael would find some work for them at his house or fixing something at the office to help get them back on their feet. Who knows how many he helped."

Yet under the shiny patina of success, Bomek was hitting some big bumps, primarily because of his lack of acumen as a businessman. At least three times he was disciplined by the Manitoba Law Society.

In November 1991, Bomek was hired to act for the City of Flin Flon in collecting monies owed by a Mr. and Mrs. D. Bomek didn't do much, and an in-house lawyer for the city took over the case. Mr. and Mrs. D were then eager to retain Bomek, but, of course, since he knew every detail of the case, he had a conflict of interest. He went ahead and prepared a Statement of Defence for the Ds anyway. He pleaded guilty to breach of duty to avoid conflict of interest, and was fined three thousand dollars and costs of five hundred dollars.[3]

On March 16, 1992, he was acting for clients who intended to purchase a business in Flin Flon. He told the vendors that he had a cheque for $53,000 that would be handed over on the day of sale. What he didn't reveal was that his client's cheque was subject to certain conditions that could not possibly be met by the closing date, or perhaps at all. Bomek was found guilty of breach of "candour, honesty, and integrity." He was fined $2,500 and costs of $5,000.[4]

In 2002 Bomek acted for five clients on estate matters. In each case he withdrew money from trust accounts for the payment of his fees and disbursements prior to performing the legal service for which he was retained. In one case, he billed a widow for $5,000 dollars, long before he actually did something about an insurance claim that she depended on for her livelihood. Bomek pleaded guilty to eight counts of professional misconduct and was fined $10,000, plus $15,000 in costs.[5]

The last of these offences signalled that he was in trouble financially. He had expanded his practice too quickly and he had invested in a Mexican vacation spa that had collapsed. Not only did he lose money, but so did many of his friends and clients in Flin Flon.

But there was another, darker cloud hanging over Bomek – the breakdown of his second marriage and his hidden sexual orientation. Bomek's sex life began at age fourteen when he had both his first heterosexual and homosexual encounters. After that he was intimate with both men and women. He finally married in 1975, because he wanted to have children (and he does have two grown-up daughters). He continued his homosexual activities after his marriage at a time when he was living in Winnipeg. "I'm not a predator," he insists. "I get my jollies otherwise, for example at gay clubs in Winnipeg . . . I don't prey on children or non-consenting adults." By the time he moved to Flin Flon, he and his wife had divorced. He married again, this time to a schoolteacher, and the two of them built a home at Bakers Narrows, right on Athapapuskow Lake, twenty kilometres south of Flin Flon. But in 2001, she moved next door, literally, and that marriage was over. It was a lonely time for Bomek, so when he ran into Daniel he was eager for a relationship.

Michael first met Daniel in prison, after the younger man had been sentenced to nine months for assaulting his common-law wife. Daniel claimed that she had come into his bedroom while he was sleeping and hit him on the head with a cup to wake him up.

He was so angry, he picked up the cup and threw it back at her. "I would never have allowed him to plead guilty," insists Bomek, "but the police had put pressure on his legal-aid lawyer. 'Oh, plead him guilty, plead him guilty. Get it over with.' His mother phoned me and said, 'My son's in jail. Is there anything you can do to shorten his sentence? We don't want legal aid any more. They're not doing a good job.'" Bomek went to the Pelican Narrows RCMP depot to pick up Daniel's pre-sentence report, and, as was his habit, he went into the cells to visit. One fellow he knew well was sleeping, and Bomek went over and sat on him as a joke. Everybody laughed. "I said, 'Which one of you is Daniel?' And this young guy replied, 'I am.'"

'Your mom says you have six kids. You look like you're barely out of puberty.'

'I have six kids, I do.' And pulling up his shirt, added, 'Look, I've got hair on my chest.' He pointed to what he later told me was his treasure trail, a little bit of fluff from his navel to his pubic hairs. I went over and tweaked it and said, 'Holy Cow, I still don't believe you have six kids.' Then Daniel gave me the report, and I left."

The next morning Bomek returned to the police depot and began to go over Daniel's statement. "'Did you really say this?' I kept asking. Suddenly he grabbed me at the back of my head and he kissed me. I jumped up from my chair because it spooked me. He stood up and grabbed the back of my neck and kissed me again. 'Would you help me out?' he said. 'Get me out jail? We could get together afterwards.' I thought, Well he's of age.

"When he got out of prison, he didn't go back to Pelican first. He didn't go back to his kids, or his common-law, or his parents. He came to Flin Flon. He came to my house. For almost two years, Daniel came to my house at least once a week. Sometimes he would come four times a week. We had a tremendous relationship. I can honestly say he's the only man I've ever loved, and I think it was mutual."

While he was still in prison, Daniel told his two cellmates that he thought his lawyer was gay. A police constable overheard him and demanded, "What do you mean your lawyer is gay? Did you promise him something in exchange for legal services? Are you paying him?" A nervous Daniel blurted out, "No, I'm not," because it was his mother who had hired and paid the lawyer. After that relations between Bomek and the RCMP deteriorated rapidly.

"When I first started practising in Pelican Narrows – and I practised there for ten years – I would go to the police station, ring the bell in the back, and they'd let me in. I'd get the key and I would go to the cells, open them, close the door with the key in my hand, and sit down and talk to my client, very relaxed. Then it seemed that my welcome at the police station got less and less. Suddenly I was only allowed into the interview room at the back. Then that stopped, and I was expected to interview through a thick glass partition with a hole about the size of a cup. I would have no part of that."

It was a tradition of Bomek's to bring a dozen doughnuts and mugs full of coffee to the police on court days. One day at the depot he happened to be using a letter opener with his firm's name printed on it. One of the staff said, "Oh, can I have one? Those are neat." Bomek said sure, and the next time he arrived with a bunch of letter openers. "The staff sergeant came into the coffee room and he threw one at me. 'Keep this,' he yelled at me. 'I don't want your goddamned charity. I don't want you distributing stuff in here. I don't want you coming into the police station except to do interviews with your clients.'

"After that I started being very difficult. If there were six or seven people in custody, I would take the whole day and interview them at the community hall/courthouse. So any matter scheduled that day for trial got set over to another day. Those in custody got priority, so it was very easy for me to tie up the court system. And I did that. We had to have special sittings. I set everything down for trial which means a lot of work for the police, and I was taxing their staff. And I think I got a little cocky, because I was victorious. The cockier I got, the more difficult they got. The more difficult they got, the more difficult I got."

Bomek was shocked, however, to find that the RCMP were taking their pique out on his clients. "I discovered that they were serving them green bologna sandwiches that they had bought off the food truck. They were returned because they were stale-dated. This is what the RCMP were buying and freezing and then reheating. . . . My clients weren't allowed to have blankets. The police said, 'You sleep in your clothes anyway. Why would you want a blanket?' They couldn't shower. Their liberties were curtailed. They were treated like second- and third-class citizens." Bomek finally contacted a deputy commissioner in the RCMP whom he had met. This officer gave him a number to phone in Ottawa. Suddenly hot breakfasts and dinners were being served to everybody in Pelican Narrows's holding cells.

All the while, the RCMP were trying to dig up dirt on Bomek, and he was giving them plenty of opportunity. Rumours spread like wildfire that he was gay. "Guys would call me up, 'I hear that you're gay? Well, I think I am too, but I've never tried it. If I come to Flin Flon, can I come to your house?' And I'd say, 'Sure. Why not?' And that's how it all started."

Quickly, though, things got out of hand. "Everybody wanted to try me. I was a white guy. I lived in a big house, I was a really good cook . . . I started getting phone calls from young guys who would say, 'Listen, if you get me out of jail, I'll give you the best blow job you've ever had.' I wasn't interested in that. I wasn't interested in getting paid. I started to get teased, I started to get taken advantage of, and I didn't like it. So I decided I was going to take a year off. But then my arrest intervened."

Ironically, the police got their first evidence on which they could lay a charge, not from one of Bomek's "guys" but from a woman. In March 2001, she was supposed to testify against her boyfriend, who had allegedly assaulted her and who was Bomek's client. She decided not to proceed with the charges, because she wanted the two of them to work things out. She wanted her boyfriend to get counselling and to understand the seriousness of abusing her, and she wanted to tell the judge this. Bomek advised her that, during the trial, she should insist that she couldn't remember anything. "If you say that," Bomek told her, "the Court can't touch you and will have to leave you alone." He told her that he couldn't tell her how to testify, but, he said (at least three times), "I'm telling you to tell the judge you don't remember anything." The police didn't lay the charge right away. They were looking for stronger stuff.

Over a couple of months the RCMP contacted every male client of Bomek's, asking them if the lawyer had ever made sexual advances or traded sex for money. A poster was pinned up on the band office bulletin board with his picture, asking anyone with information about him to contact the RCMP. "It said something like, If you ever had any dealings with him, and you have anything bad to say about him, jump on the bandwagon," says Bomek. "And a couple of guys did. Made up ludicrous stories, thinking that they were going to sue me and get some money. Cause I was reputed to be rich and famous." Eventually forty-one charges were laid. Daniel was one of the people who laid a complaint.

After his arrest on these charges on September 17, 2002, Michael Bomek was incarcerated in the Prince Albert penitentiary. He did not ask for bail, realizing that, if he was found guilty, the period spent in jail before his trial would count as double-time. "I remember writing in my notes that there were six guys in the yard that'd been in my house, in my bed. A couple would talk to me. The rest would say, 'Pretend you don't know me. Pretend you don't know me.' They were scared I might say something. Of course, I never would." Eventually, he was assigned to the carpentry shop, which he quite liked. He wrote a friend, "Would you believe I'm doing finishing work on cabinets for the RCMP. Only I would have such luck."

He contacted his friends asking them to send letters of support to the Court, and letters flooded in. "I remember with fondness and much gratitude your caring support and legal expertise when my daughter landed in trouble." "During my time as a member of the municipal council, six years as mayor [of Flin Flon], I can vouch that Michael was very involved in our community. Many of his ideas and efforts have become mainstays of community life." "I have not spoken to Michael since he was removed from Flin Flon, but like many who knew him we are shocked by the charges and are keeping him in our prayers. I have not walked in his shoes, therefore I can only support him. A note to Michael: Remember you are great because God doesn't make junk." "He has been generous in his assistance concerning personal matters. His conduct was professional." "I have not but the best to say about him. He was a gentleman in every way of the word." "He was a very clean man and did a lot for the community." "Michael has been my opposing lawyer in a divorce with my ex-husband and my own present husband's opposing lawyer in his divorce case. He most certainly goes to great lengths to help his clients to win their case, and I would rather have him as my lawyer than as an opposing lawyer." "When he was walking down the street, he always had a big smile and was always ready to stop and visit." "I think he is a very nice and good person. . . . He helped me on a couple of occasions in his profession and was of great help." "There was [sic] never any inappropriate comments or impolite behaviour displayed towards our teenaged sons or ourselves." "Being a lawyer you make a lot of enemies. I feel that he has been set up."

It was presumed by these letter writers and other supporters that he would plead not guilty at this preliminary hearing. Bomek's lawyer hired a private investigator, who discovered that several of the forty-one charges were made under duress and would likely be discredited during a trial. "I was so gung-ho to go to trial, because I knew that 95 per cent of them [the witnesses] would never show up in court. And those that came to court were going to get amnesia." The Bomek team was gearing up to fight when a near-tragedy intervened. Daniel attempted suicide. He was rushed to Flin Flon and then flown by air ambulance to Saskatoon. "He was in a coma. It was nip and tuck as to whether he was going to make it or not," says a friend. The idea that he would have to stand up in court and tell the world about his intimate relationship with

Michael Bomek sent him into a spiral of despair, for, if there is one thing that is taboo in Woods Cree society, it is homosexuality. Daniel told his former lover, "I couldn't face having to tell the court that you didn't make me come to your house, that I came on my own." Bomek could see those who did testify would be destroyed while they gave evidence and during cross-examination. He didn't want any more suicide attempts, and neither did the Crown. A deal was struck.

On July 14, 2003, none other than Chief Justice W.F. Gerein of the Court of Queen's Bench heard the disturbing details of eight of the forty-one charges against Bomek. The prosecutor, Dennis Cann, read through the list in a bored monotone. At one point he described how Bomek had asked a "traditional type" man from Sandy Bay, who could hardly speak a word of English, "Can I suck you off?" At that point the impartial expression of the judge changed. He stared at Cann intently, raising his hand to his mouth in thinly disguised shock. It seemed as though he were trying not to shake his head. Bomek was equally affected; with each charge described, he slouched a little more. The sunny blonde court clerk showed the most emotion. She was horrified.

Bomek pleaded guilty to eight counts – a mixed bag of obstructing justice, sexual assault, engaging in prostitution. He was sentenced to three and half years in prison, but, since he had already served ten months awaiting trial, this was reduced to two years less a day. He served one-sixth of his sentence, and was released in November 2003. As part of his sentencing, he promised never to practise law again. He'd been disbarred in Saskatchewan and Manitoba anyway. Elvena Pearson states clearly what most people in Pelican Narrows thought of the sentence: "It seems like they're favouring him because he's a lawyer and he's got money. That's not fair, not at all, in my opinion. The bugger should still be in jail. He should be in the pen somewhere. He deserves it for all the hurt he caused those people, men and women."

At the hearing, Michael Bomek offered this interpretation of his wrongdoing: "I recognize that I crossed the line, that I never should have invited people into my house . . . I forgot that, just because it's nine-thirty at night and the doorbell rings and someone comes to my door, that he's a client, that even though my lifestyle continues that my duty as a solicitor must continue as well. . . . But I failed to see that, my Lord. I guess I was so interested and so happy someone rang my bell, it was a lonely time for me." Chief Justice W.F. Gerein didn't show much sympathy. "What you have done is heinous and reprehensible in the extreme. You were given a great opportunity, a great blessing, a great gift. You were given an opportunity to be a member of what I consider to be the most noble profession. . . . You have brought the profession into some disrepute. You've brought the administration of justice into some disrepute."

For a long time Gordon Peter Ballantyne couldn't believe that Michael Bomek had done what he was accused of doing. He was sure the lawyer was the dupe of people who wanted to get even for some reason, or who didn't want to pay the money they owed him. (Interestingly, Bomek insists he never exchanged his legal services for sexual favours; even Daniel, or at least his mother, was presented with a bill, he says.) It was as though Gordon Peter couldn't acknowledge what had gone on with Bomek and the young men of Pelican Narrows. Perhaps it was seen as another threat to his own children. They are walking such a thin tightrope as it is. On the one side is the abyss of violence and alcoholism, on the other the traditional Cree virtues of generosity and co-operation, which he is trying so hard to instill in them. His twenty-three-year-old daughter, Vanessa, was clever at school but she dropped out of Grade 11 when she became pregnant. After having a second child, and, after years of staying home looking after them, she now wants to party. She sometimes disappears for days at a time, leaving Gordon Peter and Susan to look after her boys. The good news is that she is enrolled in Woodlands College, hoping to complete her Grade 12 next year. Peter Junior, his eldest son, has graduated from high school and now must get up the courage to leave the reserve for a post-secondary education. The sweet and handsome Ronald dropped out of school this year. He spends his time babysitting various people's children and helping around the house. The little girl he fathered came to visit the Ballantynes at Easter, and Gordon Peter was beside himself with joy. The third boy, Scott, is in Grade 9, but he's been having a hard time with the gangs that roam the reserve, and has been beaten up on occasion. Gordon Peter says Scott's often afraid to go to school, but he knows that he must. Melissa is doing the best she can in school, but she too upsets her dad, especially since he found her drinking beer one day.

Gordon Peter loves the reserve, the magnificent scenery, the friends and relatives whom he greets everywhere he goes, his work as a construction foreman – even if it does only pay fourteen dollars an hour. He tries to harness his despair at the drinking and violence that goes on, although sometimes it's hard. In April 2004 his cousin who lives nearby was stabbed to death, and his common-law wife charged. Two days later, a house nearby burnt to the ground at one-thirty in the morning. Philip Ratt's third daughter – "the pretty one, the one who looked like her mother" – perished.

Gordon Peter is also disturbed at the crony politics that inflict his band. At the lack of ambition and entrepreneurship. At the lack of any kind of economic opportunity. And even though he doesn't believe things will get better any time soon, he still nurtures the hope that his life, and his children's, will somehow become as rich and rewarding as that of the old hunter and fur trapper his great-grandfather, Chief Peter Ballantyne.

ENDNOTES

CHAPTER 1

1 Fisher, Anthony D. "The Cree of Canada: Some Ecological and Evolutionary Considerations." In Bruce Cox, ed., *Cultural Ecology: Readings on the Canadian Indians and Eskimos*, McClelland & Stewart, 1973.

2 Meyer, David. "The Prehistory of Northern Saskatchewan." In Henry T. Epp and Ian Dyck, eds., *Tracking Ancient Hunters: Prehistoric Archaeology in Saskatchewan*, Saskatchewan Archaeological Society, 1983.

3 Boldt, Menno, and J. Anthony Long. "Tribal Traditions and European-Western Political Ideologies: The Dilemma of Canada's Native Indians." *Canadian Journal of Political Science* 17 (3): 1984, p. 541.

4 Kemp, H.S.M. *Northern Trader*, Jarrolds London, 1957, p. 101.

5 Rossignol, Marius. "Property Concepts among the Cree of the Rocks." *Primitive Man* 12 (3): 1939, p. 96.

6 Ibid., p. 69.

7 HBCA. Cumberland District Reports, 1815 to 1827–28, B.49/E/1.

8 Ridington, Robin. "Technology, world view, and adaptive strategy in a northern hunting society." *The Canadian Review of Sociology and Anthropology* February 1982, pp. 469–481.

9 Interview. University of Saskatchewan Archives, papers of R.G. Williamson MG 216: Box 26-L12-2.

10 Jan, Arthur J. *Arthur Jan's Memoirs*, self-published in 1960. In possession of author, p. 24.

11 Miller, J.R. *Skyscrapers Hide the Heavens: A History of Indian-White Relations in Canada*, University of Toronto Press, 1989, p. 61.

12 Morantz, Toby. "The Fur Trade and the Cree of James Bay." In Carol M. Judd and Arthur J. Ray, eds., *Old Trails and New Directions: Papers of the Third North American Fur Trade Conference*, 1980, pp. 39–58.

13 Quoted in Arthur J. Ray, *Indians in the Fur Trade: Their Role as Hunters, Trappers and Middlemen in the Lands Southwest of Hudson Bay 1660–1870.* University of Toronto Press, 1974, p. 14.

14 HBCA. Cumberland House Journal, B.49/a/25a, fol. 21, 34, 35.

15 Rich, E.E., ed. *Cumberland House Journals and Inland Journal*, The Hudson's Bay Record Society, 1951, vol. 4, p. 27.

16 *Missions de la Congrégation des Oblats de Marie Immaculée* 64 (décembre 1878): p. 488.

17 Ibid.

18 Williamson.

19 Brightman, Robert. *Grateful Prey: Rock Cree Human-Animal Relationships*, Canadian Plains Research Centre, 2002, p. 88.

20 National Archives of Canada. RG 10, vol. 3787, file 42239.

21 Ibid.

22 Ibid., vol. 2970, file 156710-7.

23 Williamson.

24 National Library of Canada and Indian and Northern Affairs Canada. Indian Affairs Annual Report for the year ending June 30, 1904, p. 88.

25 Ibid. Indian Affairs Annual Report for the year ending June 30, 1902, p. 204.

26 Ibid., p. 202.

27 Ibid., p. 205.

28 To Surveyor General, Ottawa, from Bowman, D.L.S., July 1922, pp. 1–2, Federation of Saskatchewan Indians.

29 National Archives of Canada. RG 10, vol. 6912, file 671/28-3, pt. 3.

30 Buckley, Helen, J.E.M. Kew, and John B. Hawley. *The Indians and Métis of Northern Saskatchewan: A Report on Economic and Social Development*, Centre for Community Studies, Saskatoon, p. 5.

CHAPTER 2

1 Tough, Frank. *"As their Natural Resources Fail": Native Peoples and the Economic History of Northern Manitoba, 1870–1930*, University of British Columbia Press, 1996, p. 2.

2 Thistle, Paul C. *Indian-European Trade Relations in the lower Saskatchewan River Region to 1840*, University of Manitoba Press, 1986, p. 11.

3 Friesen, Gerald. *The Canadian Prairies: A History*, University of Toronto Press, 1987, p. 18.

4 Henry, Alexander. *Travels and Adventures in Canada and the Indian Territories Between the Years 1760 and 1776*, Charles E. Tuttle Co., 1969, p. 260.

5 Ibid.

6 Thistle. *Indian-European Trade Relations*, p. 53.

7 Rich, E.E., ed. *Cumberland House Journals and Inland Journal*, The Hudson's Bay Record Society, 1951, vol. 4, pp. 63–64.

8 Ibid., p. 157.

9 Ibid., p. 109.

10 Ibid., p. 113.

11 Ibid., p. 159.

12 Ibid., p. 327.

13 Merasty, Ron. "Pelican Lake Post 1818-1819." Research paper, 1988–89, p. 1.

14 Tyrell, J.B., ed. *Journals of Samuel Hearne and Philip Turnor*, The Champlain Society, 1934, pp. 334, 335.

15 HBCA. Cumberland House Report on District, 1819, B.49/e/2.

16 Ibid., Dec. 29, 1818.

17 Ibid., Jan. 18, 1819.

18 Rossignol, Marius. "Property Concepts among the Cree of the Rocks." *Primitive Man* 12(3): 1939, pp. 66, 67.

19 HBCA. Correspondence Book, Pelican Lake, 1891–1903, B.158/b/1.

20 Merasty, p. 1.

21 Marchildon, Greg, and Sid Robinson. *Canoeing the Churchill: A Practical Guide to the Historic Voyageur Highway*, Canadian Plains Research Centre, 2002, p. 38.

22 Friesen, Gerald. *The Canadian Prairies: A History*, University of Toronto Press, 1987, p. 197.

23 *Aski-Puko, The Land Alone: a report on the expected effects of the proposed hydro-electric installation at Witego Rapids upon the Cree of the Peter Ballantyne and Lac La Ronge Bands*, 1976, p. 175.

24 Kemp, H.S.M. *Northern Trader*, Jarrolds London, 1957, p. 45.

25 Interview. University of Saskatchewan Archives, papers of R.G. Williamson MG 216; Box 26-L12-2.

26 Quoted in Frank Tough, *"As their Natural Resources Fail": Native Peoples and the Economic History of Northern Manitoba, 1870–1930*, University of British Columbia Press, 1996, p. 51.

27 Kemp, p. 45.

28 HBCA. Correspondence Book, Pelican Lake, 1891–1903, B.158/b/1, August 3, 1892.

29 Ibid., July 21, 1891.

30 Ibid., March, 1889.

31 Ibid., October, 1896.

32 Ibid., January 23, 1897.

33 Ibid., November, 1898.

34 Ibid., November, 1896.

35 Kemp, p. 162.

36 Kemp, pp. 19, 20.

37 Jan, Arthur J. *Arthur Jan's Memoirs*, self-published in 1960. In possession of author, p. 4.

38 Ibid., p. 25.

39 Rossignol, p. 64.

40 Interview. University of Saskatchewan Archives, papers of R.G. Williamson, MG 216: Box 26-L12-2.

41 Ibid.

42 *Aski-Puko*, p. 129.

43 Goulet, Keith N. *Oral History as an Authentic and Credible Research Base for Curriculum: The Cree of Sandy Bay and Hydroelectric Power Development 1927–67, an example.* M.A. thesis, University of Regina, 1986, p. 121.

44 Ibid., p. 129.

45 Piercy, C.H. "Part I, The areas in the remote northern part of the Province of Saskatchewan." *Survey of Educational Facilities in Northern Saskatchewan*, 1944, p. 24.

46 Williamson.

47 Goulet, p. 144.

48 Indian Affairs. Sept. 15, 1926, p. 3.

49 Keighley, Sydney. *Trader, Tripper, Trapper: The Life of a Bay Man*, Watson & Dwyer, 1989, p. 167.

50 Arrowsmith, William Alfred. *Northern Saskatchewan and the Fur Trade.* Thesis, University of Saskatchewan, 1964, p. 88.

CHAPTER 3

1 Quoted in Jennifer Brown and Robert Brightman. *The Orders of the Dreamed: George Nelson on Cree and Northern Ojibwa Religion and Myth*, University of Manitoba Press, 1988, p. 83.

2 Downes, P.G. *Sleeping Island: The Story of One Man's Travels in the Great Barren Lands of the Canadian North*, Western Producer Prairie Books, 1988, p. 55.

3 Dion, Joseph F. *My Tribe the Crees*, Glenbow Museum, 1979, p. 56.

4 Friesen, Gerald. *The Canadian Prairies: A History*, University of Toronto Press, 1987, p. 15.

5 Martin, Calvin. "Subarctic Indians and Wildlife." In Carol M. Judd and

Arthur J. Ray, eds., *Old Trails and New Directions: Paper of the Third North American Fur Trade Conference*, University of Toronto Press, 1980, p. 74.

6 Cooper, Rev. John and Rev. J.M. Pénard. "Land Ownership and Chieftaincy Among the Chippewayan and Caribou-eaters." *Primitive Man* 2: 1929.

7 Brightman, Robert. *Acimowina and ācaōhīī wina: Traditional Narratives of the Rock Cree Indians*, Canadian Museum of Civilization Mercury Series, p. 214.

8 ————. *Grateful Prey: Rock Cree Human-Animal Relationships*, Canadian Plains Research Centre, 2002, p. 111.

9 Kupferer, Harriet J. *Ancient Drums, Other Moccasins: Native North American Cultural Adaptation*, Prentice Hall, 1988, p. 49.

10 Brightman, *Grateful Prey*, p. 118.

11 Interview. University of Saskatchewan Archives, papers of R.G. Williamson MG 216: Box 26-L12-2.

12 Ibid.

13 Brown, Jennifer and Robert Brightman. *Orders of the Dreamed*, p. 145.

14 Williamson.

15 Ibid.

16 Helm, June and Eleanor Burke Leacock. "The Hunting Tribes of Subarctic Canada." In Eleanor Burke Leacock and Nancy Oestreich Lurie, eds., *North American Indians in Historical Perspective*, Random House, 1971, p. 368.

17 Brown and Brightman. *Orders of the Dreamed*, p. 36.

18 Rossignol, Marius. "The Religion of the Saskatchewan and Western Cree." *Primitive Man* 11(1 and 2): 1938, p. 68.

19 Siggins, Maggie. *Riel: A Life of Revolution*, HarperCollins Canada, 1994, p. 246.

20 Canadian Press Newswire, March 15, 2000.

21 Kupferer, p. 9.

22 Williamson.

23 Rossignol, p. 69.

24 Downes, p. 86.

25 Ibid., p. 51.

26 Charlebois, Ovide. *Missions de la Congrégation des Oblats de Marie Immaculée*, No. 210, Dec. 1919, p. 281.

27 Bonnald, Etienne. *Missions de la Congrégation des Oblats de Marie Immaculée*.

28 Archives Deschâtelets. HEB 1716.E84L5, Nov. 19, 1885.

29 Ibid.

30 Ibid.

31 Gray, Mary Agatha. *The Vicar Apostolic of Keewatin, Canada*, Librairie Beauchemin, 1939, p. 59.

32 Ibid., p. 62.

33 Saskatchewan Archives Board. *Indian Education in the North West* by Rev. Thompson Ferrier, 1906, R-834.11d, p. 37.

34 Getty, Ian A.L. "The Failure of the Native Church Policy of the CMS in the North-West." In Richard Allen, ed., *Religion and Society in the Prairie West*, Canadian Plains Research Centre, 1974, p. 26.

35 Gray, p. 72.

36 Downes, p. 35.

37 HBCA. Pelican Lake correspondence, 1938–1939, B.158/a/11.

CHAPTER 4

1 Hamell, George R. "Strawberries, Floating Islands, and Rabbit Captains: Mythical Realities and European Contact in the Northeast during the Sixteenth and Seventeenth Centuries." *Journal of Canadian Studies* 21(4): 1987, p. 85.

2 Merasty, Marie. *The World of the Wetiko: Tales from the Woodland Cree*, Saskatchewan Indian Cultural College Curriculum Studies and Research, 1974, pp. 8, 9.

3 Kemp, H.S.M. *Northern Trader*, Jarrolds London, 1957, p. 197.

4 Ibid.

5 Miller, J.R., *Skyscrapers Hide the Heavens: A History of Indian-White Relations in Canada*, University of Toronto Press, 1989, p. 129.

6 Grant, John Webster. *Moon of Wintertime: Missionaries and the Indians of Canada in Encounter since 1534*, University of Toronto Press, 1984, p. 9.

7 Saskatchewan Archives. Davin, Nicolas Flood, *Report on Industrial Schools for Indians and Halfbreeds*, March 14, 1879, R1400-1e.

8 Bryce, P.H. *The Story of A National Crime*, James Hope & Sons, 1922, p. 4.

9 Saskatchewan Archives, No. 226.

10 Ibid.

11 National Archives of Canada. RG 10, vol. 6292, file 619-1, part 1, Sept. 22, 1922.

12 Ibid., Sept. 10, 1924.

13 Ibid., Aug. 25, 1928.

14 Ibid., Sept. 25, 1925.

15 Ibid., March 16, 1926.
16 Ibid., Aug. 27, 1929.
17 Ibid., May 25, 1933.
18 NAC. RG 10, vol. 6314, file 655-10, part 2, Oct. 15, 1946.
19 NAC. RG 10, vol. 6313, file 655-5, part 1, Aug. 24, 1925.
20 Highway, Tomson. *Kiss of the Fur Queen*, Doubleday Canada, 1968, pp. 77–78.
21 NAC. RG 10, vol. 6314, file 655-10, part 2, June 8, 1944.
22 NAC. RG 10, vol. 8450, file 511/23-5-040, July 11, 1929.
23 Ibid., Feb. 2, 1937.
24 NAC. RG 10, series B-8, file 518, 1915.
25 NAC. RG 10, vol. 6292, file 619-1, part 1, Nov. 8, 1938.

CHAPTER 5

1 Williams, Glyndwr, ed. *Andrew Graham's Observation on Hudson's Bay, 1767–91*, Hudson's Bay Record Society, 1969, p. 35.
2 Young, T. Kue. *Health Care and Cultural Exchange: the Indian Experience in the Central Subarctic*, University of Toronto Press, 1988, p. 34.
3 Leighton, Anna L. *Wild Plant Use by the Woods Cree (Nihīthawak) of East-Central Saskatchewan*, National Museum of Man Mercury Series, paper no. 101, 1985.
4 Interview. University of Saskatchewan Archives, papers of R.G. Williamson MG 216: Box 26-L12-2.
5 Goulet, Keith N. *Oral History as an Authentic and Credible Research Base for Curriculum: The Cree of Sandy Bay and Hydroelectric Power Development 1927–67, an example.* M.A. thesis, University of Regina, 1986, p. 105.
6 Rossignol, Marius. "Property Concepts among the Cree of the Rocks." *Primitive Man* 12(3): 1939, p. 68.
7 Williamson.
8 HBCA. York Factory Post Journal, June 10, 1782, B.239/a/80. fos. 63–64.
9 Quoted in Young, p. 35.
10 William Tomison. "Cumberland House Journals, 1775-882." In Rich, ed., *Cumberland and Hudson House Journals 1775–82*, 2d series, 1779–82, p. 240.
11 Ibid., p. 247.
12 Quoted in Young, p. 36.
13 Quoted in Helen Buckley, J.E.M. Kew and John B. Hawley. *The Indians and Metis of Northern Saskatchewan: A Report on Economic and Social Development*, Centre for Community Studies, Saskatoon, 1963, p. 6.

14 Ray, Arthur J. "Smallpox: The Epidemic of 1837–38." *The Beaver*: Autumn 1975, p. 11.

15 ———. *Indians in the Fur Trade: their role as hunters, trappers and middlemen in the lands southwest of Hudson Bay 1660–1870*, University of Toronto Press, 1983, p. 187.

16 Ibid., p. 107.

17 Gray, Mary Agatha, trans. by J.M. Pénard. *The Vicar Apostolic of Keewatin, Canada*. Librairie Beauchemin, 1939, p. 50.

18 HBCA. Correspondence Book, Pelican Lake, 1891–1903, B.158-b-1.

19 Corrigan, Cameron. "Scurvy in a Cree Indian." *Canadian Medical Association Journal*, April 1946, vol. 54, p. 380.

20 NAC. "Report of the Royal 9 NorthWest Mounted Police, 1913." *Sessional Paper*: 28, p. 107.

21 Kemp, H.S.M. *Northern Trader*, Jarrolds London, 1957, p. 71.

22 Ibid., pp. 71, 72.

23 Ibid., p. 74.

24 Waldram, James B., D. Ann Herring, and T. Kue Young. *Aboriginal Health in Canada: Historical, Cultural, and Epidemiological Perspectives*, University of Toronto Press, 1995, p. 61.

25 Ibid., p. 62.

26 Bryce, P.H. *The Story of a National Crime*, James Hope & Sons, 1922, p. 2.

27 Moore, P.E. "No Longer Captain: A History of Tuberculosis and Its Control Among Canadian Indians." *Canadian Medical Association Journal*, May 6, 1961, vol. 54, p. 1012.

28 NAC. Indian Affairs School Files, RG 101, vol. 6314, files 655-10, part 1 and part 2.

29 Cockburn, R.H., ed. "To Reindeer's Far Waters: P.G. Downes' Journal of Travels in Northern Saskatchewan." *The Journal of Polar Studies*, p. 174.

30 NAC. Report of the Royal Canadian Mounted Police, Sept. 30, 1927, p. 30.

31 HBCA. Pelican Lake Journal, 1938–39, B.158-a-11.

32 "Aboriginal Health in Canada," Health and Welfare Canada, Medical Services Branch, Minister of Supply and Services Canada, 1992, p. 33.

33 Quoted in Ray. *Indians in the Fur Trade*, p. 198.

34 Williamson.

35 Honigmann, John J. "Expressive Aspects of Subarctic Indian Culture." In June Helm, ed., *Handbook of North American Indians*, volume 6, Smithsonian Institution, 1981, p. 732.

36 Ibid.

37 Brody, Hugh. *Indians on Skid Row: the Role of Alcohol and Community in the Adaptive Process of Indian Urban Migrants*, Ottawa: Dept. of Indian Affairs and Northern Development, 1971.

CHAPTER 6

1 Boldt, Menno and J. Anthony Long. "Tribal Traditions and European-Western Political Ideologies: The Dilemma of Canada's Native Indians." *Canadian Journal of Political Science* 17 (3): 1984, p. 539.

2 Ibid., p. 542.

3 Ibid., p. 543.

4 Quoted in Miller, J.R. *Skyscrapers Hide the Heavens: A History of Indian-White Relations in Canada*, University of Toronto Press, 2000, p. 10.

5 NAC. RG 10, vol. 6912, file 671/28-3.

6 Ibid.

7 Ibid.

8 Tobias, John L. "Protection, Civilization, Assimilation: An Outline History of Canada's Indian Policy." *As Long as the Sun Shines and Water Flows: A Reader in Canadian Native Studies*, University of British Columbia Press, 1983, p. 44.

9 Quoted in Miller, p. 254.

10 NAC. Indian Affairs, RG 10, vol. 6912, file 671/28-3, pt. 2.

11 Ibid.

12 Ibid., 1922.

13 Ibid., March 18, 1924.

14 Ibid.

15 NAC. Indian Affairs, RG 10, vol. 6912, file 671/28-3, pt. 3.

16 Ibid.

17 HBCA. Pelican Lake Correspondence, B.158-a-10, 1934.

18 Ibid.

19 Cockburn, R.H., ed. "To Reindeer's Far Waters: P.G. Downes' Journal of Travels in Northern Saskatchewan." *The Journal of Polar Studies*, p. 146.

20 Miller, p. 326.

21 *Aski-Puko, The Land Alone: a report on the expected effects of the proposed hydro-electric installation at Witego Rapids upon the Cree of the Peter Ballantyne and Lac La Ronge Bands*, 1976, p. 175.

22 Ibid., p. 183.

23 NAC. Indian Affairs, RG 20, file 672/37-2-26-18.

24 Ibid., RG 20 file 672/37-2-26-16.

25 Ibid., RG 20 file 672/37-2-26-167.

26 PricewaterhouseCoopers, Auditors' report on supplementary information, Peter Ballantyne Cree Nation, for period ending March 31, 2000.

27 Ibid.

CHAPTER 7

1 NAC. RCMP 709-1907, RG 18, series A-1, vol. 344, p. 6.

2 Ibid.

3 NAC. RCMP 53-1903, RG 18, series A-2, vol. 245, p. 39.

4 Ibid.

5 NAC. RCMP 709-1907, RG 18, series A-1, vol. 344, *Rex v. Marie Linklater,* Summary of evidence given at the preliminary trial of the accused.

6 NAC. RCMP 53-1903, RG 18, series A-2, vol. 245.

7 Ibid.

8 NAC. RCMP, RG 18, series A-1, vol. 272.

9 Ibid.

10 Gray, Mary Agatha, trans. by J.M. Pénard. *The Vicar Apostolic of Keewatin, Canada,* Librairie Beauchemin, 1939, pp. 84, 85.

11 NAC. Indian Affairs, RG 10, volume 6912, file 671/28-3, pt. 2.

12 Ibid.

13 Ibid.

14 Ibid.

15 HBCA. Pelican Lake journals, 1938–39, B.158/a/11.

16 Ibid.

17 Ibid.

18 Ibid.

CHAPTER 8

1 Manitoba Court of Appeal, *Bomek v. Bomek,* 1983, M.J. 96, Suit no. 286/82.

2 Interview. University of Saskatchewan Archives, papers of R.G. Williamson MG 216: Box 26-L12-2.

3 The Law Society of Manitoba, Discipline Case Digests, Case No. 94-09.

4 Ibid., Case No. 94-02.

5 Ibid., Case No. 02-01.

INDEX